THE PEN AND THE CROSS

The Pen and the Cross

Catholicism and English Literature, 1850–2000

RICHARD GRIFFITHS

continuum

Published by the Continuum International Publishing Group

The Tower Building	80 Maiden Lane
11 York Road	Suite 704
London	New York
SE1 7NX	NY 10038

www.continuumbooks.com

First published 2010

British Library Cataloguing-in-Publication Data
A catalogue record for this book is available from the British Library.

ISBN 978-0826-49697-3

Typeset by Pindar NZ, Auckland, New Zealand
Printed and bound by MPG Books Group, Ltd

To the members of the Theological Wine,
past and present

Contents

Contents

SECTION FIVE: THREE OUTSTANDING FIGURES

SECTION SIX: NEW WINE IN NEW BOTTLES: CATHOLIC WRITERS OF THE LATE TWENTIETH CENTURY

Preface

Many years ago, I wrote a book on the Catholic revival in French literature in the nineteenth and twentieth centuries, entitled *The Reactionary Revolution*. Though it was originally aimed at explaining that French phenomenon to the British public, the unexpectedly warm reception of its French translation brought me many new friends and colleagues in France, with many of whom I have kept contact. It was in fact a query from some of these friends (at a Léon Bloy conference in Périgueux), about the nature of English Catholic literature, that gave me the idea of producing the present book.

The first thing to say is that English Catholic literature was and is vastly different from its French counterpart. A comparison of the two revivals and their historical and literary backgrounds will however do much to explain the specific nature of the English manifestation of this phenomenon. In the course of this examination, I have had three sets of readers in mind: (i) British Catholics, who may find here new insights into the Catholic authors they already know and information about Catholic authors previously unknown to them; (ii) those in Britain who without being Catholics have nevertheless read authors of universal appeal such as Gerard Manley Hopkins, Graham Greene, Evelyn Waugh, David Jones, David Lodge or Muriel Spark and would like to understand more about the specifically Catholic forces at work within them; (iii) French enthusiasts for Catholic literature, who will need explanation about the situation of British Catholicism and the nature of English Catholic literature.

Such a study cannot be a pure exercise in English literary criticism. While several of the authors with whom we will be dealing are worthy of extensive critical study in their own right, we will need to concentrate above all on those aspects of their work which are particularly affected by their Catholicism and by the Catholic literature of which they are part. In the process, we will naturally be looking at the literary quality of what they write; but even here, it is the way in which that quality is affected by Catholic concerns that will be at the centre of our interests. In undertaking this study, I have been keenly aware of the valuable work done by others in recent years, both on English Catholic literature in general and on specific authors. Among the books that I have found particularly useful I would single out Thomas Woodman's Open University text *Faithful Fictions: The Catholic Novel in British Literature*; also Ian Ker's *The Catholic Revival in English Literature 1845–1961* (which, despite its title, consists of six studies of Catholic authors – Newman, Hopkins, Belloc, Chesterton, Greene and Waugh); Conor Cruise O'Brien's *Maria Cross: Imaginative Patterns in a Group of Modern Catholic Writers*; Malcolm Scott's *The Struggle for the Soul of the French Novel*; Albert Sonnenfeld's *Crossroads: Essays on the Catholic Novelists*; Edward Norman's *Anti-Catholicism in Victorian England*; Walford Davies's excellent critical edition of the poetry of Gerard Manley Hopkins; and a number of books and essays on Catholic literature by David Lodge and Bernard Bergonzi.

Many people, over the years, have given me insights into various aspects of this subject, often from their own experience. Many of them have since died, though some are still alive. They have included the Revd Alec Vidler and Émile Poulat, with whom I had fascinating discussions on Modernism and the Integrist reaction; Fr Jean-Marie Charles-Roux, who told me much about the Rosminians and the Catholic mission to Britain in the mid-nineteenth century; Fr Michel de Certeau, SJ, with whom I discussed on a number of occasions the various forms of vicarious suffering; Fr Pie Duployé, OP, who reinforced me in my view of Graham Greene's misunderstandings of Péguy; Sir Shane Leslie, who reminisced about Robert Hugh Benson in the Cambridge of the 1900s; Richard Ellmann, for the insights he gave me into the relationship between Catholicism and French and English Symbolism; Jim Ede, who introduced me to the paintings and writings of David Jones; Monsignor Alfred Gilbey, who told me much about the social and political attitudes of many twentieth-century British Catholics; and Henri Massis, who evoked his friend Hilaire Belloc's attitudes to the Action Francaise movement.

I also owe thanks to others, alive and dead, who have helped me either by providing valuable information, or by equally useful discussions. The list cannot be exhaustive. It includes Maxime Alexandre, Nick Atkin, Dominic Baker-Smith, Alan Bell, Robert Bolgar, Bill Bush, Evan Davies, Walford Davies, Mary Douglas, Fr Edward Dowding, Roger Ellis, Bill Evans, Fr Illtud Evans, OP, Gilbert Gadoffre, Pierre Glaudes, the Rt Revd Lord Harries of Pentregarth, Geoffrey Hill, Bernard Howells, Julian Jeffs, the Hon. John Jolliffe, Fr Jean-Pierre Jossua, OP, Anthony Levi, Peter Levi, Patrick McCarthy, Dominique Millet-Gérard, Mgr Maurice Nédoncelle, the Revd Edward Norman, Fr Walter J. Ong, SJ, Hugo Perks, Sir Charles Petrie Bt, Mick Quinn, Bernard Richards, Fr Michael Richards, David Ricks, Norma

Rinsler, Joseph Royer, Robert Speaight, Freddy Stopp, Elizabeth Stopp, Brian Sudlow, Bernard Swift, Wynn Thomas, John Wain, Mary Walsh and Dan Whitehouse. Also, not least, my fellow members of the Theological Wine.

I am grateful to the following publishers and trustees for permission to quote from the following poets: John Murray, for the poetry of George Mackay Brown (from *Collected Poems*, 2006); Johnson and Alcock, and Anvil Press, for the poetry of Peter Levi (from *Collected Poems 1955–1975*, 1976, and *The Echoing Green*, 1983); David Higham Associates, and Carcanet, for the poetry of Elizabeth Jennings (from *New Collected Poems*, 2002); The Trustees of the Estate of David Jones, for the poetry of David Jones (from *In Parenthesis*, 1937, *The Anathemata*, 1952, and *The Sleeping Lord*, 1974); and Oxford University Press, for the poetry of David Gascoyne (from *Collected Poems*, 1965).

I owe particular thanks to Robin Baird-Smith, who commissioned this book. It has, as always, been a pleasure working with him. I also remember with great affection the two people who many years ago encouraged my book on French Catholicism – Richard Sadler, who commissioned it for Constable, and James Mitchell (later co-founder of the publishing firm Mitchell Beazley), who was my editor for it, and whose strong interest in religious matters led to many fruitful conversations. My greatest thanks must be, however, to my wife Patricia, for her patience in relation to my absorption in this study and for the help she has given me to distinguish the wood from the trees.

Richard Griffiths
Penarth, 2010

SECTION ONE

Introduction

1

Clearing the Decks: An Approach to English Catholic Literature

The study of 'committed literature', whether political or religious, used to be regarded with suspicion by pure literary scholars, who saw it as falling between the stools of two different disciplines in each case. Of recent years, however, the interface between literature and politics has become an important area of research, in relation to a wide range of western European countries. On the religious front 'Catholic literature', in France in particular, has for many decades been a major area of literary research. Certain problems remain, however, in relation to such a study. In it, literature is sometimes used almost exclusively as an illustration of political or religious trends. While this is of importance in itself, it neglects the *literary* dimension and fails to ask some pertinent questions. To what extent does commitment, whether political or religious, affect the literary worth of what is being written? What are the specific pitfalls that such authors need to avoid? Is there a literary genre of real value that can be produced by such means? The present study aims to answer some of these questions in relation to English Catholic literature, while at the same time using it for some insight into contemporary religious trends.

But first, why *Catholic* literature? Why has one religion been singled out in this way? One of the reasons is that, in Catholic countries, a large and identifiable body of literature grew up (particularly in France in the nineteenth and twentieth centuries) that had specifically Catholic concerns. Because the Catholic faith uses a coherent system of imagery and specific forms of expression, that literature formed a clearly defined entity, which could exist almost independently alongside the secular literature of its age. Part of its strength lay in numbers: the Catholic public in France was a vast reserve ready to read about its own concerns. Part of its strength, too, lay in the fact that its imagery, forms of expression and modes of thought were readily recognized and understood by its target public. So it was that a body of literature developed, that was a coherent expression of themes specific to itself. What has been called the French 'Catholic revival', when in the late nineteenth century a prominent series of figures from the intelligentsia, having converted dramatically to the Catholic faith, began to write in these forms, was a literary bombshell. Catholic literature now contained writing of great literary worth; and within that literature certain figures (such as Léon Bloy, Joris-Karl Huysmans, Charles Péguy, Paul Claudel and later François Mauriac and Georges Bernanos) developed high originality of their own, often transcending the confines of what Catholic literature had seemed to be up to that time.

What, then, of Britain? Why do we talk about a Catholic revival in *English* Literature? Surely the same underlying circumstances as in France did not exist? It is certainly true that the social environment for Catholicism was very different in this country, in that Catholicism was a minority religion and until the nineteenth century had been a beleaguered one. As in France, there had been a spate of conversions to Catholicism in the mid to late nineteenth century, particularly among the literate intelligentsia; and, though the nature of those conversions and the place from which the converts had come were very different, there was in both countries the same concern to convey the nature of the faith by artistic means. There was, too, a considerable interest in this country for what had been going on in France and, in an age when 'every gentleman was capable of conversing in French', the writings of the French Catholic revival were readily available to the British converts. So it is, that from the 1890s onwards a hard core of writers in the English language showed a deep involvement in Catholic religious matters while writing works of literary value; and that trend continued into the twentieth century, culminating in outstanding works by Graham Greene, Evelyn Waugh and David Jones, all three of whom, though so individual in their writings, nevertheless owed a great deal to their immediate forebears. That English revival has, moreover, still to be borne in mind when we look at the post-war generation of Catholic novelists and poets from the 1950s onwards, most of whom owed in one way or another something to the literature that preceded them, even when they seemed to be breaking free from it and to be in some respects its antithesis.

This revival had lagged in time behind its close relative, the French Catholic revival, with a gap of about twenty years. And the French and British Revivals differed greatly, both in 'importance' (in the French meaning of 'size') and in their major concerns. They were, however, fully aware of each other and there was considerable cross-fertilization of ideas and of themes, in both directions.

Let me start with one or two necessary definitions. In this book I will be taking 'English Catholic literature' to mean Catholic literature in the English language, primarily written in Great Britain.[1] This may well harm the sensibilities of the Welsh and the Scots, who can quite rightly point to indigenous and separate English-language literatures of considerable worth existing alongside the literatures in the Celtic languages in their respective countries, but it is the only convenient way to encapsulate what was written *in the English language* on Catholic themes (and which had more in common with a shared Catholic core than with any national particularities within this island) without having recourse to some artificial and meaningless concept such as 'British Catholic literature'. I shall, however, be referring to '*British* Catholics' when we talk about the exponents of that literature living in these islands.

Further sensitivities may be hurt by my use of the term 'Catholic'. For many Anglicans of the Anglo-Catholic persuasion, 'Catholic' is the term used for Anglo-Catholics (embodying the belief that theirs is the true Catholic tradition, from which the Roman Church has strayed); and the term used, by them, for members of the Catholic Church, is '*Roman* Catholic'. Nevertheless, a continual use of the term 'Roman Catholic' when the actual members of that Church use, purely and simply, the word 'Catholic' to describe themselves, would be excessively clumsy if repeated throughout the book, and would be unnecessarily Anglican-orientated. In the same way, the 'Church *in* England' will mean the Catholic Church in this country, whereas the 'Church *of* England' of course means the Established Anglican Church.[2]

But what do we mean by 'Catholic literature'? We should start from the fact that this does not mean the same thing as 'literature written by Catholics'. As I have said in another context:

> For a great many Catholics (as for a great many Anglicans, Jews, deists, positivists) the writing of a literary work has not automatically involved a deep concern with matters of faith. Compendia of Catholic literature, compiled by pious and well-meaning critics, have too often jumbled together writers whose sole point of contact is the fact that they are Catholics. [Catholic literature] has suffered much not only from becoming intermingled with non-religious literature written by Catholics, and with literature written against a backcloth of religious beliefs, but with no specifically religious preoccupations in subject or treatment; it has also been stuffed willy-nilly into the same pigeon-hole as pious literature of a very different type.[3]

Archbishop Rowan Williams, discussing in the Introduction to his book on Dostoevsky the nature of the 'Catholic novel', produces an elegant and satisfying definition of the traditional Catholic novel, which in Britain culminated in the novels of Evelyn Waugh and Graham Greene, and in France in the novels of François Mauriac and Georges Bernanos. When we call them Catholic novelists, he says, we mean 'not that they are novelists who happen to be Catholic by private conviction', but that 'their fiction could not be understood by a reader who had no knowledge at all of Catholicism and the particular obligations it entailed for its adherents.'

Williams also points, however, to another, more modern, type of 'Catholic novel', which is not so much about 'problems or dilemmas distinctive to Catholics as individuals in the contemporary world', but about 'the possibility of any morally coherent life in a culture of banality and self-deceit'.[4] In this it would be more difficult to agree with him. Many novels that match this definition could in no way be described as 'Catholic novels'. While such concerns *do* have their place in many novels of the post-war generation, such as those by Muriel Spark and David Lodge, what makes it possible to describe them as 'Catholic novelists' is an underlying concern, still, with 'problems or dilemmas distinctive to Catholics'; and without that perspective they would merely be classed as modern novelists like any other, though concerning themselves strongly with moral dilemmas in modern society.

There are, too, a number of non-Catholic writers such as Anthony Burgess (many of them lapsed Catholics) who occasionally address Catholic themes and attitudes in the course of their novels. These, and nominal Catholics like Ford Madox Ford, in whose works Catholic themes at times similarly emerge, could in no way be described as 'committed novelists' of the kind we will be studying. As Woodman has written of Ford, his 'actual religious allegiance seems to have been no more than nominal', and his stance in his novels tends to be 'theist and supernaturalist rather than specifically Christian'.[5] Novels by writers such as Ford or Burgess, then, though worthy of extensive study in another context, have been taken to be outside the remit of the present study, which deals specifically with committed literature written from a Catholic viewpoint.

What of 'Catholic poetry'? Here the problem of definition is of a different order. While it is easy enough to detect religious concerns in a piece of poetry, it is more difficult to decide to what extent it is 'literature'. There has, over the ages, been a strong tradition in all parts of the Christian Church of pious poetry of a sentimental and banal kind – what Norman Nicholson defines as 'moral uplift in rhyme, or pious verse about the Good Shepherd', in which 'the use of conventional images and worn-out phrases seems to imply that Christianity itself is no longer a living thing'[6] – but this can hardly be described as 'literature'. Yet there has also been, alongside it, a robust literary tradition of religious poetry which can stand comparison with the best of secular poetry, from Catholic poets like St Robert Southwell and Richard Crashaw to Anglicans like George Herbert, John Donne and Henry Vaughan, to Nonconformists like Isaac Watts. In the Catholic literature of our period, alongside much of the banal type described by Nicholson (which in the Catholic case often involves the use of outworn and sentimental Catholic imagery), there have been certain outstanding poets by any standard – such as Gerard Manley Hopkins or David Jones – and many others who have considerable merit – such as Francis Thompson, Alice Meynell, Lionel Johnson or Coventry Patmore. In the best of this poetry, the Catholic input does not merely consist of the external application of Catholic imagery and expression (as in many of the lesser poets), but of a profound, in depth examination of the Catholic experience, often linked specifically to the meaning and experience of the Mass (as in poetry by David Jones, Elizabeth Jennings or George Mackay Brown) or to meditation on more universal Catholic themes and issues (as in poems by Gerard Manley Hopkins).

One of the besetting dangers, in a study such as this, is to conceive of the literature of a movement as consisting entirely of the great works by the great authors. If one ignores completely the inferior works written by lesser writers one can miss much that throws light on the specific concerns of Catholic authors in the period; and, by neglecting the background from which the works by the greater authors came, one can underestimate or even misinterpret their achievement. Thus, when studying the French Revival, I had not only to read the works of the great writers such as Huysmans, Bloy, Péguy and Claudel, but also those of a multitude of lesser writers such as Baumann, Retté, Lafon, Psichari, and so on. So much so, that I was described by some of my young French contemporaries as 'the man who had read more appalling French novels than anyone known'. In this study of the English Revival, I have followed the same system, in relation both to the novel and to poetry, and have found much that throws light on the writings of the greats, and on the attitudes (religious, social and political) of the British Catholic intelligentsia. There is a danger, however, in this approach and that is the desire to cover in one's text every Catholic author, major and minor (a procedure which can reduce everything to a featureless landscape). I have therefore tended to pick out certain typical examples of work by minor authors for the kind of detailed examination that can throw light on the major authors who are the centre of the study.

Finally, what must be stressed is that this study will concentrate above all on what the French call 'la grande littérature': narrative prose, poetry and the theatre. Other genres, such as the essay, theological writings and journalism, are treated at times but usually as illustrations to fill out a picture, or to make a historical point. Such writings have always existed in religious circles: religious controversy has always flourished whether in journals and newspapers, in pamphlet form, or in theological works of a greater size. What makes the Catholic Revival in English literature, from the late nineteenth century onwards, so striking is the extraordinary flowering of literary works from 'la grande littérature' that it produced.

Notes

1   We will not be looking at the equivalent 'English' Catholic literature in the United States, as this, such as it is, exists in a very different context, and would unnecessarily complicate our study.
2   This would be further complicated, from Welsh disestablishment in the 1920s onwards, by the use of the term 'Church *in* Wales' for the Welsh Anglican Church; but luckily we have had no cause, in this study, to use that term.
3   Richard Griffiths, *The Reactionary Revolution*, p. 3.
4   Rowan Williams, *Dostoevsky: Language, Faith and Fiction*, pp. 5–6. I am grateful to Richard Harries for drawing my attention to this definition.
5   Woodman, *Faithful Fictions*, pp. 17–18.
6   Norman Nicholson, introduction to *An Anthology of Religious Verse, Designed for the Times*.

2

Catholicism and British Society in the Nineteenth and Early Twentieth Centuries

The French and British Revivals

The concerns of English Catholic literature on the whole failed to mirror those of its French equivalent. The reason for this lies mainly in the position, and history, of the Catholic Church within the two countries and the very different opponents it had to face in each.

In France the last three decades of the nineteenth century saw a strong revival in religious values, with many Catholic conversions among the intelligentsia and a flowering of literary and artistic output of a Catholic nature. To a large extent, this was a reaction against the tyranny of institutionalized atheism and anticlericalism, in the urban society of the nascent Third Republic. The vast claims of nineteenth-century positivism dominated this society, which had become imbued with the belief that Catholicism was purely for the uncultivated and ignorant and that it was impossible to be both intelligent and Christian. At the same time, politically, anticlerical laws had become the hallmark of the Third Republic. However, in the space of a few years a new Catholic intelligentsia, made up mainly of recent converts, had made religion once more respectable. The major concerns of these converts mirrored this situation. While a few of them tried to harness philosophy and things of the mind to their cause, the vast majority spurned intellectualism (which had led, in their view, to the excesses of institutionalized atheism) and stressed all those things in Catholic doctrine that flew in the face of the reign of science and of human ideas of reason and progress. There was an obsession with the miraculous, the efficacy of suffering, the complementary nature of good and evil. At the same time, their politics tended towards extreme reaction and opposition to the Republic and its institutions. A writer like Joseph de Maistre (1755–1821), who had combined counter-revolutionary politics with mystical beliefs in vicarious suffering and the equivalence of the 'sacred' and the 'de-sacred',[1] became naturally one of the major influences upon the writers of the French revival.

The British converts' situation was very different. They were mostly converts not from atheism or agnosticism, but from another form of Christianity, Anglicanism. And where in France, despite all historical vicissitudes, Catholicism had remained the religion of the vast majority of Christians, in Britain Catholicism was very much a minority religion, which had been kept by force of law in an inferior position for centuries until the early nineteenth. The major concern therefore, for British Catholic writers, was not with what differentiated Christianity from the secular society of the time, but with what differentiated Catholicism from other forms of the Christian religion. The miraculous and the mystical had a lesser part to play. In their place came a concentration on specifically Catholic views of the sacraments and of the priestly role. The authority of the Church, also, was continually contrasted with what appeared the 'free-for-all' of the Anglican position. Secular politics played a lesser role for most of these writers (with certain conspicuous exceptions), than for their French equivalents, until the interwar period. At the same time there was a concern with class and social position that would seem strange to French eyes.

Persecution and Penal Legislation

Nowadays, most people are aware of the grievous persecution that was suffered by British Catholics in the sixteenth and seventeenth centuries – the tortures and executions of priests for celebrating the Mass, and of those who harboured them, and the very large fines and punishments enacted on those (the 'recusants') who refused to attend the compulsory Anglican services. It is perhaps less well known that after the times of physical persecution, the Catholic population continued to suffer under a series of laws, known collectively as the 'penal laws', which inflicted various civil disabilities upon them. The Test Act of 1673 required all holders of office under the Crown (including the armed services) and all holders of municipal office to receive communion according to the rites of the Church of England at least once a year and to make a 'Declaration against Transubstantiation'. In 1678 this was extended to peers and members of the House of Commons. Those wishing to enter university were required to pass similar tests. These laws, which effectively removed Catholics from public life and severely restricted their religious life, received some palliation in the late eighteenth century, in the Relief Acts of 1778, 1791 and 1793 (the Emancipation Act of 1791 finally legalizing Catholic worship), but Catholics were still excluded from the highest civil and military offices and from the universities. It was only after some years of campaigning for Catholic emancipation that the 1829 Catholic Relief Act removed most disabilities.

One of the major factors (apart from growing tolerance) that led to the 1829 Act was the growing unrest in Ireland, which under the Act of Union of 1800 had become part of the 'United Kingdom of Great Britain and Ireland'. Even stricter penal laws had been exerted in Ireland, where the vast majority of people were Catholic. The pressure from Irish politicians for reform was very strong. In 1829, when Daniel O'Connell, the leader of the reform movement, had an unexpected and dramatic electoral success in a crucial by-election, the Duke of Wellington and Sir Robert Peel were led urgently to consider repeal.

This repeal did not mean that the British public had given up its anti-Catholicism, which remained as rabid as ever in many circles. This was seen in the reactions of a large section of the Tory Party against Wellington and Peel on this issue, followed by the downfall of the Government in the 1830 election.[2]

Nineteenth-Century Anti-Catholicism

The Catholic literary revival began against this background of anti-Catholicism, which had remained an integral part of the British psyche right up to the nineteenth century. As Edward Norman has pointed out:

> Catholic beliefs, especially the sacerdotal nature of the Christian ministry (which the Protestant Archbishop Whately called 'religion by proxy'), the primacy of St Peter and the See of Rome, the invocation of saints, veneration of the Virgin, transubstantiation, popular miracles and so on, seemed to some Protestants mildly derisory, to others downright wicked, and to some, even perverted.[3]

Far more dangerous was the belief that the Catholic Church was conspiring to give itself greater power and influence, by whatever means came to hand. These fears were expressed most clearly in works such as those of the Revd Charles Kingsley. His historical novel *Westward Ho!* was concerned with the 'dastardly plots' of Elizabethan Catholics and in particular the Jesuits. Like many, he believed such 'plots' still to be a feature of the Church's activities in this country and in Europe as a whole, in the nineteenth century. As he put it, when Napoleon III was instrumental in reinstating the Pope into his temporal possessions, the French Emperor was 'a notorious tool of the Jesuits, the most frightful incarnation of Antichrist's triple power – money, sword and priestcraft – which our age has seen.'[4] An introductory essay to a

1875 edition of *Foxe's Book of Martyrs*, written by a Protestant clergyman and entitled 'An Essay on Popery', had this to say of Catholicism: 'Let us then hold up the inhuman system to merited execration; let parents teach their children, and children teach their children, to dread and to oppose this abomination of desolation.'[5]

As Edward Norman has pointed out, the two decades succeeding Catholic emancipation saw a series of events that exacerbated these anti-Catholic feelings. There were two main issues: the effect of the Oxford Movement within the Church of England and then in 1850 the 'Papal Aggression' – the creation of a Catholic Hierarchy in England.

The Oxford Movement was a group of Anglicans, based mainly in Oxford, which set out to restore the Church of England to what they saw as its mainline position in the universal Church. They reacted against the extreme Protestantism, and the latitudinarianism, of much nineteenth-century Anglicanism and aimed to restore the High Church character of the seventeenth-century Church. In the process, they stressed those characteristics that the Church of England and Catholicism had in common. They believed 'that the Church of England held an intermediate position, represented by the patristic tradition, as against modern Romanism on the one hand and modern Protestantism on the other'.[6] Leading lights in the movement included John Henry Newman, Edward Bouverie Pusey, John Keble and Hurrell Froude. Though at the start questions of ritual played a very minor part in their concerns, the movement eventually became strongly associated with elaborate ritual on the Catholic model and became pilloried by its opponents as 'Ritualism'. Despite all the controversies that it faced, the 'Tractarian' movement (so called because of the *Tracts for the Times,* published from 1831 onwards, which had encapsulated its early teachings) had an enormous influence upon the Anglican Church, and many of the customs that are now taken for granted in that Church have their origins in this movement.

From the start, the Tractarians had aroused considerable opposition among the Protestant majority of the Church of England, which inevitably linked them with the dangers of Roman Catholicism. As Bishop Bagot of Oxford put it in 1845, 'The rude, unthinking, and unjustifiable manner in which some have allowed themselves to speak of the Reformation has a direct tendency to produce that frame of mind which underestimates the intolerable evils and errors of the Romish system'.[7] Lord John Russell, in an open letter in *The Times* to the Bishop of Durham on the dangers of the 'Papal Aggression' in 1850, declared that any outward threat from Catholicism was as nothing compared to 'the danger within the gates from the unworthy sons of the Church of England herself'.[8] Such views were reinforced by a large number of lurid anti-Tractarian novels.[9]

Opponents of the Oxford Movement had felt themselves vindicated in their fears when a spate of Tractarian conversions to Roman Catholicism took place from 1845 onwards, headed by John Henry Newman. Feeling against Catholicism, and against Anglican 'Ritualism', became even stronger in the second half of the nineteenth century.

The Pope's decision to create a Catholic hierarchy in England was another factor which helped revive virulent anti-Catholicism. The move had, innocently, been seen by Rome more as an administrative measure than any kind of provocation. Until then, Vicars Apostolic had served the United Kingdom, under the auspices of the Sacred Congregation of Propaganda. Matters had been complicated, however, by the accession of Ireland (which had a regular Catholic episcopal hierarchy of its own) to the Union. Petitions were made to the Holy See for an English hierarchy and in September 1850, in the Letters Apostolic *Universalis Ecclesiae*, England and Wales became an ecclesiastical province of the Catholic Church, with a hierarchy consisting of an Archbishop and twelve suffragan Bishops, each with a territorial title. Nicholas Wiseman was created a Cardinal and became the head of this new hierarchy as Archbishop of Westminster.

The change was mishandled and the situation was not helped by the apparently provocative wording of the documents concerned, which exacerbated an already inflammatory situation. The Prime Minister, Lord John Russell, in his open letter to *The Times*, agreed with the Bishop of Durham that 'the late aggression of the Pope upon our Protestantism' was 'insolent and insidious', and went on:

> There is an assumption of power in all the documents which have come from Rome; a pretension of supremacy over the realm of England, and a claim to sole and undivided sway, which is inconsistent with the Queen's supremacy, with the rights of our bishops and clergy, and with the spiritual independence of the nation . . .. I have little hope that the propounders and framers of these innovations will desist from their insidious course. But I rely with confidence on the people of England; and I will not bate a jot of heart or hope, so long as the glorious principles and the immortal martyrs of the Reformation shall be held in reverence by the great mass of a nation which looks in contempt on the mummeries of superstition.[10]

Such anti-Catholicism was not universal, particularly in educated circles; but it was always there in the background, emerging to the front of the stage at times of crisis. It lasted, in a diluted form, right into the twentieth century. Some of the conventional upper middle-class characters in Maurice Baring's novels of the interwar period provide good examples of the (by that stage) almost off-hand dismissal of Catholics and their attitudes to religion.

The Class Structure of the Catholic Population

The class structure of British Catholicism presents a very different picture from that in France, where Catholicism remained a national religion with representation from almost all classes of society, despite the loss of belief among the intelligentsia, the politicians and the new urban working class. By the early nineteenth century, what remained of Catholicism in Britain presented a very specific class profile.

On the one hand, there were a number of aristocratic recusant families, many of which had maintained the faith through all the vicissitudes since the sixteenth century, living in comparative retirement from the world of government and of commerce. On the whole, by keeping a low profile, they had survived – and, old habits dying hard, even after Catholic emancipation they tended to remain fairly retiring. In the nineteenth century they were joined by a number of aristocratic converts, such as the Third Marquess of Bute. On the other hand there were the poor, mainly in London and South Lancashire, the latter having been, from the sixteenth century onwards, a centre of the faith.[11] For them survival had been far harder, unless they lived in the vicinity of one of the great houses.

In the late eighteenth and early nineteenth centuries there was to be considerable growth in the working class Catholic population, which soon greatly outnumbered the old aristocratic families. It has been calculated that in 1845, out of 450,000 Catholics in England and Wales, about 385,000 were working class, of whom about 315,000 lived either in London or in Lancashire.[12] There had been a vast influx into England, Wales and Scotland of Irish labourers, who came to work on the major projects of the industrial revolution, and by the 1840s this had been further swollen by those fleeing the Famine. This invasion was to continue throughout the nineteenth century, eventually making Irish Catholics one of the major forces in British Catholicism. There was, in the first half of the nineteenth century, still very little in the way of a successful Catholic bourgeoisie, possibly because of the inhibiting effects of the penal laws.

Though the aristocratic Catholics were a comparatively small proportion of the Catholic population, their influence had been disproportionately large. Until the early nineteenth century very few public places of worship were available and those that existed were restricted to the towns and totally inadequate for the urban Catholic population.[13] With no diocesan or parish system, worship had been maintained mainly through the provision of private chapels in the houses of the great, to which the local population could come to worship. It was the landed families, too, who tended privately to employ the priests. In these circumstances, powerful members of the laity exerted a great deal of influence in the English Church.

The situation of the Catholic Church in Britain in the early nineteenth century was later to be graphically described by Cardinal Vaughan:

> Marks of persecution were fresh upon her body, the smell of fire was still upon her clothing. Her organisation was abnormal and missionary, reduced to its lowest form, as though England had been China or Japan. After ten centuries of public praise her voice was low; her divine services cut down to their bare essentials; many of her distinctive devotions and practices were either forgotten or conducted in private, and, as it were, in silence, and with closed doors. No kind of uniform, no outward mark of distinction in her ministers was visible. The English Church was like a ship on an angry sea, close reefed and battened down, exposing as little surface as possible to the stiff gale which was still only lessening.[14]

This situation was to change dramatically from the 1830s onwards. First, there was the large influx of Irish, which I have already noted. It is interesting to observe that, unlike the French situation, these urban, working class immigrants remained inherently religious.[15] They swelled enormously the number of practising Catholics in the working class of Great Britain.

The most important development, however, was the large number of converts from Anglicanism in the wake of the Oxford Movement. These tended mostly to be from the middle classes, who from now on played a greater part in British Catholicism. These converts were often viewed with mistrust and disdain by the longstanding members of the Catholic Faith (particularly as a good number of these 'Oxford' men had been Anglican priests before their conversion). This disdain was often reciprocated by them, particularly with regard to what they saw as the religious ignorance of so many of the old Catholics. W. G. Ward, for example, once said, 'Speaking in argument with English Catholics is like talking with savages'.[16] The 'Oxford Catholics' formed a vital new element in British Catholicism and brought considerable intellectual distinction. Many of the early writers of the Catholic Revival were of their number, as were the ecclesiastical historians who revised the popular vision of the history of the Catholic Faith in this country. A later generation of converts were very much in their image.

A further development was the result of the creation of the Catholic Hierarchy in 1850. The influx of priests from abroad and the introduction of 'Italianate' forms of dress and worship[17] aroused grave suspicion among the old British Catholics, yet for the new 'Oxford' converts 'the details of Roman custom in all these matters were held a part of orthodoxy just because they were Roman'.[18] Far more serious aspects of the new situation were the centralization and regimentation of what had often been a fairly disorganized but relatively free ecclesiastical situation, and the old Catholics' mistrust of the ultramontanism which they saw as invading the English Church – that tendency which favoured the centralization of authority in the Papal Curia as opposed to national or diocesan independence. The nineteenth century was the age of the triumph of ultramontanism in the Church, culminating in the declaration of Papal Infallibility in the Vatican Council of 1870. This tendency was particularly strong among many of the new British converts. While many British Catholics (particularly the old Catholics) failed to see the necessity or the desirability of centralization in the Church, or of rule from Rome, others, such as the converts Father Faber and W. G. Ward, embraced the new situation with ultramontane fervour. The immediate social result, of course, of the creation of the new hierarchy was the diminishing of the power of the lay recusant families.

So, all in all, the nineteenth century was a time of great and often disconcerting change in British Catholicism. This translated itself, in the case of many, into concerns for form and authority which lasted well into the twentieth century. It was not until after the Second World War that any significant change took place in British Catholic attitudes.

Notes

1 See Richard Griffiths, 'Le sacré et le dé-sacré dans le roman catholique' in *Dimensions du sacré dans les littératures profanes.*
2 Edward Norman, *A History of Modern Ireland*, p. 83.
3 Edward Norman, *Anti-Catholicism in Victorian England*, p. 14. I am indebted to this book for much of the information about Victorian anti-Catholicism contained in this section.
4 Quoted in Malcolm Day's introduction to the 2009 edition of Kingsley's *Westward Ho!* p. xi.
5 Ingram Cobbin, 'Essay on Popery', in *Foxe's Book of Martyrs* (London, 1875), p. iv, quoted in Norman, *Anti-Catholicism*, p. 13.
6 *Oxford Dictionary of the Christian Church.*
7 Quoted in Norman, *Anti-Catholicism*, p. 105.
8 *The Times*, 7 November 1850.
9 See Margaret Maison, 'Surpliced Vipers and Silly Women', in *The Victorian Vision*, pp. 71–88.
10 *The Times*, 7 November 1850.
11 Bernard Bergonzi, in his novel *The Roman Persuasion*, p. 15, notes that his hero Wilfrid Cartwright, originally the son of a small shopkeeper in Lancashire, came

of a family that 'had been Catholic for generations, like so many in Preston, the most traditionally Catholic town in England'.

12 Jean Alain Lesourd, *Les Catholiques dans la société anglaise, 1765–1865*, Vol. 1, 630–1.

13 The situation in Liverpool, as described by Purcell, was typical. 'In Liverpool, for instance, there were only four chapels and fourteen priests . . . Of the Catholic population of Liverpool, there were 39,000 adults for whose spiritual wants there was no adequate provision' (Edmund Purcell, *Life of Cardinal Manning*, Vol. 1, 647).

14 *Reply of the Archbishop-Elect to the Address of the Clergy and Laity of the Diocese of Westminster* (1892), p. 6 (quoted in Purcell, Vol. 1, 646).

15 It is worth noting the strength, too, of Christian nonconformism in industrial areas in Britain, particularly in the Welsh mining valleys, where it was the dominant culture among both workers and employers. The phenomenon of anti-religious tendencies in industrial areas, so typical of the French urban scene, does not appear to have existed in many parts of Britain.

16 Quoted in Purcell, p. 656. Purcell defends these old Catholics thus: 'They were content, if without doubt or question, without intellectual understanding or philosophical defence, to hold the faith of their forefathers, burnt into their souls by the fire of persecution. If they neglected its intellectual bulwarks and outposts, they all, through the evil days, held the citadel of the Spiritual Kingdom. They had handed down the Torch of Faith from generation to generation . . . The fool in his folly mocked at them because, foresooth, their intellectual vision had grown dim in the prolonged darkness of 300 years.'

17 For example, veneration of the Blessed Sacrament, together with Benediction (though a simpler version of the latter had been introduced into Britain by émigré priests at the time of the French Revolution); veneration of the Sacred Heart; excessive devotion to the blessed Virgin Mary; and, at a more prosaic level, the use of cottas in place of surplices, and the use of the 'Roman collar' (introduced by the Rosminians in the 1850s).

18 Maisie Ward, *The Wilfrid Wards and the Transition*, Vol. 1, p. 9.

SECTION TWO

The Beginnings

3
The Preparatory Ground, 1840–1890

The full literary impact of the Catholic literary revival in Britain was to be felt from 1890 onwards. Nevertheless, there was considerable literature written by Catholics before this date, some of which can qualify as 'Catholic literature'. Though much of it was of poor quality, one figure at least stands out not merely as a good (and possibly great) writer, but also as a major influence on those who were to follow later. This was John Henry Newman, one of the most influential religious figures in the nineteenth century, who was also to have a considerable literary impact.

John Henry Newman

Newman (1801–90) was, as we have seen, a leading spirit of the Oxford Movement. In 1845, however, he had converted to the Roman Catholic Church, deeply dividing the Tractarian Movement and setting off a spate of Tractarian conversions. After ordination in 1847, he established the Oratory in Birmingham in 1849. He spent 1854 to 1858 as rector of the new Catholic University in Dublin. Newman would have remained in comparative obscurity had it not been for the powerful impact of his ideas and his writings. This was partly because of his strained relations with that other great convert from Anglicanism, Henry Manning (who became Cardinal Archbishop of Westminster in 1865) and partly because of his views on the developing nature of religious truth, and his clear discomfort at the ultramontane attitudes of the Church under Pius IX. However in 1879, towards the end of Newman's life, the new Pope Leo XIII (elected the year before) made him a cardinal. Newman has been described as 'unsuccessful in most of his undertakings in the RC Church during his lifetime', but as having had a vast influence upon the restoration of Roman Catholicism in England.[1]

Newman was, as well as a thinker and theologian, a consummate communicator. His literary skills are evident in his essays and works of persuasion, of which the best are his contributions to the *Tracts for the Times*; the *Essay on the Development of Christian Doctrine* (1845), which was a defence of his change from Anglicanism to Catholicism in that year; *The Idea of a University Defined and Illustrated* (1873), which brought together his ideas on Christian education, from his Dublin experience onwards; and *A Grammar of Assent* (1870). His masterpiece in this genre is, however, generally accepted to be the *Apologia pro Vita Sua* (1864), a powerful response to unjust criticisms that had been levelled at him by the Revd Charles Kingsley (who had suggested that Newman did not feel it necessary, as a Catholic, to speak the truth). The response, after the initial exchange of letters, took the form of a moving autobiography, written in a clear and accessible style.

One must not forget Newman's devotional writings and in particular those that were posthumously collected in the volume *Meditations and Devotions* (1893). These are simple, straightforward expressions of Christian truth, encapsulating profound and often complicated concepts within forms of expression that are easily understood. As in his early sermons from his Anglican period, the teacher and communicator can be sensed in these texts.[2]

Newman wrote successfully in the genres of 'la grande littérature' too. His is among the best Christian poetry of its time and his two novels are not negligible. At its best, his poetry combines a profound religious sensibility with a firm and controlled sense of literary taste and moderation. There is not a touch, here, of the crass sentimentality that was to mar so much Catholic poetry then and since. His masterpiece, the long poem *The Dream of Gerontius* (1865), was inspired by the Requiem Offices, which play a large part within it. It is a depiction of a just soul leaving the body at death and being received into heaven. Its incorporation of the liturgy into the body of the poem is very effective, as for example in the opening juxtaposition of the words of the dying man and the intercessions of the 'Assistants'. Interwoven with these liturgical episodes, we have Newman's powerful and effective depiction of the dying man's feelings and experiences. Take, for example, the man's panic at approaching death:

> I can no more; for now it comes again,
> That sense of ruin, which is worse than pain,
> That masterful negation and collapse
> Of all that makes me man; as though I bent
> Over the dizzy brink
> Of some sheer infinite descent;
> Or worse, as though
> Down, down for ever I was falling through
> The solid framework of created things, and needs must sink and sink

Into the vast abyss. And, crueller still,
A fierce and restless fright begins to fill
The mansion of my soul . . .
O Jesu, help! pray for me, Mary, pray!
Some angel, Jesu! such as came to Thee
In Thine own agony . . .
Mary, pray for me. Joseph, pray for me. Mary, pray for me.[3]

Newman also inserted, within the text of *Gerontius*, poems that were to become two of his most famous hymns, 'Praise to the Holiest in the height', and 'Firmly I believe and truly'. *Verses on Various Occasions* (1868) contains many examples of successful Christian poems from his earlier, pre-conversion period, including 'The Pillar of Cloud' ('Lead, kindly light').

Newman's novels are not on the same level as his poetry; but one of them is certainly far better than most other English Catholic novels written in the second half of the nineteenth century. *Loss and Gain: The Story of a Convert* (1848) was Newman's response to aspersions Elizabeth Furlong Shipton Harris cast upon the recent Oxford converts in her novel *From Oxford to Rome: And How It Fared With Some Who Lately Made The Journey* (1847). This novel, though indescribably boring, was rightly seen by Newman as a challenge to his own integrity, and that of his fellow-converts. It described Tractarian clergymen who, after many uncertainties and agonies, were finally converted to Catholicism – and only then realized 'that the image showing so fairly in their minds, of a Church whose stones were silver, and out of whose hills they might dig fine gold – a Church abounding with olive-oil and honey', had turned out to be a mirage, which was merely 'the result of an unclear atmosphere playing over a lake of water less pure, or a land whose soil was less wholesome than that they possessed already'.[4] As with Kingsley's attack, Newman's response was immediate. As he later wrote, he decided that 'the suitable answer lay . . . in the publication of a second tale; drawn up with a stricter regard to truth and probability, and with at least some personal knowledge of Oxford, and some perception of the various aspects of the religious phenomenon, which the work in question handled so rudely and so unskilfully.'[5] This, though a 'conversion novel' of the type common in both French and English Catholic literature from now on, was also a weapon of controversy. As such, its depiction of the dilemmas facing the potential converts is convincing, as are the dialogues, which are often lively and entertaining, when the depiction of such complex arguments might so easily have become unwieldy. Above all, Newman shows the dilemmas such converts faced: the losses they sustained, the uncertainties as to whether they had taken the right path – and finally (as opposed to Elizabeth Harris's ending) the inestimable gains of coming home to the bosom of Mother Church. Newman had managed to turn a weapon of controversy into a very readable novel. There are moments in it that are profoundly moving, such as the hero's experience at Benediction at the end of the novel, where in the presence of the Blessed Sacrament he becomes fully aware of the Catholic truth that has been beckoning to him:

> A cloud of incense was rising on high; the people all suddenly bowed low; what could it mean? The truth flashed on him, fearfully yet sweetly; it was the Blessed Sacrament – it was the Lord Incarnate who was on the altar, who had come to visit and to bless His people. It was the Great Presence, which makes a Catholic church different from every other place in the world; which makes it, as no other place can be, holy.[6]

Callista: A Sketch of the Third Century (1856) is less successful. It was one of a series of stories of the early Christian martyrs that had been commissioned, as weapons of propaganda, by Cardinal Wiseman (whose own *Fabiola: A Tale of the Catacombs* had appeared in 1854). *Callista*, with its story of the difficulties faced by a girl living in pagan society who is attracted to Christianity but uncertain about conversion to what was deemed a subversive religion, is a kind of historical counterpart to some of the problems faced by a Catholic convert from Anglicanism in *Loss and Gain* – though of course the stakes were far higher, and for Callista included martyrdom. It has however none of the living immediacy of Newman's other novel. It is written in a ponderous, pseudo-historical style, epitomized by addresses to the reader such as the following:

> We are in hopes the reader, as well as Agellius, is attracted by the word Callista, and wishes to know something about her fate; nay, perhaps finds fault with us as having suffered him so long to content himself with the chance and secondhand information which Jucundus or Juba has supplied. If we have been wanting in due consideration for him, we now trust to make up for it.[7]

Despite this, *Callista* is one of the better examples of the genre, at times containing lively conversations and even humorous effects. Nevertheless, amid Newman's outstanding literary output in essay form and poetry, it has to be admitted that his two novels stand on a lower level.

Newman's reputation grew as the years went by. In France, in particular, there was great interest in his writings in the twentieth century. Their major impact in France was in the 1900s, at the time of the Modernist crisis,[8] when Catholic thinkers such as Henri Bremond found much to admire in Newman's ideas and attitudes.[9] But not only Modernists found Newman's writings appealing. That firm traditionalist Paul Claudel often referred to Newman's works (theological, poetic and novelistic) with approval.[10] Newman's appeal was also strong in British Catholicism. His shadow falls over many later Catholic writers – both for the power of his thought and his spirituality and for the literary inspiration of his writings. Sadly, the literary quality of most of the Catholic writing that immediately succeeded him, both in poetry and in fiction, tended to be singularly poor.

Lesser Catholic Novelists: sentimentality and overt didacticism

The 'Catholic novel' was to become, in the twentieth century, one of the most successful genres in English Catholic Literature. Its beginnings in the nineteenth century (apart from Newman's *Loss and Gain*) were not auspicious. Most of the novels written in this period were eminently forgettable (and have been forgotten). One of their besetting sins was sentimentality. Cardinal Wiseman's *Fabiola* is a case in point. As one eminent Jesuit, who edited a reprint of *Fabiola* in 1962, has said: 'The dialogue is stilted and the Roman martyrs are out of place in the world of Little Lord Fauntleroy . . .. I find the dialogue cloying and the atmosphere of Wiseman's Rome almost too chaste'.[11]

Around the same time, a number of fairly un-literary authors attempted Catholic novels of modern life which were of a similar kind. The atmosphere of these novels is usually indicated by their titles: Cecilia Caddell's *Home and the Homeless* (1858) and *Never Forgotten* (1871), J. C. Heywood's *How will it end?* (1872) and Agnes Stewart's *The Cousins: or Pride and Vanity* (1849) and *Eustace, or Self-devotion* (1860) are all good examples. The last of these titles illustrates that such sentimentality was not restricted to Catholic literature, as it clearly aped the title of Dean Farrar's moral tale *Eric, or Little by Little*, which had appeared two years before. There is no doubt that virtuous Catholic literature of this kind reflected more general Victorian tastes.

Novelists such as Emily Agnew (*Geraldine: A Tale of Conscience*, 1839 and numerous other novels stretching into the 1860s) combined this tone with an extreme form of didacticism. Her *Rome and the Abbey: A Tale of Conscience* (1849), which is typical of her output as a whole, provides many examples of the unrealistic and often clumsy episodes of 'teaching' that permeated a number of novels of this period. Much of this novel consists of the lessons given to characters, such as a young girl named Lilia, by various figures including the Jesuit Father Duago. A typical exchange is as follows:

'It was nearly a year ago, [said Lilia] that Father Duago taught me the doctrine of the Trinity in the Unity of God. He then said that God's contemplation of his own perfection was not a barren abstraction, but a fruitful production, for that the perfect image of Himself was the instantaneous consequence . . . I further learned at that time that the mutual love of these two Divine Persons produced instantaneously a third Divine Person; so that the Divinity has contained from all eternity three Persons – all holy, wise and powerful, one as the other – God being in three parts.'

'The last expression is your own, I conclude?', said Mr Terrison.

'Yes', replied Lilia. 'When I think that God has chosen to be in three parts, I find it easier to understand the equality of His Trinity.'

'Perhaps the expression "God *is* in three parts" may be admissible', said Mr Terrison, 'but you must be careful not to say that God is *divided* into three parts, for the Church adores the holy and undivided Trinity.'[12]

Such grotesque excesses are the extreme, but there is no doubt that a desire to inform pervades the Catholic novels of the late nineteenth century, as does a very Victorian penchant for a literature of pious sentiment. Of these authors and others like them, one can only repeat what a Catholic reviewer said one such novel in *The Month* in 1874: 'A bad novel is a bad novel . . . Trash is trash, in whatever form it presents itself, and Catholic trash is the worst of all.'[13]

Margaret Maison and Thomas Woodman have rightly pointed out that certain novelists such as Edward Dering, Canon William Barry and 'John Oliver Hobbes' (Pearl Craigie) did manage in differing ways to rise above much of the Catholic narrative fiction around them,[14] but even they failed to compete with the secular literature of their time and are little remembered today. It is worth singling out two typical, if late, examples to illustrate the weaknesses that existed in such literature: Canon William Barry's *Arden Massiter* (1900) and Pearl Craigie's *Robert Orange* (1900).

Two Typical Novels: *Arden Massiter* and *Robert Orange*

One must beware of classifying as Catholic novels what are merely novels written by Catholics, containing little in the way of religious content, or else merely using Catholic details as picturesque props. Canon William Barry's *Arden Massiter* is an exotic tale of dark intrigue, set in Italy, involving the secret society the Camorra. Its sensational and over-complicated plot, featuring sinister castles full of dark memories ('Udolpho' being evoked on a number of occasions by the first-person narrator),[15] is written in a grandiose style, stuffed with obscure allusions. It has been suggested that 'social

Catholicism' is viewed sympathetically in the novel, yet the theme of the plight of the poor (here mainly associated with a Protestant Socialist hero) has little place in the main plot of the novel (the hero's socialism appearing mainly to be used as an explanation for how he had met the anarchist villain in London).[16] The novel deals above all with the political situation in post-unification Italy, with anarchists, aristocratic papal state traditionalists and many other disaffected groups reacting, at times together, against Piedmontese rule. One of the most striking scenes features the popular riots in Rome at the time of the Italian defeat by the Abyssinians at Adowa.[17] Catholicism is introduced into the novel in the form of 'local colour', much as in other contemporary secular novels set in Italy, such as, in more whimsical vein, Henry Harland's *The Cardinal's Snuff-Box* (1900). The supernatural is mostly invoked here in the form of belief in the 'evil eye' and unavoidable destiny, and in the Camorra members' allegiance to a Neapolitan shrine of the Virgin Mary. It is true that the virginal heroine Costanza is depicted as extremely devout and as having withstood the sexual demands of the villain by going into a deep faint or coma (which those hearing of it describe as 'a miracle') but nothing further is made of this. No religious message is ever proffered. Indeed, contemporary reviews made no mention of religion, the author's aims being described in one of them as follows:

> It is a story of lust, rapine and bloodshed, of Anarchists and banditti, of secret compacts, of miracles and superstitions; but it aims, in a rather highly coloured fashion, to picture some of the forces at work in modern Italy and to contrast the survival of rank mediaevalism with the bustle and practicality that may be seen on the surface of things in the capital.[18]

The major strand of Catholic narrative fiction in the late nineteenth century consisted of novels of modern life, often containing crises of conscience by the main characters, when their Catholic belief and duty came into conflict with their human desires. These have been classified by Woodman as 'renunciation novels'.[19] As Margaret Maison has put it:

> The renouncement of earthly affection proved a popular theme, and tales of a conflict between passion and principle, describing a kind of heroine-lover-faith triangle, were in great demand throughout the century.[20]

Sadly, most of the novels of this type tended to have boring, clumsily-contrived plots and unconvincing characterization. As the century progressed, however, a small number of writers began to write rather more successfully, though continuing weaknesses tended to mar the genre, as in *The School for*

Saints (1897) and its sequel *Robert Orange* (1900), by the recently converted 'John Oliver Hobbes' (the pseudonym of the female writer Pearl Craigie). These two novels appear, at first sight, to have a certain amount to offer us. Craigie sets out to create a Trollopian study of English upper-class life and high politics revolving around the House of Commons. Into this she inserts two further themes: the conversion to Catholicism of the central character, the up-and-coming politician Robert Orange and his eventual decision to become a priest; and Robert's love for a devout young girl named Brigit and their renunciation of each other, on the very day of their wedding, because her husband, thought to be dead, turns out to be alive. Stated so baldly, these themes sound very promising but that promise is not fulfilled. Orange's motivation, in relation to his renunciation of Brigit when her husband's survival is revealed, is never properly explored. Indeed, the depiction of this dilemma seems to have more to do with social convention (including the social shame of the situation) than with religion. The treatment of renunciation, a favourite theme of Craigie's throughout her career (pre-dating her conversion), differs little from the way it was dealt with in her earlier secular novels.[21] When, at the end of *Robert Orange*, the husband eventually really dies, Orange has already made his decision to become a priest and he does not know of the husband's death. Brigit decides not to get in touch with him and this form of Christian renunciation is one of the most convincing and well-motivated religious moments in the novel. Throughout the rest of the two books, however, there is no clear or coherent explanation of motives. A duel towards the end of *Robert Orange*, in which Robert kills a man, has tenuous connection to the main plot (and appears not to raise any ethical issues for this Catholic convert). A Ruritanian-style subplot, revolving around the 'Alberian' embassy, adds unnecessary 'aristocratic' glamour to the plot, as does the fact that Orange is in fact a French nobleman, and Brigit an Alberian princess. The political issues of the day are rarely properly explored and the emotional relationships between the various characters seem to alter at whim. All in all, these two novels make puzzling reading, even though one commentator has reported of *Robert Orange* that 'the sincerity and spiritual power of this story made its impact at once', and that 'it was hailed as one of the finest Catholic novels of the age'.[22]

The appearance of Mrs Wilfrid Ward's *One Poor Scruple* in 1899, one year before *Robert Orange*, was to open a new age of the Catholic novel. A number of similar works henceforth competed reasonably successfully with the secular literature of the day.[23]

Problems of Nineteenth-Century Catholic Poetry

Over the ages, there has been a lot of successful religious poetry, capable of vying with the best in secular literature. However, there is a tendency for religious poetry to descend, without due care, into depths of banality and sentimentality. Run-of-the-mill Catholic poetry, in the nineteenth century in both England and France, was only too prone to such dangers. Taut, allusive, *literary* religious poetry of Catholic import has existed throughout the ages, but only too often in the mid-nineteenth century the apparatus of contemporary Catholic 'Italianate' piety could lend itself to sugary vulgarity.

A rather better poet than most, who nevertheless could at times give way to such weaknesses, was Aubrey de Vere (1814–1902). His Catholic poetry is on the whole far less impressive than his secular poetry. This product of the Anglo-Irish Protestant ascendancy came under the influence of Newman in Oxford, though he was not converted to Catholicism until 1857. In the meantime the Irish famine years of 1845–9 had brought home to him his country's plight and he wrote extensively on this, particularly in his book *English Misrule and Irish Misdeeds* (1848). His country was to inspire some of his most powerful poetry. A very good example is the poem 'Róisín Dubh' (Black Rose). This had been the title of a famous song written in the sixteenth century, in which the female figure of the Black Rose is a metaphor for Ireland in her struggle against England. De Vere's poem makes the Black Rose a much less overtly political, but far more tragic figure, with the losses of the Great Famine very much in mind. The Biblical allusions are particularly effective: the Massacre of the Innocents, followed by the suggestion that the dark Rose will eventually be able to rejoice as Miriam did after the engulfing of Pharaoh's host in the Red Sea. This vision of a future time carries over into the last stanza – but the last two lines bring us back to the ghastly present:

> O who art thou with that queenly brow
> And uncrowned head?
> And why is the vest that binds thy breast,
> O'er the heart, blood-red?
> Like a rose-bud in June that spot at noon,
> A rose-bud weak;
> But it deepens and grows like a July rose:
> Death-pale thy cheek.
>
> 'The babes I fed at my foot lay dead;
> I saw them die;

> In Ramah a blast went wailing past;
> It was Rachel's cry.
> But I stand sublime on the shores of Time,
> And I pour mine ode,
> As Miriam sang to the cymbals' clang,
> On the wind to God.
>
> 'Once more at my feasts my bards and priests
> Shall sit and eat:
> And the Shepherd whose sheep are on every steep
> Shall bless my meat;
> Oh, sweet, men say, is the song by day,
> And the feast by night;
> But on poisons I thrive, and in death survive
> Through ghostly night.'[24]

'Róisín Dubh', with the female figure at its centre, lends itself well to comparisons with de Vere's Catholic poetry, in which, as in so many nineteenth-century Catholic poets, a Marian devotion is central. The dangers we have noted take over in poems such as 'Mater Salvatoris', 'Sancta Maria' and 'Mater Christi'. In them, the liberal use of exclamation marks draws our attention to the shortcomings of the content and tone:

> O heart with His in just accord!
> O Soul His echo, tone for tone!
> O Spirit that heard, and kept His word!
> O Countenance moulded like His own!
>
> Behold, she seemed on earth to dwell;
> But, hid in light, alone she sat
> Beneath the Throne ineffable,
> Chanting her clear Magnificat.[25]

One is tempted, on looking at the decline in de Vere's poetic gift, to think of the pop singer who, asked if he could think of a title for a piece of Christian pop music, suggested, 'I found Jesus and lost my talent'.

If de Vere shows us the deleterious effect of stock Catholic expression in the work of an otherwise effective poet, Father Frederick William Faber (1814–63) provides a rather more complicated picture. Faber left the Anglican priesthood for the Catholic Church one month after John Henry Newman and in 1847 was ordained priest. In 1848, when Newman founded the Oratory of St Philip Neri in Birmingham, Faber placed himself under him as a novice. In 1849 Newman sent him to found the Oratory in London and Faber remained Head of that community until the end of his short life. In the years 1850–63 he wrote a series of works on the spiritual life, which were printed, reprinted and translated, so that throughout Western Europe, rightly or wrongly, he became known as 'a master in mystical theology'.[26] His was a spirituality which owed a great deal to the Italian influence in the English Church of the 1850s, with its concentration on liturgical pomp and its intense devotion to the Blessed Sacrament and to the Blessed Virgin Mary. For this and for many other reasons, Faber's writings commended themselves particularly to the writers of the French Catholic Revival. Léon Bloy's diary, for example, is full of quotations from these works.

When it comes to poetry, Faber had one advantage: he did not see himself as a poet. His numerous hymns were written for a purpose. As he said in his preface to *Jesus and Mary* (1849), he had felt the need for a collection of hymns suitable for singing. But he had at first believed that 'the Author's ignorance of music appeared in some measure to disqualify him for the work of supplying the defect'. Nevertheless, eleven were written for special occasions and proved very popular. Modestly, while mentioning the numerous applications that had been made for copies of them, he expressed surprise that this was so, 'in spite of very glaring literary defects, such as careless grammar or slipshod metre', and presumed that this must be because 'people were anxious to have Catholic hymns of any sort.' So he wrote many more and having been informed by a musical friend that almost all these hymns 'would do for singing', had decided to publish them.[27]

Many of Faber's hymns remain popular to the present day. While much of his output shares the same sugary approach that we have seen in de Vere's Marian poems, there are also one or two grand statements which accord more with modern taste, such as 'My God, how wonderful thou art' and 'Hark! Hark, my soul'. In some other hymns, an almost childlike form of expression can palliate what would otherwise be mawkish effects, as in the moving post-Communion hymn 'Jesus, gentlest Saviour'. Father Faber was not a great poet and knew himself not to be; but in his hymns he created something fitted to a purpose; and some of his verse has lasted better than that of far more accomplished poets of his time.

Coventry Patmore

Coventry Patmore (1823–96) – a name to conjure with in Catholic circles in his time – is now almost unread (except in Paul Claudel's excellent French prose and verse translations of some of his poems, which came out in 1911,[28] and which are still read by Claudel enthusiasts). This modern neglect is in some respects unjust.

Patmore had written a great deal of poetry before his conversion in 1864, two years after the death of his wife. In 1844 he had published a volume simply entitled *Poems*, and between 1854 and 1856 he had produced a long sequence of poems, *The Angel in the House*, a paean of praise for married love, which was dedicated to his wife. While much of this early poetry does not particularly appeal to modern taste, the Victorian public was very enthusiastic about *The Angel in the House*. One critic has said that in it 'Patmore captured the Victorian fancy with his somewhat too slippered description of love and married life'.[29]

His post-conversion collection *To the Unknown Eros* (1877–8) was unlikely to have appealed to the same public. With it, however, Patmore became a central figure in Catholic literary circles and particularly in the group that gathered around Alice Meynell, where he also became friendly with Francis Thompson.[30] Alice Meynell was in part responsible for the public interest in Patmore's Catholic poetry. Patmore, who was obsessed with achieving formal and intellectual perfection in his poetry, entered, in the 1880s, into an extended correspondence with Gerard Manley Hopkins, whose advice he sought upon a number of his drafts.

To the Unknown Eros contains poetry of high seriousness, written in a form of free verse that looked forward to the poetry of the twentieth century. In both these respects it was a considerable improvement on his secular poetry. Though it has little in the way of overt Catholic imagery and symbolism, it addresses recognizable Catholic themes, particularly in the poet's concern to relate human love (even erotic love) to Divine Love. This concern echoes the French Dominican Lacordaire's statement 'There are not two forms of love', a statement that was highly influential on Paul Claudel. Patrick McCarthy, who has written of the relationship between Claudel and Coventry Patmore, Alice Meynell and Francis Thompson, has suggested that it was this that provided Claudel's enthusiasm for Patmore: 'Central to Patmore, as to Claudel, is the notion of human love as foreshadowing the love of God.'[31]

One of the shorter poems, 'Vesica Pescis',[32] is a good example of Patmore's art. It echoes the story of one of Christ's miracles, in which the fishermen, having toiled all night in vain, are told to cast their nets once more. The poem elaborates on the story, with this fisherman finally catching the hidden Divinity, who tells him the poet's task. The verse form is typical of the best of Patmore in its skilful use of the effects that can be created by free verse and in its gradual and dramatic build-up to the words 'But Thee!':

In strenuous hope I wrought,
And hope seem'd still betray'd;
Lastly I said,
'I have labour'd through the Night, nor yet
Have taken aught;
But at Thy word I will again cast forth the net!'
And, lo, I caught
(Oh, quite unlike and quite beyond my thought,)
Not the quick, shining harvest of the Sea,
For food, my wish,
But Thee!
Then, hiding even in me,
As hid was Simon's coin within the fish,
Thou sigh'd'st, with joy, 'Be dumb,
Or speak but of forgotten things to far-off times to come.'[33]

The best-known of all the poems in *To the Unknown Eros* is 'The Toys', which appears in many anthologies. In it the poet, who has dealt severely with his child, goes to his room and finds him surrounded by his favourite toys, 'to comfort his sad heart'. The poet prays to God that when we die, he should remember 'of what toys we made our joys', and how weakly we had understood what he wished of us:

Then, fatherly not less
Than I whom Thou hast moulded from the clay,
Thou'lt leave Thy wrath, and say,
'I will be sorry for their childishness.'[34]

Despite its element of Victorian sentimentality, this poem succeeds in its moving message of Christian humility and of God's forgiveness. Claudel, who included it in his translations, was clearly influenced by it (both by its tone and message and by its use of the image of childhood toys), in his own poem 'Le jour des cadeaux' (so untypical of all the rest of Claudel's powerful and often declamatory verse).[35]

Patmore struck quite a figure among his Catholic contemporaries. The quality of his Catholic poetry is a cut above most of their work (with the exception of that of Gerard Manley Hopkins, at which we will be looking in the next chapter).

It has to be said that the beginnings of the Catholic literary revival were not particularly auspicious. Newman's brilliant contributions to literature were in no way matched by his immediate successors. The Catholic novel got off to a disastrously bad start and there was little in the way of effective Catholic poetry published in the years 1850–90 (the only major Catholic poet, Gerard Manley Hopkins, being unknown and unpublished in his own lifetime). The first outward signs of anything of literary value came in the realm of poetry, first with Patmore and then in the 1890s, in the writings of Francis Thompson, Lionel Johnson and Alice Meynell. The novel had to wait a few years longer, until the new century, when it became a major genre which was to go through many transformations.

Notes

1 *Oxford Dictionary of the Christian Church*.
2 A. N. Wilson includes extracts from some of Newman's most inspiring devotional writings in his anthology *John Henry Newman: Prayers, Poems and Meditations* (2007).
3 John Henry Newman, *The Dream of Gerontius*, 1866, reprinted in *Verses on Various Occasions* (1868), pp. 293–340.
4 Elizabeth Furlong Shipton Harris, *From Oxford to Rome*, p. 170.
5 Newman, 'Advertisement to the Sixth Edition', in *Loss and Gain* (1874).
6 Newman, *Loss and Gain*, part 3, chapter 10. As Woodman points out (*Faithful Fictions*, p. 6), 'Anglicans found a special impressiveness about the service of Benediction, a ceremony fostered by the Italian party and quite unlike anything in the contemporary Church of England'. It was clearly not just the ceremonial that impressed Newman, however, but above all the deeper meaning of the service and the actual presence of Christ in the Host (so different from contemporary Anglican beliefs). As Ian Ker observes, 'It is striking how it is the reservation of the Sacrament in the tabernacle in Catholic churches that more than anything else impressed and moved Newman.' (Ian Ker, *The Catholic Revival in English Literature, 1845–1961*, p. 19).
7 Newman, *Callista*, p. 213.
8 See C. J. T. Talar, 'Newman in France during the Modernist period', *Newman Studies Journal*, 22, 1 (Spring 2005).
9 See Maurice Nédoncelle and Jean Dagens (eds), *Entretiens sur Henri Bremond* (Paris – La Haye: Mouton, 1967). See particularly the contributions 'Newman selon Bremond' by Maurice Nédoncelle and 'Bremond et le modernisme' by Émile Poulat.
10 In his diaries he quotes many of the ideas expressed in Newman's *Meditations and Devotions*. He advised Gide to read *An Essay on the Development of Christian Doctrine* and was bowled over by the *Apologia pro Vita Sua*. He often quoted from *Loss and Gain*; and, as a poet and dramatist, he particularly savoured *The Dream of Gerontius*, describing it as 'An admirable psychagogical poem' and noting its similarity with his own dramatic procedures. A number of critics have drawn attention to *Gerontius'* influence on certain specific scenes in Claudel's *Le Soulier*

de Satin; but it is also possible to see a more general influence of it upon Claudel's methods of incorporation of the liturgy into his early dramatic works.

11   Bernard Basset, SJ, introduction to Nicholas Wiseman, *Fabiola* (1962 edition), p. viii.

12   Emily C. Agnew, *Rome and the Abbey: A Tale of Conscience*, pp. 79–80.

13   *The Month*, 1894, quoted in Margaret Maison, *The Victorian Vision*, p. 155.

14   Margaret Maison, *The Victorian Vision: Studies in the Religious Novel* (1961); Thomas Woodman, *Faithful Fictions: The Catholic Novel in British Literature* (1991).

15   Ann Radcliffe's *The Mysteries of Udolpho* (1794) was a prime example of the 'Gothic' novel, centring round a mysterious castle. Jane Austen's *Northanger Abbey* is a parody of such literature, in which the heroine's over-heated imagination has been fired by reading *The Mysteries of Udolpho*.

16   Typically, the only 'Catholic' comment on the social question occurs when a political Cardinal, asked by Massiter to get the Church to support the values of the Sermon on the Mount, uses this as an occasion to comment on the way in which the Church, whose priests are 'victims' themselves, and 'eat our scanty bread with tears', has been despoiled by the Italian State (William Barry, *Arden Massiter*, pp. 16–17).

17   Up-to-date material indeed, as Adowa took place in 1896, only four years before this novel appeared.

18   *New York Times*, 5 May 1900.

19   See Woodman, *Faithful Fictions*, pp. 9–19 and passim.

20   Margaret Maison, *The Victorian Vision*, p. 159.

21   See, for example, *Some Emotions and a Moral* (1891) and *A Study in Temptations* (1893).

22   Margaret Maison, *John Oliver Hobbes: Her Life and Work*, p. 41.

23   For Mrs Wilfrid Ward, see pp. 62–5.

24   Aubrey de Vere, 'Róisín Dubh'.

25   Aubrey de Vere, 'Mater Salvatoris', *May Carols* (1857).

26   'Frederick William Faber', *Catholic Encyclopedia*.

27   Father Faber, preface to *Jesus and Mary* (1849).

28   Paul Claudel, *Poëmes de Coventry Patmore* (Paris: NRF, 1912). These translations had appeared the previous year in the *Nouvelle Revue Française*, Sep–Oct 1911.

29   Francis Beauchesne Thornton, *Return to Tradition*, p. 85.

30   For Alice Meynell and Francis Thompson, see pp. 54–6.

31   Patrick McCarthy, 'Claudel, Patmore and Alice Meynell: some contacts with English Catholicism', p. 177. See also Marius-François Guyard's study of the influence of Patmore upon Claudel, 'De l'Eros Inconnu aux Grandes Odes' (1963), passim.

32   This was one of the poems translated by Claudel.

33   Coventry Patmore, 'Vesica Pescis', in *The Unknown Eros* (1877); in *The Poems of Coventry Patmore*, p. 390.

34   Coventry Patmore, 'The Toys', in ibid., pp. 365–6.

35   Paul Claudel, 'Le jour des cadeaux', *Corona Benignitatis Anni Dei* (1915). I am grateful to the late Gilbert Gadoffre for drawing to my attention these two poems by Patmore and Claudel.

4

A Solitary Genius,
Gerard Manley Hopkins

Gerard Manley Hopkins (1844–89) stands as a poet outside time. He was almost unknown in his lifetime, but was to become a major influence upon the poets of the twentieth century, where he was recognized to be revolutionary in his poetic techniques and highly original in the subject matter he treated. Though he wrote most of his poetry between 1876 and 1889, it was not until 1918, almost thirty years after his death, that his friend the poet Robert Bridges finally produced an edition of most of his verse. Apparently Bridges had waited until he felt the public was ready for Hopkins' unusual poetry. It is true that this poetry was to have a far greater appeal for a twentieth-century readership than it would have had in its own day.

He came from an Anglican family and had a brilliant undergraduate career at Balliol College, Oxford (one of his tutors being Walter Pater). While at Oxford he came under the influence of the Tractarian movement, before being received by John Henry Newman into the Catholic Church in 1866. After taking his degree he became for a short time a schoolmaster at the Oratory School under Newman, but in 1868 he decided to train to become a Jesuit priest and also to burn all the poetry he had written up to that time. The last stage of his Jesuit training (1874–7) took place at St Beuno's College, North Wales. This was to be crucial to his development as a poet. While there, he learned Welsh and came to appreciate the forms of medieval Welsh verse. In 1875 he was inspired, by the shipwreck in which a group of nuns exiled by Germany's penal laws had perished, to start writing poetry once more, with the famous poem 'The Wreck of the *Deutschland*', of which David Jones has said that it is 'one of the most exciting poems in the English language.'[1]

Over the next seven years, 1877–84, he was to fill a series of posts either as curate or schoolmaster, and continued to write poetry. In 1884 the Order sent him to be Professor of Greek and Latin literature at the Royal University of Ireland, Dublin (the Catholic University). There he felt keen misery and his poetry from the period shows a sense of deep despair. He died of typhoid there in 1889. Robert Bridges published eleven of his poems as part of an anthology in 1893, and six poems in 1915; but it was not until 1918 that he produced *Poems of Gerard Manley Hopkins*, and that Hopkins became generally known.

Hopkins's poetry was revolutionary in form. The most striking thing about it, at first sight, is its rhythms. He had developed a new method of writing poetry, which he called 'sprung rhythm'. This rejects the regularity of usual English verse and scans, as Hopkins said, 'by accent or stress alone, without any account of the number of syllables, so that a foot may be one strong syllable, or it may be many light and one strong'.[2] In this way traditional metrical patterns are removed and one can have any number of syllables in each line. The only constraint is that it should *sound* right – and Hopkins was particularly keen that his poetry should be read aloud. At times he used accent marks over certain syllables, in order to produce the right effects.

This type of verse is closer to the patterns of ordinary speech than traditional English verse. Various sources for his inspiration have been pointed to: the patterns of Hebrew poetry, as found in the Psalms; the quantitative metre of Greek verse, with which Hopkins was so well acquainted;[3] the highlighting of stress in the cynghanedd form of medieval Welsh poetry;[4] Old English poetry; the liturgy. The fact remains that this form was highly original in the nineteenth century context. Hopkins wrote, in a letter to Robert Bridges:

> Why do I employ sprung rhythm at all? Because it is the nearest to the rhythm of prose, that is the native and natural rhythm of speech, the least forced, the most rhetorical and emphatic of all possible rhythms, combining, as it seems to me, opposite and, one would have thought, incompatible excellences, markedness of rhythm – that is rhythm's self – and naturalness of expression.[5]

Within these rhythms, further powerful effects are achieved by extensive use of alliteration, assonance and onomatopoeia.

Focus on form can, however, distract attention from what Hopkins was writing about – which was equally original. His keen observation of nature (his journals are full of closely described details of the natural scene around him) led him to use nature to express profound truths. Usually, this expression was not direct, with natural objects being used as intellectual symbols, so much as indirect, with what he called 'inscape' evoking 'the individual or essential quality of the thing'. In this he was influenced by his reading of the medieval philosopher Duns Scotus, who believed that however distinctive individual 'particular' things may appear to us in their 'thisness', they only make sense when we place them in relation to their essence, or 'whatness'. In other words, their particularity can reveal their essence. 'Inscape' was, in Hopkins's view, facilitated by 'instress' – those characteristics within an 'inscape' that make an effect upon the mind of the person observing it.[6]

This is where Hopkins's Catholicism is most fully expressed in his poetry. The presence of God in the nature he has created is stressed in poem after poem. In 'Pied Beauty', for example, the poet's detailed list of all the things in nature that share the characteristic of being 'dappled' ends with a clear reference to the creator of the world, whom we must praise. The poem also owes to Duns Scotus the concept of the particularity of these individual parts of creation, in contrast with the unchanging nature, 'past change', of God, who created their essence:

> Glory be to God for dappled things –
> For skies of couple-colour as a brinded cow;
> For rose-moles all in stipple upon trout that swim;
> Fresh-firecoal chestnut-falls; finches' wings;
> Landscape plotted and pieced – fold, fallow and plough;
> And áll trádes, their gear and tackle and trim.
> All things counter, original, spare, strange;
> Whatever is fickle, freckled (who knows how?)
> With swift, slow; sweet, sour; adazzle, dim;
> He fathers-forth whose beauty is past change;
>   Praise him.

Alongside simpler poems that evoke individual scenes from nature, there are others that explore quite complicated issues, using Nature always as their touchstone. A good example is 'That Nature is a Heraclitean Fire and of the Comfort of the Resurrection'. This poem, written in the last year of Hopkins's life, deals with the philosopher Heraclitus's belief that everything in the material world stems from the element of fire, and is therefore perpetually changing and moving. The poem starts with a powerful evocation of this perpetually changing world, through the effects cast by passing clouds (note the effective use of alliteration):

> Cloud-puffball, torn tufts, tossed pillows | flaunt forth, then chevy
>   on an air-
> built thoroughfare: heaven-roysterers, in gay-gangs | they throng;
>   they glitter in marches.
> Down roughcast, down dazzling whitewash, | wherever an elm arches,
> Shivelights and shadowtackle in long | lashes lace, lance and pair.

Further descriptions of ever-changing nature are now given, ending with a clear reference to Heraclitus: 'Million-fuelèd, | nature's bonfire burns on'. We now turn to man, as a part of the same nature. But suddenly, the poet rebels at this: 'Enough!', man is not like the rest of nature. Christ's resurrection has brought him stability and immortality. The world's Heraclitean fire is now just ash and from being a mere 'Jack', or joke, Man has become an 'immortal diamond':

> Enough! The Resurrection,
> A heart's-clarion! Away grief's gasping, | joyless days, dejection.
>   Across my foundering deck shone
> A beacon, an eternal beam. | Flesh fade, and mortal trash
> Fall to the residuary worm; | world's wildfire, leave but ash:
>   In a flash, at a trumpet crash,
> I am all at once what Christ is, | since he was what I am, and
> This Jack, joke, poor potsherd, | patch, matchwood, immortal diamond,
>   Is immortal diamond.

As can be seen, many of the beliefs and philosophies underlying Hopkins's poetry are Catholic, that of Duns in particular. Hopkins evokes him in the last line of 'Duns Scotus's Oxford', as the man who 'fired France for Mary without spot'. (Duns, lecturing in Paris, had called for the adoption of the doctrine of the Immaculate Conception – a doctrine dear to Hopkins's heart). There are, however, a small number of poems on specific themes of nineteenth-century Catholic spirituality; these use Catholic imagery in a way that transcends the often mawkish use made of it by other nineteenth-century poets. Two poems on Marian themes, 'The May Magnificat' and 'The Blessed Virgin compared to the Air we Breathe', are as far as one could wish from the run-of-the-mill Marian poetry of the period.

'The May Magnificat' is a beautifully simple poem, in quatrains of short lines, in which the poet conversationally asks himself why May has been called 'Mary's month': 'May is Mary's month, and I / Muse at that and wonder why.' The celebrations of the main events in the Virgin's life, such as Candlemas and Lady Day, have been placed by the Church at times of the year that match the events concerned. So why May? Hopkins suggests asking Mary herself, and the reply is clear:

>   Ask of her, the mighty mother:
>   Her reply puts this other
> Question: What is Spring? –
> Growth in everything.

This is the marvellous time of year when we begin to see everything around us growing:

> Flesh and fleece, fur and feather,
> Grass and greenworld all together;
>   Star-eyed strawberry-breasted
>   Throstle above her nested
>
> Cluster of bugle blue eggs thin
> Forms and warms the life within;
>   And bird and blossom swell
>   In sod or sheath or shell.
>
> All things rising, all things sizing,
> Mary sees, sympathising
>   With that world of good,
>   Nature's motherhood.

Each of these creatures and plants is magnifying the Lord, as Mary did for the child growing within her.

'The Blessed Virgin compared with the Air we Breathe' is based on a conceit (very similar to the kinds of religious conceit used by one of Hopkins's heroes, the Elizabethan Jesuit poet-martyr St Robert Southwell), which casts the Virgin as being, like the air that gives us physical life, the force that maintains our spiritual life. Like 'The May Magnificat', it forms a robust contrast to much of the Marian poetry of its time.

A number of other poems, too, use specifically Catholic imagery. In 'The Bugler's First Communion', we have an example of that mixture of the banal and the holy, the material and the spiritual, which is so typical of the best in Catholic spirituality. The priest fetches the Host (the young boy's 'treat') from the cupboard, while marvelling at the mystery of the presence of Christ in it:

> Here he knelt then in regimental red.
> Forth Christ from cupboard fetched, how fain I of feet
>   To his youngster take his treat!
> Low-latched in leaf-light housel[7] his too huge godhead.

And later in the poem, musing on giving communion to the soldiers, the priest once more speaks of the Host in words of common practicality (the 'ration' being a term suitable for the soldiery, but the 'ration' in this case being royal). The banality of the rhyme scheme, and the obvious word-play and repetitions of the same word, which are so contrary to nineteenth-century concepts of what is suitable to poetry, remind one of sixteenth-century poetic conventions, and of Southwell:[8]

> Then though I should tread tufts of consolation
> Dáys áfter, só I in a sort deserve to
>   And do serve God to serve to
> Just such slips of soldiery Christ's royal ration.

While specifically Catholic themes do appear on the surface of Hopkins' poetry, his Christian spirituality, of a clearly Catholic bent, is expressed most movingly in its depths. Hopkins is a very modern poet in his form, and also a very modern Christian in much of his content. This is most evident in the 'terrible sonnets', which he wrote in Ireland while at his lowest: 'I wake and feel the fell of dark, not day', 'No worst, there is none', 'Not, I'll not, carrion comfort, Despair, not feast on thee'. They combine the mixture of faith, doubt and despair that modern man has found to be an integral part of the religious experience.

In 'No worst, there is none', Hopkins seems to echo the words of Newman's Gerontius as he felt the approach of death and called out for heavenly help.[9] Images of falling are at the centre of this experience in both poems, as are helpless cries to the Blessed Virgin (coupled by Hopkins with the Holy Spirit, 'The Comforter'). But, unlike that of Gerontius, Hopkins' despair is not answered in this poem and there is no transition to light:

> No worst, there is none. Pitched past pitch of grief,
> More pangs will, schooled as forepangs, wilder wring.
> Comforter, where is your comforting?
> Mary, mother of us, where is your relief?
>   My cries heave, herds-long; huddle in a main, a chief-
> woe, world-sorrow; on an age-old anvil wince and sing –
> Then lull, then leave off. Fury had shrieked 'No ling-
> ering! Let me be fell: force I must be brief'.
>   O the mind, mind has mountains; cliffs of fall
> Frightful, sheer, no-man-fathomed. Hold them cheap
> May who ne'er hung there. Nor does long our small
>   Durance deal with that steep or deep. Here! creep,
> Wretch, under a comfort serves in a whirlwind: all
> Life death does end and each day dies with sleep.

The only comfort in this 'whirlwind' is that death will come. 'Not, I'll not, carrion comfort, Despair, not feast on thee', however, presents us with a more positive note. In the first quatrain Hopkins rejects that despair which feasts off his dead emotions and provides a kind of distorted comfort. He will not cry 'can no more'. He *can* hope, *can* look to a new dawning, *can* reject the idea of suicide (evoked in a reference to Hamlet's 'To be or not to be'):

> Not, I'll not, Carrion comfort, Despair, not feast on thee;
> Not untwist – slack they may be – these last strands of man
> In me ór, most weary, cry *I can no more*. I can;
> Can something, hope, wish day come, not choose not to be.

In the second quatrain he turns to God himself, who has 'cast him down'. The imagery from farming is powerful: he, the victim, who was frantic (and here we have a foretaste of Thompson's 'Hound of Heaven') to flee and to avoid God's power, is 'heaped there' like grain on the threshing floor, waiting to be 'fanned':

> But ah, but O thou terrible, why wouldst thou rude on me
> Thy wring-world right foot rock? Lay a lionlimb against me? Scan
> With darksome devouring eyes my bruisèd bones? And fan,
> O in turns of tempest, me heaped there; me frantic to avoid thee and flee?

And now we come to the turning point of the poem: 'Why?' This stark word starts the sestet. In an attempt to explain why God has done this to him, the poet continues to use the image of the threshing-floor. In St Matthew's Gospel we read that God's 'fan is in his hand, and he will thoroughly purge his floor, and gather his wheat into the garner; but he will burn up the chaff with unquenchable fire'.[10] Hopkins uses the same imagery to suggest that perhaps God has put him through all his suffering in order to get rid of all that is impure (the chaff), so that what is left will be his grain, 'sheer and clear'.

The final image of the poem is highly dramatic. Like Jacob wrestling with the angel (or with God), the poet has, since he 'kissed the rod' (the rood, or Cross), been struggling with Christ, 'the hero'. The last line of the poem, with its sudden exclamation in brackets repeating the phrase 'my God!', shows a dawning realization, in Hopkins, that the dreadful struggles of 'that night, that year' in which all had been black for him, had been struggles with God. The emergence, here, from the dead despair of the other 'terrible sonnets' is shown by the phrase 'that year of now done darkness':

Why? That my chaff might fly; my grain lie, sheer and clear.
Nay in all that toil, that coil, since (seems) I kissed the rod,
Hand rather, my heart lo! lapped strength, stole joy, would laugh, chéer.
  Cheer whom though? The hero whose heaven-handling flung me, fóot
  tród,
Me? or me that fought him? O which one? is it each one? That night,
  that year,
Of now done darkness I wretch lay wrestling with (my God!) my God.

Hopkins's powerful later poetry, of which these are two examples, looks forward to the tortured verse of David Gascoyne, and to the mixture of faith and doubt that we find in R. S. Thomas. Here, finally, we find a powerful, original content which matches the revolutionary forms of expression he had devised and points decisively forward to the twentieth century. As the greatest British Catholic poet of the twentieth century, David Jones, has said, Hopkins was:

'as one born out of due time', but before his time (yet how very much *of* his time!) . . . Hopkins stands over so many later artists, saying, in the words of another and pre-eminent living artist: 'And I Tiresias have foresuffered all'.[11]

Notes

1 David Jones, preface to *Epoch and Artist* (1959), p. 15.
2 Quoted in Walford Davies, introduction to Gerard Manley Hopkins, *Poetry and Prose* (1998), p. xiii.
3 Sister Louis-Marie, while a research student of mine, drew attention to Greek verse and the Psalms, as major influences not only on Hopkins, but also, completely independently and coincidentally during the same period, on Paul Claudel's 'verset claudélien', which was equally based on the rhythms of the spoken language. (Claudel had produced excellent translations of plays by Aeschylus.)
4 Walford Davies, introduction to *Poetry and Prose*, pp. xxv–xxvi. See also David Jones's assessment of the influence of Welsh verse-forms upon Hopkins, at various points in *Epoch and Artist*.
5 Letter from Hopkins to Bridges, 21 August 1877.
6 I am particularly indebted to Walford Davies's excellent introduction to his edition of Hopkins's writings, for his succinct account of these issues.
7 The housel is the consecrated elements at the Eucharist and, by extension, the reserved Sacrament.
8 See, for example, a stanza from Southwell's poem 'The Nativity of Christ':
        Gift better than himself, God doth not know:
        Gift better than his God, no man can see:

This gift doth here the giver given bestow:
Gift to this gift let each receiver be.
God is my gift, himself he freely gave me:
God's gift am I, and none but God shall have me.

9   See p. 22–3.
10 Mt. 3.12.
11 David Jones, preface to *The Anathemata*, p. 26. The quotation is, of course, from
    T. S. Eliot's *The Waste Land*.

5

The Generation of the Nineties

A False Start: aesthetic Catholicism

The French converts of the late nineteenth century were often accused of having an 'aesthetic' approach to Christianity. Huysmans, whose secular writings and particularly his novel *A Rebours*, had been at the forefront of the writings of 'decadence', was accused, after his conversion, of being a shallow believer of purely aesthetic leanings. Léon Bloy attacked Huysmans as someone who had 'suddenly discovered Catholicism in a stained-glass window'.[1] Yet while there is no doubt that in Huysmans's writings and in those of a number of his French contemporaries, the beauties of Catholic art are very much to the forefront, for Huysmans these things were clearly allied to a profound religious sense.

The English decadents owed much to French influences, as the allusions to modern French literature in their writing clearly shows; and the works of Huysmans's secular period, before his conversion, were to be very important to them. *A Rebours* (1884), in particular, haunts the writings of Oscar Wilde, from *The Picture of Dorian Gray* to *Salome*. Other secular writings of the French Symbolist generation were regularly quoted, translated and imitated by young British writers such as Ernest Dowson, Vincent O'Sullivan, Theodore Wratislaw, Lord Alfred Douglas and John Gray, while Arthur Symons reflected a French influence not only in his own verse, but also in his groundbreaking study of the French poetic movement, *The Symbolist Movement in Literature* (1899).

It is hardly surprising, then, that Catholicism too should have become a major component in these people's writing. Its aesthetic attractions were merely a part of the hold it had on them; there was also the lure of the exotic and, in a country where anti-Catholicism had become even more prevalent of late, the *frisson* caused by the knowledge that what you were embracing was anathema to much of 'respectable' society.

To what extent was the impact of Catholicism upon the English decadents purely an extension of their admiration for the French writers of the Symbolist generation, so many of whom (Huysmans, Verlaine and Nouveau, for example) had become fervent converts? To what extent was it merely a fascination with the colourful, the artistic, the exotic? Was there any real religious involvement on the part of these authors? The picture is a very mixed one.[2]

The attitudes towards religion taken by Oscar Wilde's hero in *The Picture of Dorian Gray* (1890) could just as easily have been a description of Wilde himself. It tells us much about the impact of Catholic liturgy upon the aesthetic sensibility:

> It was rumoured of him once that he was about to join the Roman Catholic communion; and certainly the Roman ritual had always a great attraction for him. The daily sacrifice, more awful really than all the sacrifices of the antique world, stirred him as much by its superb rejection of the evidence of the senses as by the primitive simplicity of its elements and the eternal pathos of the human tragedy that it sought to symbolise. He loved to kneel down on the cold marble pavement, and watch the priest, in his stiff flowered vestment, slowly and with white hands moving aside the veil of the tabernacle, or raising aloft the jewelled lantern-shaped monstrance with that pallid wafer, . . . or, robed in the garments of the Passion of Christ, breaking the Host into the chalice, and smiting his breast for his sins. The fuming censers, that the grave boys, in their lace and scarlet, tossed in the air like great gilt flowers, had their subtle fascination for him.[3]

It is fascinating to note Wilde's obvious familiarity with the details of Catholic ritual: at Benediction, the priest in his humeral veil opening the veil of the tabernacle behind the altar, placing the Host within the monstrance and then exposing it, and, at Mass, the priest in his chasuble breaking the Host at the Fraction and placing a part of it in the chalice and then, immediately afterwards, beating his breast at the Agnus Dei. The emotional appeal of this ceremonial is clear, but it is balanced by a kind of detachment. Wilde is aware of the meaning that lies behind it, but is looking from outside rather than from inside. His hero is 'fascinated'; he enjoys the experience but he is intellectually uninvolved:

> He never fell into the error of arresting his intellectual development by any formal acceptance of creed or system, or of mistaking, for a house in which to live, an inn that is but suitable for the sojourn of a night, or for a few hours of a night in which there are no stars and the moon is in travail. Mysticism, with its marvellous power of making common things strange to us, moved him for a season.[4]

This kind of dilettantism owed much to the influence, upon the whole 'decadent' generation, of the Oxford don and literary critic Walter Pater (1839–94). Pater's philosophy stressed the importance of beauty and aesthetic sensations. In his novel *Marius the Epicurean* (1885), set in ancient Rome, he developed fully this ideal of the aesthetic life. Among the things that Marius 'tastes' in his pursuit of beauty and sensation are various forms of religion, including Christianity. C. S. Lewis has summed up Pater's attitudes to religion in *Marius* admirably:

> It interests me as showing just how far the purely aesthetic attitude to life can go, in the hands of a master, and it certainly goes a good deal further than one would suppose from reading the inferior aesthetes like Oscar Wilde and George Moore. In Pater it seems almost to *include* the rest of spiritual life: he has to bring in chastity, he nearly has to bring in Christianity, because they are so beautiful. Perhaps it is his *patronage* of great things which is so offensive – condescending to *add* the Christian religion to his nosegay of spiritual flowers because it has a colour or scent that he thinks would just give a finishing touch to the rest.[5]

Attitudes like Pater's, so common among those of the generation of the nineties who saw in Catholic liturgy something purely picturesque, exotic and aesthetically pleasing, were brilliantly satirized by Mrs Wilfrid Ward in her novel *One Poor Scruple* (1899), with her character the young aesthete Mark Fieldes. Bernard Bergonzi has written of Fieldes: '[He] is Paterian in his enjoyment of religious emotion without committing himself to religious belief; he appreciates nicely bound editions of *The Imitation of Christ*; and kneeling at Mass . . . he experiences all the refined spiritual feelings of Pater's Marius . . . Real belief is beyond Fieldes.'[6] A typical effusion by Fieldes comes when he sees, at a railway station, a monk in his habit:

> 'Did you see the monk?' he exclaimed immediately. 'What a face! And the dress all completely white. Could renunciation wear a more exquisite appearance? . . . He certainly was picturesque, sitting on a "returned empty" in the midst of the bustle, reading his Office, with his white hood half over his face, and his white beard reaching his leather belt. There was an aloofness, an unconsciousness about him in the midst of you all; it was as if Fra Angelico had been hung in the Salon.'[7]

One must beware, however, of ascribing all the religious aspirations of the decadent generation to dilettantism. A number of young poets, including Ernest Dowson, Lionel Johnson and John Gray, were converted to

Catholicism and there is no reason to doubt their sincerity in this. Yet, particularly in Dowson and Gray, it is the aesthetic impact of the Catholic faith that still appears to have been the major influence upon them.

Ernest Dowson (1867–1900) spent a great deal of his short life in France and the rest in London, in the circles around Wilde. His poetry reflects the influence of the French Symbolists and particularly of Verlaine. Dowson translated a number of Verlaine's best-known poems,[8] and a number of his own poems are conscious imitations of Verlaine's style. In 1891 or 1892, Dowson was received into the Catholic Church. He wrote a number of devotional poems, most of which appear to be based upon an attraction to Catholic ritual. In 'Extreme Unction' for example, the spreading of 'the atoning oil' on eyes, lips and feet is described in detail.[9] Dowson's earlier comment on this particular ritual, made before his conversion, is very much in the line of Pater's Marius (the use of the word 'epicurean' is very revealing):

> I think if I have a deathbed (wh. I don't desire) I must be reconciled to Rome for the sake of that piece of ritual. It seems to me the most fitting exit for the epicurean – after all one is chiefly that – and one would procure it – (it seems essentially pagan) without undue compromise or affectation of a belief in 'a sort of something somewhere', simply as an exquisite sensation.[10]

Of course, such pre-conversion flippancy says nothing about what may well have been a perfectly sincere post-conversion faith; but it is interesting to see just how important ritual is in Dowson's Catholic poetry, and also the awe felt at monks and nuns, those mysterious beings who have given up everything for God. This comes out particularly in 'Nuns of the Perpetual Adoration' (1896) and in 'Carthusians' (1899).

If there is one thing that gives Dowson's Catholic poetry a note of felt experience, it is the theme of religion as an escape, a place of calm outside the noise, bustle and sin of the world. It is perhaps significant that, among his Verlaine translations, the one taken from the Christian collection *Sagesse* stresses the theme of life in heaven, far from the noises of the street: 'How peacefully are borne up there / Sounds of the street'.[11]

The Nuns of the Perpetual Adoration are 'calm, sad and secure' within the convent walls, they do not heed the 'wild and passionate' calls of the world outside: 'There, beside the altar, there, is rest'.[12] Similarly, in 'Carthusians' the monks exist within 'austere walls' where 'no voices penetrate', and 'nothing finds entry here of loud or passionate'. Here, 'a sacred silence only, as of death, obtains'.[13]

At his best, Dowson produced some fine poetry and is generally regarded (with Lionel Johnson and John Davidson) as one of the most gifted of the poets associated with the Rhymers' Club.[14] Sadly, his religious poems do not on the whole compete with the best of his secular verse. However, one poem, 'Benedictio Domini', combines Dowson's desire to escape the world with his love of the liturgy and brilliantly evokes a particular place and time. It is a depiction of the liturgy of Benediction but, unlike the magnificent treatments of that rite in so much Catholic prose literature of the time,[15] it is a muted picture of a celebration in a dim church, taken by an aged and tremulous priest, while the world flows noisily on to perdition outside:

> Without, the sullen noises of the street!
> The voice of London, inarticulate,
> Hoarse and blaspheming, surges in to meet
>   The silent blessing of the Immaculate.
>
> Dark is the church, and dim the worshippers,
>   Hushed with bowed heads as though by some old spell,
> While through the incense-laden air there stirs
>   The admonition of a silver bell.
>
> Dark is the church, save where the altar stands,
>   Dressed like a bride, illustrious with light,
> Where one old priest exalts with tremulous hands
>   The one true solace of man's fallen plight.
>
> Strange silence here: without, the sounding street
>   Heralds the world's swift passage to the fire:
> O Benediction, perfect and complete!
>   When shall men cease to suffer and desire!

This scene is based on the church of Notre Dame de France, just off Leicester Square, which Dowson used to frequent. A letter of his, describing a magnificent Mass at this church, produces a typical contrast with the street outside ('To come outside afterwards – London again – the sullen streets and the sordid people of Leicester Square') and also consciously places his liturgical enthusiasm firmly within the context of the aestheticism of the decadence, through a specific reference to Wilde's depiction of censers at the Mass in *Dorian Gray* ('tossing his censer up "like a great gilt flower"').[16]

The poetry by John Gray (1866–1934) which appeared in the 1890s appears at first sight to share many of the characteristics of Dowson's, though it is considerably weaker. Gray is nevertheless important in any study of Catholicism and the decadence, if only because his conversion appears to have been far more fundamental than that of many others and would bring him to a life of a completely different kind, as a Catholic priest. He was a young man of humble origins, an intimate of Oscar Wilde's circle, who was presumed to have been the original for Dorian Gray,[17] though he later reacted against such suggestions. By early 1893, however, he had broken with Wilde. A new friend, André Raffalovich, a rich expatriate Russian Jew from Paris, became a strong influence on his life from 1892. Raffalovich was a homosexual who was much exercised by the moral aspects of his sexuality, writing many pamphlets upon the subject, including his book *Uranisme et Unisexualité* (1896) and who entered the Catholic Church in 1896.

Gray had been received into the Church in 1890, but appears to have lapsed soon afterwards, entering into what he was later to describe to Raffalovich as 'a course of sin compared with which his previous life had seemed innocent.'[18] However in 1898, possibly under Raffalovich's influence, he decided to train for the priesthood. He was ordained priest in December 1901. By 1906 he had been appointed as rector of a new church, St Peter's, in the fashionable Edinburgh suburb of Morningside, where he was to remain (eventually becoming a Canon) for almost thirty years. Raffalovich, who moved to Edinburgh to be near Gray, purchased the site and funded the building of the new church. They continued to live in Edinburgh until they both died, within months of each other, in 1934.

What of Gray's literary output? Like so many of the decadent generation, he was strongly influenced by contemporary French literature. His critical writings include perceptive studies of the Goncourt brothers and of Laforgue (the latter then almost unknown). His translations include four short stories by Paul Bourget and a play by Théodore de Banville, as well as many Symbolist poems. Gray's first volume of verse, *Silverpoints* (1893), bears the mark of these interests. The majority of the poems are translations from the French of Baudelaire, Verlaine and Mallarmé. Sadly, these translations too often tend to that effusive and sentimental style common in English decadent circles. A good example (one of a couple of poems on religious themes) is his translation of Verlaine's 'Un Crucifix', from the Catholic collection *Amour*. The original is admittedly a bit sugary (as so much of Verlaine's Catholic poetry can be), but it contains nothing as banal as the following evocation of the figure of Christ's 'unutterable charm':

> Against a wall where mystic sunbeams smile
> Through painted windows, orange, blue, and gold,
> The Christ's unutterable charm behold.[19]

Gray's next collection of verse, which came out in 1896, was entitled *Spiritual Poems, Chiefly Done Out of Several Languages'*, and was affected by his growing attraction to the Church. Again, most of the poems are translations, this time mainly from religious writers from earlier centuries in Italy, Spain, France and Germany: Iacopone da Todi, Vauquelin de la Fresnaye, St John of the Cross, Andreas Gryphius, Madame Guyon and so on. Here the tone is more robust and at times quite effective.

In Edinburgh in the 1920s, Gray produced a number of hymns for use in his church,[20] which served their purpose and within the limits of the genre are quite effective. And then, in 1931, he published *Poems*, eighteen examples of a new, simpler, more spiritual form of religious poetry, such as his moving evocation of the inn at Emmaus in 'Mane Nobiscum Domine': 'Stay with us, Lord, the day is travelled far; / We meet thee at its close. / Lord, at our humble table sit and share'. These are not specifically Catholic in content, but belong to a far wider Christian tradition. He had always been a figure of fine sensibility and in these poems his simple Christian faith is expressed very effectively.

His remarkable novel *Park* (1932) shows us a new Gray, sparking off in all kinds of new directions (though it also harks back to the Gray of the 1890s in its concentration, at various points, on colourful Catholic ritual and liturgy).[21] His sophisticated mind could express itself to the full in this prose fantasy of high quality and much wry humour.[22]

One of the most extraordinary figures to have been produced by the 'aesthetic' approach to religion was Frederick Rolfe (1860–1913), also known as 'Baron Corvo' (an early contributor to *The Yellow Book*). He was obsessed with the priesthood and cruelly disappointed when he was found unsuitable for ordination. The external manifestations of the Church, above all its ritual, were central to his interests. A 'grand exaspéré' of the type of Léon Bloy, he spent his time (and his pages) railing at the 'conspiracies' he believed to be being levelled at him and at the inadequacies of the contemporary Catholic Church. He could also have qualified for the description of Bloy as the 'mendiant ingrat'. Anyone who did him a favour, financial or otherwise (and there were many), seemed to qualify for even worse abuse than other people. Robert Hugh Benson, with whom he had a stormy relationship in the mid-1900s, was a case in point. Yet Rolfe was a consummate artist, whose novel *Hadrian the Seventh*[23] (in which an autobiographical character who, like him, had been refused for the priesthood, suddenly becomes elected Pope) is a minor masterpiece.[24] His idiosyncratic, ornate and mannered style is strangely effective and he stands as one of the most curious and original figures in the literature of the period.

A Catholic Flowering: three remarkable religious poets

In contrast to the aesthetic dilettantism of the circle around Wilde, we find at this time something of a revival in serious religious poetry. The three major Catholic figures in this revival were Lionel Johnson (1867–1902), Francis Thompson (1859–1907) and Alice Meynell (1847–1922). Despite their differing ages, all three produced their major collections of verse in the 1890s.

Judging Lionel Johnson by his life history, he could well have been counted among the 'aesthetic' Catholic poets in Wilde's circle, but his poetry belies this. Much of it is of a very high quality, mostly avoiding the affected sensibility of the period. W. B. Yeats greatly admired it, as did, significantly, Ezra Pound, who wrote an Introduction to the 1915 edition of Johnson's collected poetry. As Yeats put it, Johnson 'brooded on sanctity', and some of his religious poetry has an anguished note linked to a very real sense of personal guilt.

It was Johnson, while at New College Oxford, who had introduced Wilde to his cousin, Lord Alfred Douglas. After his conversion in 1892, however, Johnson repudiated Wilde. His two collections of poetry were published shortly afterwards: *Poems* (1895) and *Ireland and Other Poems* (1897). He died in 1902 of a stroke induced by an accident in the street (though the legend arose, as he was by now a serious alcoholic, that he had fallen from a barstool).

Some of Johnson's Catholic verse is reminiscent of the aesthetic predilections of Dowson, it must be admitted. In 'Our Lady of France' (dedicated to Dowson), he describes the atmosphere in the little church off Leicester Square, in tones reminiscent of Dowson's depiction of Benediction in the same place:

> Leave we awhile the turmoil of the town;
> Leave we the sullen gloom, the faces full of care:
> Stay we awhile and dream, within this place of prayer.[25]

The description of an old priest celebrating the Mass in 'The Church of a Dream' also has echoes of Dowson's 'Benediction' (indeed, the use of the word 'tremulous' seems to point to an actual imitation of his friend's poem). It fails, however, to match the tautness of that poem:

> Only one ancient Priest offers the Sacrifice,
> Murmuring holy Latin immemorial:
> Swaying with tremulous hands the old censer full of spice,
> In gray, sweet incense clouds; blue, sweet clouds mystical.[26]

Indeed, in its use of superfluous words redolent of the sugary expression of decadent poetry (such as the repetition of 'sweet'), this also contains echoes of John Gray. Most of Johnson's religious poetry, however, contains sterner stuff. 'To a Passionist', for example, is far from Dowson's musings on the haven from the world provided by the religious life. It is a vivid consideration of the contrast between our human passions and desires and the stern commitment of the Passionist:

> We love the joys of men: we love the dawn,
> Red with the sun, and with the pure dew pearled.
> Thy stern soul feels, after the sun withdrawn,
> How much pain goes to perfecting the world.[27]

Some of Johnson's other religious poetry is of a very high order indeed. One outstanding example will suffice. 'A Burden of Easter Vigil', in which Johnson places himself in the position of the disciples after the Crucifixion and before the Resurrection, brilliantly captures the disciples' mood of uncertainty, fear and doubt. Much of the disturbing effect is achieved by the voice that is used and the complex viewpoint from which the poem is written:

> Awhile meet Doubt and Faith:
>   For either sigheth and saith,
>   That He is dead,
>   To-day: the linen cloths cover His head,
> That hath, at last, whereon to rest; a rocky bed.
>
> Come! For the pangs are done,
>   That overcast the sun,
>   So bright to-day!
>   And moved the Roman soldier: come away!
> Hath sorrow more to weep? Hath pity more to say?
>
> Why wilt thou linger yet?
>   Think on dark Olivet;
>   On Calvary stem:
>   Think, from the happy birth at Bethlehem,
> To this last woe and passion at Jerusalem!
>
> This only can be said:
>   He loved us all; is dead;
>   May rise again.

> *But if He rise not?* Over the far main,
> The sun of glory falls indeed: the stars are plain.[28]

Most of Johnson's religious poetry has a similar subtlety and complexity to this. And at its best it partakes of a very modern uncertainty, where 'Doubt and Faith' come together as natural companions.

Were it not for Gerard Manley Hopkins, Francis Thompson would be counted as the most outstanding English Catholic poet of the late nineteenth century. A Catholic from Lancashire, he was a candidate for the priesthood, but was rejected because of his nervous timidity. He studied to become a doctor like his father, but failed to qualify. In 1885, after being declared medically unfit for the army, he left home and went to London, where he lived as a down-and-out, homeless opium addict. In February 1887 he sent some of his poems, including 'The Passion of Mary', to the Catholic editor Wilfrid Meynell. Wilfrid published his poems and he and his wife Alice rescued Thompson from his life of destitution, organizing his life for him and providing constant encouragement. Three volumes of verse were published in the years 1893–7 and were very well received. Thompson never, however, entirely rid himself of his addiction. He died of tuberculosis in 1907.

There is a power in the best of Thompson's verse that is unmistakable. His best-known creation, the long poem 'The Hound of Heaven', depicts the poet's attempts to escape from the call of God. The rhythm of the verse takes one, from the start, headlong down the chase:

> I fled Him, down the nights and down the days;
> I fled Him, down the arches of the years;
> I fled Him, down the labyrinthine ways
>   Of my own mind; and in the midst of tears
> I hid from Him, and under running laughter
>   Up vistaed hopes I sped;
>   And shot, precipitated,
> Adown Titanic glooms of chasmed fears,
> From those strong Feet that followed, followed after.
>   But with unhurrying chase,
>   And unperturbèd pace,
>   Deliberate speed, majestic instancy,
>   They beat – and a Voice beat
>   More instant than the Feet –
> 'All things betray thee, who betrayest Me.'

It must be admitted that Thompson's poetic output was uneven, but in the best of it one gets, as here, the sense of a profound religious experience, expressed in powerful and original ways. In one of his best poems, 'The Kingdom of God', he shows us that God's kingdom is not a distant, thing, difficult to approach; it surrounds us in the everyday world we live in, if we are only prepared to look and to perceive. 'O world invisible, we view thee, / O world intangible, we touch thee'. The destitute, vagrant Thompson, who had so often slept rough in the centre of London, is keenly aware that he is surrounded even there by mystery. God is in everything in the material world; he is revealed by our cries of sadness and despair, which bring him closer to us. The dramatic last two stanzas produce startling images based on his London experiences, which show that the miraculous is here and now:

> But (when so sad thou canst not sadder)
> Cry; – and upon thy so sore loss
> Shall shine the traffic of Jacob's ladder
> Pitched betwixt Heaven and Charing Cross.

> Yea, in the night, my Soul, my daughter,
> Cry – clinging Heaven by the hems;
> And lo, Christ walking on the water
> Not of Gennesareth, but Thames![29]

Thompson was to exert a profound influence on later generations of Catholics. One has only to read Antonia White's *Frost in May* to see the kind of effect he could have upon young Catholic minds in the inter-war period. For the first time a Catholic poet was speaking directly to those looking for faith.

Alice Meynell (1847–1922) is a very different poet from those we have been examining. Reading her poetry, one has an impression of quiet under-statement. The best of her small output was collected in three volumes: *Poems* (1893), *Later Poems* (1901) and *Poems: Collected Edition* (1913).

Her life was as quiet and retiring as her verse. Born Alice Thompson, she converted to Catholicism in 1868 and in 1875 produced her first vol-ume of poetry, *Preludes*, which brought her to the attention of the Catholic author and editor Wilfrid Meynell. They married in 1877. Their domestic life was very happy and they formed a wide circle of literary friends, includ-ing George Meredith and the Catholic poets Coventry Patmore and Francis Thompson. They were possibly the best-known figures in Catholic literary society of the period.

The best of Meynell's poetry is meditative, a series of ponderings on the implications of the Incarnation, the Crucifixion, the Resurrection. Often, as with the best poetry of Johnson and Thompson, these things are not intimately bound up with specific Catholic imagery, or aspects of Catholic liturgy. The poetry is spare, short and to the point, but its simplicity is deceptive and the overtones are infinite. In 'Advent Meditation', for example, she speaks of the time of waiting for the birth of Jesus. The central idea is the paradox whereby God, the Creator of the Universe, is about to create a baby who is himself. In other words, he is both the Creator and the created. He was to come into the world just like every other baby, formed gradually during his mother's pregnancy. The slow, burdensome waiting is described. And this natural process was just like that undergone by all the other mothers and all the other children, 'of the year'.

The insights into the nature of the Incarnation given by that poem are typical of Alice Meynell at her best. Among the many short poems with a similar impact, I would single out the dramatic 'Easter Night', in which, after all the noise and public nature of Good Friday, the Resurrection and its Victory

> Were hushed within the dead of night,
> The shuttered dark, the secrecy.
> And all alone, alone, alone,
> He rose again behind the stone.[30]

Alice Meynell's poetry can become an addiction. Its never-ending complexity behind the apparent simplicity of its form and utterance makes it something that can be continually read and re-read in moments of quiet and tranquillity.

While Catholic themes and imagery can serve a well-defined and often aesthetically satisfactory purpose in Catholic literature as a whole, one of the paradoxes of the Catholic poetry of the late nineteenth century was that the use of specifically Catholic imagery could at times lead to banality and that some of the most effective religious poetry by Catholic authors was that which eschewed such surface characteristics. To make a generalization of this would, of course, be faulty. Even in the late nineteenth century there were poets whose use of Catholic themes, Catholic imagery, or of the language of the liturgy was outstandingly effective – and who in fact stand higher than most other Catholic poets of whatever hue. One only has to think of the moving poetry and the liturgical power of Newman's *Dream of Gerontius*, or the use both of Catholic expression and underlying Catholic philosophy in Gerard Manley Hopkins's poetry, to realize that effective and highly literary expression *can* be achieved in Catholic poetry that uses Catholic language and imagery in this way. And of course, in the twentieth century, poets such as David Jones and Elizabeth Jennings were able to use these materials in an equally effective way. Nevertheless, in the 1890s it appears to have been by avoiding such specific imagery that writers such as Patmore, Johnson, Thompson and Meynell were able in some of their best poetry to avoid the banal extremes of de Vere and achieve a more universal and profound expression of Christian experience.

Notes

1   Léon Bloy, *La Femme pauvre*, part 2, chapter 8.
2   I am grateful to the late Richard Ellmann for a number of very interesting conversations on the religious dimension of the relationship between the French and British Symbolists.
3   Oscar Wilde, *The Picture of Dorian Gray* (1890), in *The Works of Oscar Wilde*, 1948, pp. 105–6.
4   Ibid., p. 106.
5   C. S. Lewis, letter to Arthur Greeves, 10 January 1932, *The Collected Letters of C. S. Lewis*.
6   Bernard Bergonzi, introduction to Mrs Wilfrid Ward, *One Poor Scruple*, p. x.
7   Mrs Wilfrid Ward, *One Poor Scruple*, p. 36.
8   For example, 'Tears fall within mine heart, / As rain upon the town', 'Colloque sentimental', 'Spleen' and 'The Sky is Up Above the Roof', in *Decorations* (London: Smithers, 1899).
9   The details of the content of this poem appear to be based on the scene of Emma's death in Flaubert's *Madame Bovary* (1857). What Dowson does not seem to have realized is the atrocious irony with which Flaubert had infused this parody of the conventions of the deathbed scene – instead, he sees the imagery as deeply moving.
10 Dowson, letter to Arthur Moore, 1889, quoted in R. K. R. Thornton and Caroline Dowson, *Ernest Dowson: Collected Poems*, p. 241.
11 'The Sky is Up Above the Roof', in *Decorations* (1899).
12 'Nuns of the Perpetual Adoration', in *Verses* (1896).
13 'Carthusians', in *Decorations* (1899).
14 W. B. Yeats and Ernest Rhys founded the Rhymers' Club in 1890, as a dining club for poets. Some of the best poets of the era were members, and two collections of their work were published: *The Book of the Rhymers' Club* (1892) and *The Second Book of the Rhymers' Club* (1894).
15 See Wilde's depiction earlier in this chapter; also the many treatments of this theme in the Catholic novel (see pp. 106–10).
16 Letter to Arthur Moore, 19 October 1890, quoted in Thornton and Dowson, p. 230.
17 Ernest Dowson and Lionel Johnson both referred to him as Dorian in letters at this time (Ellmann, p. 291). He himself signed himself 'Dorian' in letters to Wilde.
18 Brocard Sewell, *In the Dorian Mode: A Life of John Gray 1866–1934*, p. 13.
19 John Gray, *Silverpoints*. Verlaine's original is far more robust:

> Contre le mur que vient baiser le jour mystique
> D'un long vitrail d'azur et d'or finement roux,
> Le Crucifix se dresse, ineffablement doux.

20 *St Peter's Hymns* (London: The Cayme Press, 1925).
21 See pp. 106–13.
22 For *Park*, see pp. 89–91.
23 See pp. 114–15.
24 For *Hadrian the Seventh*, see pp. 86–7.
25 'Our Lady of France', in *Poems* (1895).
26 'The Church of a Dream', in *Poems* (1895).
27 Johnson, 'To a Passionist', in *Poems* (1895).
28 Johnson, 'A Burden of Easter Vigil', in *Poems* (1895).
29 Thompson, 'The Kingdom of Heaven'.
30 Alice Meynell, 'Easter Night', in *Later Poems* (1901).

The Catholic Novel before Greene and Waugh, 1899–1938

6

Moral Dilemmas: The Novel of Contemporary Life

In Britain, the Catholic novel had a very slow start compared to its French counterpart. Where, in France, Catholic novels were flourishing by the early 1890s and, moreover, were being written by authors of distinction such as Bloy and Huysmans, it was not until the turn of the new century that any such novels, with appreciable literary merit, began to appear in Britain. Even then, the authors concerned were in what one might call the 'second eleven' when placed alongside their secular contemporaries. Three authors, of varying quality, stood at the forefront of the new existence of the Catholic novel in Britain: Mrs Wilfrid Ward, Robert Hugh Benson and Maurice Baring. Possibly the best, in literary terms, was Mrs Ward, whose subtle and often ambiguous treatment of what would otherwise have been stock Catholic subjects makes of her work something of a cut above many of her contemporaries. Benson, though vastly popular in his day, falls into many of the traps of the over-zealous proselytizer and his works have many faults, both psychological and structural. He is well worthy of study, though, standing as he does centrally in the tradition of the English Catholic novel. Baring, whose novels at first glance appear to be slight and lacking in structure, does in fact stand for a new departure. He wrote in the 1920s and his work was very much in harmony with new techniques of the novel that were being developed by his secular contemporaries.

The major thing that differentiates the English Catholic novel, in this period, from its French counterpart is the fact that, as Bernard Bergonzi puts it, 'English Catholic writers were relatively restrained and tentative in showing the manifestations of the supernatural in the natural'.[1] English Catholic novels tended to be about the problems facing Catholics in the modern world and about crises of conscience caused by conflict between the Church's teachings and their own human desires, rather than the explicit irruption of the supernatural into the material order.

Mrs Wilfrid Ward (1864–1932)

In 1899 there appeared one of the most remarkable of English Catholic novels. This was *One Poor Scruple*, by Mrs Wilfrid Ward (Josephine Mary Ward), a member of the recusant aristocracy who had married the Catholic publicist Wilfrid Ward (son of W. G. Ward). It takes a major human dilemma (the conflict between Catholic morality and human desire), which had been treated extensively in novels by a number of writers in the late nineteenth century, but its skilful and sympathetic depiction of the drama is masterly in comparison to theirs. The characters are real, complicated human beings rather than marionettes. It also provides us with a convincing picture of late nineteenth-century British upper-class society.

In the novel a Catholic recusant family, the Riversdales, living as they have for generations in the country, are contrasted with the more worldly, 'fast' society of London. Madge Riversdale, who has married into the family and then been widowed, is caught between the two and though her heart appears to be with the 'bright lights', she retains an underlying consciousness of what Catholic morality demands. A crisis is caused by her wish to marry Lord Bellasis. There is one impediment: Bellasis has a wife whom he has divorced, who is still alive. This causes Madge some concern, but nevertheless she accepts Lord Bellasis and the date for the marriage is fixed. She dares not announce this to the Riversdales. Meanwhile her sister-in-law Mary, a girl of great piety, has had the realization that God is calling her to the religious life. She tells Madge of this. Overcome, Madge confesses her secret to her. That evening she goes to confession and writes to Bellasis to break off her engagement. She feels calm and at peace. But that peace is broken by the awful realization that by her unthinking and selfish actions another woman, Cecilia Rupert, has been brought to commit suicide. The old priest, to whom she had made her confession the evening before, is horrified by her tortured appearance at Mass the next morning.

Told baldly like this, one can see how this plot might well have lent itself to the kind of mawkish treatment so common in earlier novels of renunciation. But this novel stands out for its realistic and unsentimental treatment of its characters, a kaleidoscope of late nineteenth-century figures from old George Riversdale, the recusant squire, to Mrs Hurstmonceaux, the worldly busybody, to Cecilia Rupert, the outwardly independent New Woman, to Mark Fieldes, the *fin-de-siècle* aesthete. And Madge herself is thoroughly convincing. The moral of the tale is not pushed at the reader. Indeed, it is only on reflection that one sees how Cecilia's suicide (and Cecilia is depicted with sympathy and understanding) brings home the nature of the society with which Madge has become embroiled, which contrasts so greatly with the simple faith of Mary Riversdale. Bernard Bergonzi has said of this novel:

> In *One Poor Scruple* Mrs Ward brings together the traditional interests and pieties of the English Catholics, and the uncertainties of the age when she was writing, and makes a satisfying work of art out of them. I believe that the novel stands up well when compared with later works of English fiction on Catholic themes, notably in the very difficult matter of rendering what a Catholic would see as the working of grace in human life without sacrificing physical or psychological plausibility . . . In this novel Mrs Ward nicely integrated faith and art and knowledge of humanity.[2]

Mrs Ward was to write several other novels over the next three decades. A number of those written between 1900 and 1913 possess similar sterling qualities to *One Poor Scruple*. Three stand out in particular. *Out of Due Time* (1906) depicts with sympathy and understanding the dilemma of people with Modernist leanings in the face of the need for obedience to the Church's authority.[3] *Great Possessions* (1909) is a return to the theme of contemporary society and of a moral dilemma caused by a conflict between its values and eternal values. It is a story of guilt and repentance. In a society depicted as being ruled by money, a young girl named Molly Dexter keeps a fortune that has been left to her, by failing to reveal that there is a later will in her possession that leaves the money to others. She lives a life of great luxury until, eventually, she decides to confess the truth and give up the money. As with Mrs Ward's other novels, the psychology is convincing. Molly has been brought up as an orphan, dependent upon unsympathetic relatives; her desire for things of this world is in part the result of her sense of initial rejection. At one point, this insecurity leads her to slander unnecessarily a young priest in whom she has confided, thus threatening his future within the Church. But she also has instincts for good, revealed in her care for those who suffer, from her childhood onwards. When, despite her initial delight in her new social position, she has decided to give everything up, she has a great sense of relief – much as another of the characters, Edmund Grosse, a rich man who becomes ruined during the course of the novel, feels that his life can finally become worthwhile, as he leaves indolence behind. The society surrounding them is brilliantly and satirically depicted, in all its pretensions and false values.

The most outstanding of these pre-war novels is undoubtedly *Horace Blake* (1913). It is a riveting story, in which one's judgement has to be reserved until the very last pages. It starts with the eponymous hero, a fiercely anticlerical playwright, suffering from terminal cancer. He decides to go to Brittany, accompanied not by his wife Kate (who is as strongly anticlerical as him and, despite his ill-treatment of her, devoted to him and to his fame), but by his daughter Trix, who he hardly knows. In Brittany, he is converted to the faith of his youth shortly before he dies. Told like this, it sounds a recipe for a banal 'conversion novel'. But Horace Blake's death takes place less than halfway through the book, the rest of which is taken up with the repercussions of the conversion. Was it real, or was it the fear of death that had brought it on?[4]

Trix and Stephen Tempest, a young man who is preparing to write Blake's biography (and who is depicted as some kind of Christian), witnessed his last days and believe in the reality of the conversion. Predictably, Kate Blake believes the opposite and disapproves of Stephen's plan to juxtapose in the biography depictions of Horace's Catholic youth with that of his eventual reversion to the faith, and to end the book with a heartfelt essay by Trix on the author's last days. But soon, faced with documentation on the vileness and cruelty of many of Horace's activities, Stephen becomes convinced that the conversion can have been nothing but 'an ignoble clinging to superstitious rites, and a pose by which he sought to deceive himself', because 'the serene atmosphere of a real moral conversion was absolutely impossible for a man as rotten as Blake'.[5] He revises his plan and decides to concentrate on that aspect of Blake's life. Meanwhile, Trix has discovered even worse things, which concern herself, about her father's activities. She now hates her father and cannot, after all she has heard, believe in his conversion.

Things are further complicated by the fact that the old Breton curé, despite his sympathy for Horace, finds it difficult to assess the reality of his conversion (and even more so that of Trix, who at her father's death had asked to be received into the Church), and asks himself 'how to distinguish imagination from faith'.[6] We, the readers, are in complete uncertainty of the truth and of what is eventually going to happen.

Finally, Kate Blake receives from the curé a notebook in which Horace had put down his experiences over his last weeks. It is full of Christian meditation on works he has been reading, including Pascal and, tellingly, Huysmans's conversion novel *En route*, in which the autobiographical hero Durtal reaches peace despite his sins. Kate, whose secular and atheistic upbringing had been of a highly moral kind (so different from her husband's attitudes), is not only convinced by what she reads, but realizes that she has a moral imperative to act upon it. Horace's conversion was a sincere one, she realizes, and bore in it the seeds of redemption. In her last interview with Stephen, she asks how he, a Christian, could have failed to understand that according to his religion redemption is available to even the vilest human being:

You were better, I knew, by instinct, than other men I had met. You are good and you are a Christian. I have been reading the Gospels for the first time, and I see that the main notion in them is that sin is not irremediable. I was taught that there was no such thing as sin, but that there were noble characters and base characters. I never dreamt of the base elements being transmuted into the noblest. But why did *you* not understand? Trix was not brought up a Christian as you were. Why, when you read the horrible things I sent you for the Life, did not you, who had seen him near the end, you who had read Trix's story, say to me, 'Both are true, the vileness and the nobility that came out of that awful cleansing'?[7]

Stephen is partly convinced. They decide that the biography will not be written. 'I cannot readjust my ideas quickly enough to see how far I could follow you', he says, 'but even if I could see to some extent with your eyes, I could not do the work as it ought to be done.'[8] In other words, the upright agnostic is further on the path to God's truth than the tepid Christian. Kate decides not to put the task in the hands of anyone else, because she sees no possibility of making the truth understood by the many.

Horace Blake is typical of Mrs Ward's best techniques. A situation is put before the reader and the author does not come immediately down on one side or the other. All options remain open. Only gradually do we begin to realize the Christian message lying beneath the surface. Here, it is the Christian, and Catholic, message of redemption; the ability of the sinner, however heinous, to repent and be accepted, and the contrast between this and the judgement of non-believers and a non-Catholic Christian.

Mrs Ward's writings during the war and its aftermath tended to be of lesser quality but her last important novel, which appeared in the year of her death, broke new ground. *Tudor Sunset* (1932) broke across some of the simplistic stereotypes contained in Catholic historical novels such as those of Benson. In it, alongside typically harrowing depictions of the torture and killing of the Elizabethan Catholic martyrs, she gave a compelling picture of the ageing Elizabeth, fearful of death, and of the mixture of attraction and repulsion felt for her by those Catholics among her household.

If there are two qualities, above all, which stand out in Mrs Ward's fiction, they are a keen insight into human motivation and an ability to depict contemporary society in all its complexity. At the same time she manages, far more subtly than most Catholic novelists of her time, to convey a religious message; on the one hand about moral dilemmas faced by Catholics and on the other about the nature of religious vocation and the workings of grace. She has the rare quality of never pushing a conclusion at the reader, as so many of the other English Catholic novelists of this period did. She has been an unfairly neglected figure in studies of Catholic literature.

Robert Hugh Benson (1871–1914)

The same could not be said of Robert Hugh Benson (1871–1914), the Catholic priest who wrote prolifically in the years 1904–14 and whose novels received wide acclaim in his own day. Benson was the youngest son of the Archbishop of Canterbury, Edward White Benson, and had, after a short period as an Anglican priest, converted to Catholicism in 1903. He spent several years in Cambridge, as curate of the parish church of Our Lady and the English Martyrs, and there exerted an enormous influence on the University's undergraduates, as Sir Shane Leslie has described in various books.[9] This produced many conversions.

Benson became a prolific writer, writing fifteen novels in ten years, up to his death in 1914, though he also spent much energy on Catholic apologetics. Indeed, novels and essays both served the same purpose. As Leslie has put it:

> With fecundive fervour he poured forth a series of novels which may be described as the Epistles of Hugh the preacher to the Anglicans – to the Conventionalists – to the Sensualists, etc.[10]

The novels achieved considerable public acclaim and at the time Benson seemed to many observers to be a major literary figure. There is little doubt, however, that he wrote far too fast (alongside many other activities). This, and the fact that his novels are almost entirely lacking in human insight and are clearly works of straightforward and often obvious proselytism, have meant that they have not lasted well.

In his novels in certain genres these lacks are not immediately obvious. His five historical novels, for example, from *By What Authority?* (1904) to *Oddsfish!* (1914), succeed, at their best, in immersing the reader in exciting action and compelling and dramatic historical situations; though the perils and suffering of Catholic martyrs appear to leave him little space for in-depth depiction of character or motivation. This does not really matter, given the 'adventure story' nature of the narrative and the resultant simplification of historical issues. The same can be said for the novels of the future, *Lord of the World* (1907) and *The Dawn of All* (1911), where, as in most novels of this type, the main emphasis is on ideas, both political and religious. And the historical pastiche, *The History of Richard Raynal, Solitary* (1905), supposedly transcribed from a mediaeval manuscript, by its nature gives little scope for realistic characterization.

When Benson turned to writing novels of his own time, his weaknesses became clearer. Characters are unreal; moral issues, though clear-cut, are often puzzlingly simplistic and inhuman; the author's standpoint allows for no ambiguity as to motivation or meaning. In the first of these novels, *The Sentimentalists* (1906), the central character, 'Chris Dell', is a shallow *poseur* who, though a Catholic convert, is incapable of deep belief or consistent behaviour. He is weak in relation to his desires and continually returns to what is all-envelopingly called 'vice' in Paris. His friend Father Dick Yolland, a young Catholic priest, tries to help him in various ways, but these attempts are doomed to disappointment. Finally, after his engagement to a young Anglican girl, Annie Hamilton, has been broken off, Dell is persuaded, through subterfuge, to entrust his future to a mysterious Mr John Rolls, an old, wealthy landed gent who is described as a 'mystic' and a penitent (his sins having, we are told, killed his wife many years before). At his ancient moated recusant manor, Rolls has set up a kind of colony for the 're-creation' of people whose lives have apparently failed: ex-priests and all manner of strange people, ranging from tramps to ex-actresses. Rolls's recipe for Chris' redemption is that he must be 'broken', as he explains to Dick Yolland:

> He needs one thing, just as you and I do, Father. I need not tell you what that is. But the way by which Grace comes, is another matter, and in our hands. That way may be Love or Wrath. And I think it to be wrath here. Remember he has lived a gross and filthy life . . . This man must be broken to pieces, I think.[11]

This 'breaking' is particularly brutal and eventually leads Dell to the verge of suicide. In a dramatic scene, Yolland accompanies Rolls to the house where Dell is and they creep up to his room. Yolland begs Rolls to stop Dell, but Rolls says they must wait: 'I must take him in the act . . . We may have to wait an hour or two.'[12] Finally, as Rolls breaks in, Yolland sees in the room 'a hook above a window, and a noosed rope hanging from it'.[13] The final scene of the novel takes place some time later. Chris is a changed man; humble and at peace. And Dick Yolland is ecstatic: 'Chris is all right. Old Rolls is going to settle something on him . . . Good Lord! How pleased I am!'

One can see from this synopsis that not only is the scenario unreal, but the message is extremely doubtful. And the treatment of Chris's ventures into 'vice' is particularly naïve. The depiction of human love, too, seems to be beyond Benson's capabilities. As Benson's biographer Father Martindale has pointed out, 'Love . . . was frankly hysterical in Annie and maniac in Chris'.[14] The characters are very unreal. Yet we have been told, both by Benson and others, that they were based on real people. How can this be? Martindale points to the answer, describing the way in which Benson failed to see beyond externals:

Benson's very quick eye took in at once certain salient and usually external characteristics of a person who might meet him, and from these his even quicker dramatic imagination constructed a personage often quite unlike what a longer study of the person would have revealed . . . Chris is not only a caricature, but a dual personality which will not work harmoniously within itself.[15]

One can only presume that 'Mr Rolls', who was, we are told, also based on a real person, underwent a similar process.

However, the use of caricature actually helps one of Benson's comparatively successful achievements in this and in other novels: that is, the mocking of attitudes of which he disapproved and above all of the 'conventionality' and ignorance of the average Anglican, whether priest or lay. Mrs Hamilton, the mother of the girl Dell loves, is the first of a series of women depicted ironically in Catholic literature (right down to Ida in Greene's *Brighton Rock*), whose conventional views contrast with the greater insight given to Catholics. And the local Anglican priest, whose opinions Mrs Hamilton values so much, is shown to be a shallow, self-important bigot. He sees the Hamiltons as 'sound Churchpeople' ('whatever that means', says Dick Yolland).[16] His attitude to Catholics is brilliantly summed up thus:

> His attitude towards those whom he would have called his brethren of the Roman Communion was one of polite suspicion; he was accustomed to say that their training was of such a character in the seminary that it was impossible to be quite certain of the behaviour of even their most English-minded men; and in this manner he was able to preserve a certain reputation among his small and devoted flock for the generally incompatible virtues of charity and shrewdness.[17]

Satirical ability does not on its own produce a good novel. *The Sentimentalists* epitomizes many of Benson's weaknesses as a novelist. He wrote a sequel to it, *The Conventionalists* (1908) in which these weaknesses were magnified still further. It is the story of a young and apparently worldly man, Algy,[18] and other characters' perception of his vocation to monasticism. We have already seen these characters in *The Sentimentalists* – Annie, now Lady Brasted, who has become a Catholic convert of a sort; Dick Yolland, who has become a Monsignor; and, above all, Chris Dell, who has become a kind of Catholic mystic, on whom, we are told, Mr Rolls' mantle has descended. To these essentially unreal characters is added Benson himself, writing in the first person (and he is, paradoxically, an even more unreal character). The story line is not particularly edifying, as the three friends (Yolland, Dell and

Benson), convinced, as Benson puts it, that Algy is 'a born Contemplative',[19] push him by various means into the religious life. Even Catholic readers were shocked by this aspect:

> What lends itself to a somewhat widely felt disapprobation would appear to be the method pursued by Chris, Dick Yolland and Father Benson in view of ensuring Algy's coming beneath the Carthusian spell. He was jockeyed into it, people declare.[20]

The last interview between Algy and the girl he realizes he loves, but must give up, is a harrowing one; but then, as Dick Yolland says later, 'What a confounded nuisance these women are!'[21] This comment illustrates the whole tenor of the novel and of its depiction of the most serious human issues.

Most of Benson's novels[22] on contemporary subjects share many of the characteristics of these two, though their plots are very different from each other. They are on the whole disappointing. Yet there was much in Benson's output that attracted the audience of his time. He was so much of his time, however, that this appeal has not lasted into the twenty-first century.

Maurice Baring (1874–1945)

Maurice Baring, whose prolific output of novels began in the early 1920s, was on the face of it an unlikely figure for a Catholic novelist. He was a scion of a famous banking family (the seventh son of Lord Revelstoke), who became a diplomat in Paris, Rome and Copenhagen, a war correspondent in Manchuria during the Russo-Japanese War of 1905 and a special correspondent in St Petersburg before the First World War. His autobiography, *The Puppet Show of Memory* (1922), depicts his privileged childhood and these subsequent adventures.

In 1909, however, Baring was received into the Catholic Church. By the 1920s, he had become strongly associated in the public eye with his friends Belloc and Chesterton, though his outlook and writings were very different from theirs and he was in no sense a proselytizer or publicist for the Catholic religion. There is no doubt, however, that his Catholic faith was central to his existence. Princess Bibesco[23] has described how this apparent salon butterfly (he was very popular in French high society) had been changed by his religious experiences: 'He was a man who had for so long been taken for a salon clown, a society amuser, before being recognized for what he really was, a true poet who had become a poor pilgrim on the road to Damascus'.[24] He was a close friend of the Abbé Mugnier (to whom he dedicated his novel

The Coat without Seam), the society priest who had been the friend and confessor of Huysmans.[25]

Baring was urbane and civilized and his many novels, written from the early 1920s, shared these characteristics. They depicted the pre-war high society in which he himself had moved. The plots are complicated and often seem to lead nowhere, as the various characters, caught in a web of human relationships which never seem to end in happiness, move as in a dream through a series of social and emotional situations. Love never seems to be requited; ambition leads nowhere. All this is described in a laconic, almost emotionless style, made up mainly of short, inconsequential sentences. Piers Paul Read has described these novels as 'stylistically impeccable, but shapeless, with thin characterization and trivial preoccupations'.[26] But this is to underestimate them. Baring's novels *are* uneven, but at times their apparent triviality and shapelessness reflect some of the most profound concerns of the literature contemporary with him, and Baring's literary approach is very much in tune with the changes that had been occurring in the secular novel of his time. These include uncertainty, on the part of his characters, as to their perceptions both of other people's feelings and views and of their own; the conveying, often through apparently trivial details, of the complexity of life's reality; the refusal (as in Baring's contemporary André Gide) to go along with art's reorganization and ordering of what is disorganized and disordered in life. In this context, the apparent lack of 'proper' characterization merely means that the reader is left to come to his or her own conclusions, through a battery of often apparently aimless bits of factual information (books on shelves, pictures on walls, etc.). In the Catholic context, at their best these novels can be taken to reflect the aimlessness of life without God (while at the same time depicting the doomed society of pre-war Europe); occasionally a positive Catholic message, delivered unobtrusively, does make its mark, though, sadly, in some more obtrusive cases it can detract from the literary value of what is being written.

In a number of these novels, such as *Comfortless Memory* (1928), there is little or nothing in the way of a Christian message. In other novels, such as *A Triangle* (1923), the Catholic input is slight and not particularly well integrated into the story. (One is surprised, for example, when the heroine of *A Triangle*, who has until now shown little sign of Catholic faith, declares on the last page that she is 'going to ask some one to hear my confession – after all these years').[27] But the more one reads Baring's novels, the more it becomes clear that, often quite elusively, a Christian message is being gradually introduced into the action. Let us examine two novels, both typical of Baring's best writing, in which the introduction of Catholic themes into what appear otherwise worldly novels, though at times subtle and effective, can also end up being considerably less so. These are *C* (1924) and *Daphne Adeane* (1926).

C takes the form of a *Bildungsroman*, though the subject is not so much the development of a character's career, as its stagnation. Caryl Bramsley (known as 'C'), is depicted as a young man of great promise, whose promise is never fulfilled. A career as a diplomat is beyond him; his desire to be an author eludes him. His emotional life is torn between the simple and saintly Beatrice Fitzclare and the powerful influence (which always wins) of the flighty, enthralling, unreliable Leila.[28]

The background to C's story is the aristocratic and leisurely society of England and of the British diplomatic service, prior to the First World War. We are led to see C himself as the symbol of the vacuity of that society. And the only hint we get of any aspiration, on C's part, to anything more meaningful, comes in his correspondence with the Catholic girl Beatrice, in which he shows the attraction that her religion has for him.[29] He is attracted, yes, but it is typical that he is never convinced enough to accept that religion. As in everything else, he is the master of indecision.

Were it not for its last twenty pages or so, *Daphne Adeane* would possibly be the most remarkable of all Baring's novels. Daphne Adeane never appears in the novel, as she has died before it begins but her influence hangs over all the protagonists. She was a fascinating woman of Creole blood, who had been married to a prosaic city gent, Ralph Adeane. The novel starts in an art gallery, in which a portrait of her is hanging. A private view is in progress and we fleetingly see a number of people who are going to recur at various points in the plot, though here we are unaware of their importance.

As the novel progresses, the plot takes a series of unexpected turns and some characters we had expected to play a leading role fade out, while others unexpectedly emerge. At first, it appears that the plot is to revolve around the triangular relationship between Hyacinth Wake, her husband Basil and her long-standing lover Michael Choyce. Almost immediately, however, that relationship ends and Michael, an MP who needs to make an advantageous marriage, marries the young Fanny Weston. She is madly in love with him, but he is not in love with her. She becomes aware of Michael's relationship with Hyacinth (though Hyacinth now spends her time avoiding Michael) and she suffers greatly. Hyacinth unexpectedly dies. Fanny becomes very friendly with an author, Leo Dettrick, and this platonic friendship restores her confidence. Michael now realizes he is in love with his wife but it is too late, she no longer loves him. Their life continues on this uneven keel and we learn a lot about the strong influence Daphne Adeane had had on both Dettrick and a friend of his, Francis Greene, both of whom had been madly but platonically in love with her. Throughout the novel people keep remarking that, though Fanny does not exactly look like Daphne Adeane, she has a *feel* of her. The war comes. Fanny goes to France as a nurse and Michael joins the Royal Flying Corps. Fanny meets Francis Greene in France and falls in love with him (and he with her). Michael is reported missing. Two years later, the war ends. Michael is presumed dead. Francis and Fanny plan their wedding. Suddenly, the news comes that Michael is alive, and has regained his lost memory. Fanny's immediate reaction is that they must go ahead and she must divorce Michael. But she learns that Michael is still not well and will rely on her. She decides to devote herself to him and to give up her plans of marriage.

No plot outline can convey the subtleties of this novel. In its depiction of high society, and even more in its raw assessment of the changing nature of human emotions and the transience of love, one can sometimes feel looming over it the figure of Proust (whom Baring had not only read, but had met in the Paris salon society where he was so much at home). This is, of course, in no way to compare Baring's achievements with those of Proust, which are of a completely different order. Baring's style, with its clipped understatement, was the antithesis of Proust's but, in their dispassionate assessment of the nature of human relationships and the transience of love, the two authors did have something in common. In the untidy picture portrayed of the arbitrary nature of human activities one can sense the figure of Gide, too, lurking in the background. One must not forget, either, that it was Baring who had 'discovered' Chekov's works when in Moscow and he was one of the first to introduce them to the West.[30] Something of the tone of the apparently aimless conversations of Chekov's characters (the reality of human discourse, rather than a literary re-creation of it) can be found in Baring's novels.

But what about the Catholic dimension? This is at first introduced subtly and apparently without pattern. Fanny becomes aware that Daphne Adeane was a Catholic, as was Hyacinth Wake. A woman loved by another character is shown as having given everything up in order to enter a convent. These things do not at first appear (like so many other things in the novel) to have any connected meaning. Gradually, however, we realize that Fanny is becoming influenced by the legacy of these women.

After this, sadly, the techniques of introducing a Catholic message become rather more obvious. The well-tried didactic subterfuge of an interview with a Catholic priest (Father Rendall) occurs on two occasions. In the first, before the crisis, the conversation is almost entirely about Hyacinth Wake and the nature of faith. Fanny ends up by feeling instinctively that 'Hyacinth had made a great renunciation in her life and that in making it, her religion had perhaps played a part'.[31] This is the first time in the book that we are given an inkling that Hyacinth's rejection of Michael might have been a result of religious misgivings.

The second interview takes place when Fanny is debating her future, after discovering that Michael is alive. Fanny, though she calls herself a 'pagan', wants to know what Father Rendall would advise one of his flock to do. After much discussion, Rendall, who has taken the straightforward Catholic line about the sinfulness of divorce and the need for self-sacrifice, speaks of the personal after-effects of each type of decision:

> Now believe me that in every act of sacrifice we make there is a balm, and in every act of *self* that we make there is an aftertaste of fire, smoke, dust and ash.[32]

When Fanny has, with much agony, made the decision to give Francis up, she finds among Michael's books a Roman missal on the flyleaf of which Hyacinth's name is written. She reads the missal and finds that she has not only found the meaning of her sacrifice, but that she is also being inexorably brought to the Church:

> She read the *Hebdomada Major* . . . the rites and ritual of Holy Week – Palm Sunday, Maundy Thursday, Good Friday, The Mass of the Pre-sanctified, Holy Saturday, Easter Sunday . . . and then, as she laid down the book – and it was past midnight – she said to herself, 'But surely all this is the incarnation of the Greek idea . . . this *is* sacrifice . . . this *is* the very thing . . . what I have been groping for all my life . . . here it is. But then, if that is so, then I . . . then I . . . must I one day be a . . . Catholic?' . . . and her premises seemed to have led her to a conclusion so tremendous, so vast, so glorious, and so overwhelming that she could barely bear to face it – as if all of a sudden she had been brought face to face with the sun rising out of a starless night over a snowy mountain and flooding the world with glory . . . She shut her eyes, and she lay motionless for a long time, and she felt the sense of balm of which Father Rendall had spoken.[33]

The final irony is that Francis Greene, who has seen once more the portrait of Daphne Adeane, has realized that though he 'loved Fanny as much as ever' the ghost of Daphne would forever have been between them. This is, for Fanny, 'the crowning bitterness . . . Daphne Adeane has taken him back from me'. And yet, she thinks, 'it is right that it should be so; I have deserved it.'[34]

The manifest weakness of this Catholic ending, made up as it is of the clichés of the novels of renunciation produced by Baring's predecessors,[35] detracts from the worth of this novel. This should not blind us to Baring's virtues as a novelist, or to the more subtle introduction of Catholic themes that is to be found in some of his other novels, or indeed in the major part of *Daphne Adeane* itself. If read hastily, Baring can appear superficial or even vacuous. It sometimes takes a second or third reading of one of his novels to gauge the many subtleties that are often contained within this apparent simplicity. This makes it all the more regrettable that an otherwise excellent example of his art, such as *Daphne Adeane*, should have been dragged down at the end by the clichés of another genre.

Baring was essentially a writer of the second division. His writing nevertheless at times achieved some distinction – particularly in his often delicate treatment of themes that were important in the secular literature of his time. His works were, no doubt for this reason, strongly appreciated by the French public and indeed his writings often seem closer to the French secular literature of his time than to anything English, or to any Catholic literature. Ten of his books were translated into French and published by the fashionable publisher Stock; with *Daphne Adeane*, which as we have seen was close to French contemporary models, going through twenty-three printings. His treatment of Catholic themes in his novels is often very subtle and far more effective than a more up-front treatment would be. On rare occasions, however, there is a puzzling reversion to a banal use of traditional Catholic themes.

The Periphery: some novels by Catholics

In the first forty years of the twentieth century, there were a number of other Catholics who wrote novels, most of which were not strictly speaking 'Catholic novels'. There was, of course, Hilaire Belloc, whose political novels *Emmanuel Burden* (1904), *Mr Clutterbuck's Election* (1908), *A Change in the Cabinet* (1910) and *Pongo and the Bull* (1910), have little or nothing in the way of Catholic content, unless one counts that hatred of 'usury' and of the Jews which was a characteristic of continental Catholicism (of which Belloc was so much a part).[36] These novels are highly satirical. They are historical documents of some value, but make for hard reading. The incessant irony (with the author/narrator continually pretending to be on the side of the Jewish financier Barnett and his accomplices and claiming the best motives for them) begins to wear the reader down, the issues concerned are dated and the attitudes are out of tune with our times, so that their appeal has not lasted. Above all, for our purposes, they have little claim to figure in a study of Catholic literature.

The same could be said of Chesterton's brilliant fantasies (written before his conversion) *The Napoleon of Notting Hill* (1904) and *The Man who was Thursday* (1908), even though the latter has occasionally been interpreted as a Manichaean picture of the elemental struggle between good and evil, with the central figure being a depiction of God. Chesterton himself dismissed such ideas, describing his book as 'a very melodramatic form of moonshine', and mocking those who had inferred that the 'equivocal being' at the centre of it 'was meant for a serious description of the Deity', as opposed to a 'sort of elemental elf' rather like a 'pantomime ogre'.[37] In a far less successful novel, *The Ball and the Cross*, Chesterton did explore the nature of belief and unbelief, but with that heavy-handed use of paradox that has so often been associated with him. Such paradoxes were to be accommodated far more effectively in his detective short stories, the Father Brown stories, which had a distinct religious content. We will be looking at them in the next chapter.

One of the most extraordinary figures in early twentieth-century English literature, whose novels contained Catholic themes, was Ronald Firbank (1886–1926). A purveyor of 'high camp', Firbank used the appurtenances of Catholicism as props in a series of wild fantasies, from *Valmouth* (1919), through *Prancing Nigger* (1924) to *Concerning the Eccentricities of Cardinal Pirelli* (1926). As an undergraduate in Cambridge from 1905 to 1909, Firbank was strongly influenced by the writers of the decadence and his attitudes to religion may, from the first, have been affected by the dilettantism that characterized the attitudes of so many writers of the 1890s. Be that as it may, while in Cambridge he was converted to Catholicism by Robert Hugh Benson. It may have been Benson, too, who introduced him to the writings of Huysmans (whose influence has been traced in Firbank's style by critics such as Anthony Powell).[38] It is hard to be certain whether Firbank's conversion had any lasting effect on him; he appears to have had both affection and scorn for the Catholic religion, in varying quantities. But whatever his actual views, the absurd parodies, the outrageous and often blasphemous expressions and actions in his novels, are clearly coupled with a fascination for the outward trappings of religion.

Firbank is of literary importance for other reasons. Anthony Powell notes that his depiction of his *dramatis personae* of 'society ladies and ecclesiastics, lesbians, crowned heads and blackamoors, promenading against their backcloth of cathedral close, Greek mountains or Caribbean sea', was accomplished in an innovative form which made of him, not a writer harking back to the 1890s, but a member of the literary avant-garde. Noting Firbank's 'extraordinary facility in giving the impression of a crowd of people "making conversation" in a room', Powell draws our attention to the clear influence of his style upon a later writer like Evelyn Waugh.[39] And, indeed, Waugh himself, very early in his own career, praised Firbank to the skies as one of the greatest technical innovators in the twentieth-century novel. Waugh's description of Firbank's style could almost be a description of his own:

> His compositions are built up, intricately and with a balanced alternation of the wildest extravagance and the most austere economy, with conversational *nuances* . . . His art is purely selective. From the fashionable chatter of his period, vapid and interminable, he has plucked, like tiny brilliant feathers from the breast of a bird, the particles of his design . . . The talk goes on, delicate, chic, exquisitely humorous, and seemingly without point or plan. Then, quite gradually, the reader is aware that a casual reference on one page links up with some particular inflexion of phrase on another until there emerges a plot; usually a plot so outrageous that he distrusts his own inferences.[40]

Waugh was not the only Catholic writer to be influenced by Firbank. We will find traces of Firbank's style, and at times of his attitudes to religion, in such diverse writers as John Gray and Alice Thomas Ellis.

Among other novelists who wrote on Catholic themes in English in the inter-war period, mention must be made of two Scots: Compton Mackenzie, in his trilogy *The Altar Steps* (1922), *The Parson's Progress* (1923) and *The Heavenly Ladder* (1924), depicts a gradual conversion from Anglicanism to Catholicism; these novels lie in a long tradition of such semi-autobiographical writings. Bruce Marshall's *Father Malachy's Miracle* (1931) is on the other hand a strange mixture of sentimentality and silliness, which depicts the Catholic religion, through the simple priest Father Malachy, as a twee and rather quaint oddity.

One of the most striking novelists to emerge in the thirties was, however, someone whose writings prefigured what was to be one of the major themes of post-war Catholic writing – the problems faced by those who were brought up in Catholic institutions. This was Antonia White, whose *Frost in May* (1933) was a semi-autobiographical novel whose heroine, Nanda Grey, is brought up by nuns in a Catholic girls' school. The novel is critical of the attitudes of the nuns, both towards their pupils and in their own concept of their religion. But this criticism is never open. They are just allowed to speak for themselves, their statements and attitudes often being hair-raising; as in, for example, the following exchange with Nanda:

> 'You are very fond of your own way, aren't you, Nanda?'
> 'Yes, I suppose so, Mother.'

'And do you know that no character is any good in this world unless that will has been broken completely? Broken and re-set in God's own way. I don't think your will has been quite broken, my dear child, do you?'[41]

Even Nanda's admiration for the Catholic poet Francis Thompson is seen as dangerous:

'Francis Thompson was a great Catholic poet, but he did not write for little girls of eleven . . . [He] was a mystic and no one expects little girls to understand the secrets of the saints. Not that Francis Thompson was a saint. He was not always a Catholic, you know, and there is always something a little morbid, a little hysterical in his work . . . I think it would be better for you to let older people judge what is best for your little understanding.'[42]

Nanda herself, of middle-class parentage and the daughter of a convert, is seen as out of place in this school full of the Catholic glamour of the old families. The Mother Superior points this out to Nanda:

'Your father is a convert, is he not? Conversion is a great grace, but the Catholic outlook, Catholic breeding, shall we say, does not come in one generation, or even two, or three.'[43]

Yet, though White had left the Church by the time she wrote this novel, she nevertheless depicts her heroine as having a sense of *belonging* which is only broken by her enforced banishment, owing to a misunderstanding, at the end of the novel. And the author's sharing of that sense is shown by her humour (so typical of the Catholic authors of this period) at the expense of Nanda's mother, with her inability to comprehend what all these Catholic things are about.[44] White was to re-enter the Church during the War, and to resume her career as a novelist with three semi-autobiographical sequels to *Frost in May* in the 1950s (which are examined in Chapter 15).

The novels of Benson, Ward and Baring graphically illustrate the tightrope that an early twentieth-century 'Catholic novelist' writing on modern themes had to tread. On the one hand, he or she had a message to communicate; on the other hand, the more heavy-handed the message, the less satisfactory the novel was in literary terms. Not only that, but the message itself could be harmed. In the best Catholic novels, there is a degree of subtlety in the way the message is conveyed, or suggested. In the worst, it hits one like a sledgehammer.

Benson, like many of his predecessors, had no qualms in being above all a propagandist. This worked rather better in his historical novels and his novels of the future; in those genres propaganda appears less seriously out of place. Mrs Ward, on the other hand, shows us that it is possible to provide a more nuanced picture, with the Catholic message being skilfully introduced into a plot where all appears uncertain and where real characters cope with real situations.

Mrs Ward was still writing, like Benson and the nineteenth-century novelists, almost exclusively for a Catholic readership. Maurice Baring was the first in a new trend. He was basically a popular novelist, writing for a secular audience, who introduced Catholic themes into his novels. Where he did so subtly and obliquely, as in *C* and in the bulk of *Daphne Adeane*, this was remarkably successful. Where he began to use the more obvious techniques of his Catholic predecessors, however, as at the end of *Daphne Adeane*, the effect could be disastrous.

With Waugh and Greene, and with their successors Lodge and Spark, we will see the trend started by Baring becoming the most successful form of the English Catholic novel. All four are as well known to secular audiences as to Catholic ones. All four introduce Catholic themes subtly and often obliquely into their writings – and when, as in Greene and Waugh, stock Catholic techniques are introduced, they are usually either subtly undermined by irony and uncertainty, or introduced in a way which gives the reader various possibilities for interpretation. All four also wrote, alongside their Catholic works, purely secular novels. Yet, as we shall see, all four succeed in conveying a far more effective message than their predecessors.

But first, it will be worth looking at various other forms of the Catholic novel in the period before Greene and Waugh and also at some of the major themes and characteristics on which these later novelists would build.

Notes

1 Bernard Bergonzi, 'The Decline and Fall of the Catholic Novel', in *The Myth of Modernism and Twentieth Century Literature*, p. 174.
2 Bernard Bergonzi, introduction to *One Poor Scruple*, pp. xii–xiii.
3 For a discussion of this novel, see pp. 132–3.
4 The question is posed in much the same way as in Roger Martin du Gard's *Jean Barois*, a secular novel which appeared in the same year, and which shows a similar uncertainty right to the end.
5 Mrs Ward, *Horace Blake*, p. 307.
6 Ibid., p. 388.
7 Ibid., pp. 418–9.
8 Ibid., p. 421.

9   For example, Shane Leslie, *The End of a Chapter* and 'The Cambridge Apostolate' (in *Memorials of Robert Hugh Benson*).

10   Shane Leslie, *The End of a Chapter*, p. 76.

11   R. H. Benson, *The Sentimentalists*, p. 139.

12   Ibid., p. 221.

13   Ibid., p. 223.

14   C. C. Martindale, *The Life of Monsignor Robert Hugh Benson*, Vol. 2, p. 60.

15   Ibid., p. 54.

16   *The Sentimentalists*, p. 22.

17   Ibid., p. 49.

18   Amazingly, according to Sir Shane Leslie, 'Algy' was modelled in part on Ronald Firbank, who Benson had converted, at Cambridge in 1907. (Sir Shane Leslie, in conversation with the present writer, in the early 1960s.)

19   Benson, *The Conventionalists*, p. 133.

20   Martindale, *Life of Benson*, Vol. 2, p. 64.

21   *The Conventionalists*, p. 291.

22   *None Other Gods* (1911), *The Coward* (1912), *An Average Man* (1913), *Initiation* (1914), *Loneliness* (1915).

23   Princess Marthe Bibesco (1886–1973) was a Romanian aristocrat who married Prince George Bibesco. The Bibescos lived a cosmopolitan life, much of it in Paris. Marthe became very friendly with authors Maurice Barrès and Marcel Proust. and became known as 'the toast of Belle Époque Paris'. Her great friend the Abbé Mugnier converted her to Catholicism.

24   Princesse Bibesco, *Le Confesseur et les poètes*, p. 221.

25   Mugnier's life was a mixture of the secular and the religious. On the one hand, he was a 'society priest', the confessor of the Faubourg Saint-Germain; on the other, he was able to exert a profound religious influence on an author such as Huysmans.

26   Piers Paul Read, 'What's become of Baring' (Review of Maurice Baring, *Letters*, ed. Jocelyn Hillgarth and Julian Jeffs), *The Spectator*, 13 October 2007.

27   Maurice Baring, *A Triangle*, p. 193.

28   In its cynical up-ending of the normal progress of a *Bildungsroman*, and in the hero's perpetual failure to fulfil his promise owing to his entanglements with women of contrasting character, this novel has echoes of Flaubert's *L'Éducation sentimentale*.

29   See pp. 111–12.

30   See Baring, *Landmarks of Russian Literature* (1910), and *An Outline of Russian Literature* (1914).

31   Maurice Baring, *Daphne Adeane*, p. 264.

32   Ibid., p. 299.

33   Ibid., p. 316.

34   Ibid., p. 317.

35   The final situation appears remarkably similar to that in *Robert Orange*.

36   See pp. 144–6.

37   G. K. Chesterton, *Illustrated London News*, 13 June 1936.

38   Anthony Powell, introduction to *The Complete Firbank* 1988), p. 7.

39   Ibid., pp. 10–11.

40 Evelyn Waugh, 'Ronald Firbank', *Life and Letters*, March 1929, quoted in David
    Lodge, 'The Fugitive Art of Letters', in *Working with Structuralism*, p. 130.
41 Antonia White, *Frost in May*, p. 145.
42 Ibid., pp. 104–5.
43 Ibid., p. 145.
44 See pp. 136–7.

7

Gripping Adventures and Sensational Fantasies: Four Popular Narrative Genres

Catholic writers of narrative fiction in the early twentieth century wrote in four major genres other than the novel of modern life. These were the historical novel, the novel of the future, the ghost story and the detective story. In each case, they built upon an already existing fashion within secular literature. Robert Hugh Benson, in particular, harnessed historical and futuristic novels and ghost stories to his own religious aims in a way that brought Catholic concerns effectively before the public. Indeed, he had a talent for writing gripping adventure stories of this type, in which his lacks with regard to psychological depiction and realistic motivation mattered far less than in the novel of contemporary life. In the detective story, there was only one major Catholic exponent, G. K. Chesterton. His was a remarkable addition to the genre on any terms and brought the Catholic faith before a very wide public.

Visions of the Past: the historical novel

In the late nineteenth and early twentieth centuries, Catholic historical writing concentrated above all on the Elizabethan period, depicting the heroic example of the Catholic martyrs of that reign. This was in some respects a revelation to the general public. Until the early twentieth century, the view that had prevailed in Britain, regarding the sixteenth century, was that of the justified triumph and acceptance of Protestantism in the country and also that of Queen Elizabeth's heroic stance, supported by the vast majority of loyal British people, against the subversive forces of 'international' Catholicism. It was believed that there was a contrast to be drawn between the excessive cruelty of the repression of Protestants under the Catholic Queen Mary, 'Bloody Mary', and the more enlightened reign of Queen Elizabeth. As Evelyn Waugh put it, 'It was still generally believed in England that Elizabeth's anti-Catholic legislation was remarkable for its leniency and that in an age of savage intolerance she and Cecil stood out as unique examples of enlightenment and moderation.'[1] The truth about the barbaric treatment of the Catholic martyrs in that reign was not part of the national consciousness.

Indeed, amid the anti-Catholic hysteria of the mid-nineteenth century a literature of hate had developed in Britain, of which one of the best examples is the Revd Charles Kingsley's *Westward Ho!* (1855), with its attacks on the sixteenth-century Jesuits as deceitful traitors to the Crown. This novel stressed the cruelties of the Inquisition and played down any idea of similar cruelties by Elizabeth and her ministers. The martyr St Robert Southwell and his companions were described as having 'bullied the long-suffering Elizabeth and her council into giving them their deserts . . . insist[ing] on being hanged, whether Burleigh liked it or not', and the heroism and sufferings of the clandestine priests were grotesquely mocked as being almost entirely imaginary, as they 'skulked in and out all the year round, . . . and found a sort of piquant pleasure, like naughty boys who have crept into the store-closet, in living in mysterious little dens in a lonely turret and going up through a trapdoor to celebrate mass in a secret chamber in the roof, where they were allowed by the powers that were to play as much as they chose at persecuted saints.'[2] Loathsome Jesuits were the mainstay of much of the Protestant literature of this period,[3] with Jesuitical perversion of Protestant society being related as much to the nineteenth century as to the sixteenth. Such literature did nothing to lead the British public into any greater understanding of the complexities of sixteenth-century history.

Pope Leo XIII's beatification of fifty-four English martyrs in 1886 enhanced the perception, among British Catholics (though not among the nation as a whole), of what these people had undergone. Nine more were beatified in 1895, and these events sparked off a spate of new biographies, including John Hungerford Pollen's *Acts of English Martyrs Hitherto Unpublished* (1891) and a number of reprints of early works on the martyrs.[4] Within the next decade, Dom Bede Camm OSB (a former Anglican priest, like Pollen) had produced his *Lives of the English Martyrs Declared Blessed by Pope Leo XIII* (1904) and *Forgotten Shrines* (1910), a study of the great recusant families and their houses; and further individual biographies of martyrs were published.[5]

The historical novels of Robert Hugh Benson were the first literary shots fired in this campaign.[6] *By What Authority?* (1904) shows the strong influence of Bede Camm, to whom it was dedicated. This novel and *Come Rack! Come Rope!* (1912) compellingly and dramatically depicted for the general public the perils and suffering of the Catholic community during Elizabeth's reign. Their continuing loyalty to the Crown (particularly against the Spanish threat) was stressed and accusations of treachery rejected. Often, the events leading up to arrests were depicted in an exciting and suspenseful manner. These gripping stories were a religious version of the vastly popular secular yarns, by authors such as G. A. Henty, that flourished in the late nineteenth and early twentieth centuries. (As early as the 1870s, Cecilia Caddell had written that 'the private history of the Catholic families of England' was rich in 'all the materials for a "sensation novel"', consisting as it did 'in hairbreadth escapes, in daring rescues, in lifelong imprisonments and heroic deaths'.)[7] These characteristics ensured Benson's novels' popularity with the reading public. The national press greeted them as a completely new insight into that period of British history. A 1912 review of *Come Rack! Come Rope!* in *The Times*, for example, asked 'why Englishmen [ignored] the history of Catholic Recusancy in their near past', and commented 'It is such a noble page of the history of England.'[8]

Less successful were Benson's attempts to get to grips with other periods of early Catholic history. Immediately after *By What Authority?*, he wrote *The King's Achievement* (1905), a study of the reign of Henry VIII. In this novel the depiction of the suppression of the monasteries, though harrowing, provided nothing to match the drama of the Elizabethan novels. Benson then decided to write a novel on the reign of Queen Mary, *The Queen's Tragedy* (1906). The reason he gave for writing this was that 'several kindly critics' of his previous books had 'remarked that the reign of Mary Tudor told a very different story with regard to the Catholic character'.[9] This novel is, however, marked by the author's inability to get to grips with the problem of justifying the Protestant martyrdoms in that reign (they are merely mentioned in passing and little in the way of a clear stance is taken); and the novel itself, filled with the depressing sight of Mary's sufferings as a monarch, is static, monochrome and – frankly – boring. It took *Come Rack! Come Rope!* (1912) and *Oddsfish!* (1914), the latter of which dealt with the persecutions of the seventeenth century, to recapture the excitement of his earlier writings.

While Benson did much to set the record straight as far as the British public's perception of the sufferings of the Catholic martyrs were concerned, the general picture that emerges from the range of his historical novels appears at times to ignore certain other aspects. The cruelty of Elizabeth's reign is rightly depicted, but the equivalent cruelty of Mary's reign is left unexplained. And, as Benson's lengthy justification of papal thinking behind the Bull releasing Queen Elizabeth's subjects from their allegiance shows, the Pope could for him do no wrong, even in an act like this, which caused British Catholics so much suffering.[10] But the fact that Benson's historical account could at times be partial cannot detract from the effect of his writings in setting the general picture straighter than it had been up to this time.

Hilaire Belloc was greatly enthused by Benson's historical work, writing in 1907 that it was 'unique' and that he believed that Benson might well be the person to 'give us some sort of idea what happened in England between 1520 and 1560'.[11] Belloc himself was to write extensively on that earlier period, producing studies of Wolsey, Cromwell and Cranmer, culminating in his *How the Reformation Happened* (1928). But the subject of predilection for British Catholics, both as historians and as novelists, remained the great persecution that took place in Elizabeth's reign, as in, for example, Christopher Hollis' historical work *The Monstrous Regiment* (1930). Mrs Wilfrid Ward's novel *Tudor Sunset* (1932) was to be a far more nuanced picture of the clash of loyalties in the period, though none of the horrors were spared. The best, and one of the last, of the profuse literature dealing with the Elizabethan martyrdoms was Evelyn Waugh's *Edmund Campion* (1935), a life of the great Jesuit martyr which outshines all its predecessors on that subject.

The main impression one gains from this martyrdom literature is one of a claustrophobic, clandestine society, perpetually having to take precautions against hostile authority and against informers and spies. The heroism of the priests who, knowing what awaited them if caught, nevertheless returned time and again from the continent in order to serve the Catholic community by providing them with the sacraments, is constantly underlined, as are the great risks taken by the households that harboured them. And the barbarous punishments – the torture on the rack and then the hanging, drawing and quartering while still alive – are at times described in harrowing detail. Part of the impact of these novels was that they drew heavily on actual historical events. Benson's *Come Rack! Come Rope!*, in particular, deals with the scandal of the betrayal of the Fitzherbert brothers by their son and nephew Thomas Fitzherbert (a story so awful that it figures, in passing, in much of the Catholic literature of this time, as an example of the extremes to which human treachery could go in Elizabeth's reign).[12] But even in the novels whose main characters are fictional, real characters are usually visible in the background. Mrs Wilfrid Ward, in *Tudor Sunset*, produces an array of real-life figures that are richly interwoven into her fictional plot and lists, at the end of the book, the sources that she has so closely followed. Among the historical characters she uses is the Countess of Arundel, Mrs Ward's own ancestor and widow of the martyred Philip Howard, Earl of Arundel.

Prominent among these real figures, in such novels, are the great exemplary heroes and villains of Catholic history. The heroes include Edmund Campion, who makes striking appearances in both of Benson's Elizabethan novels. A popular villain is Richard Topcliffe, the dastardly 'poursuivant' whose methods of spying and of torture had become a byword. As the man who had suborned young Fitzherbert to betray his family, he naturally plays a large part in Benson's *Come Rack! Come Rope!* But he also appears as an evil force in the background of *By What Authority?* and in Mrs Ward's *Tudor Sunset* he plays a central and sinister role. Christopher Hollis, in his history *The Monstrous Regiment*, uses Topcliffe prominently in order to illustrate the viciousness of the period.[13]

The exemplary figure who epitomized the Catholic public's view of sixteenth-century history was, however, Mary Queen of Scots. She stood, in the literature of this period, for Catholic martyrdom. All the other details of her tempestuous and erratic life were subordinated to her suffering and imprisonment, her betrayal by intermediaries and her execution and death. Even Fr. Rolfe, who exhibited such scorn for most aspects of his contemporary Church, shared in this cult for 'that predestined victim of countless treasons, of unnumbered wrongs, wrongs which warped and maddened and bewildered her noble nature, but never quenched her courage, . . . never made her false to her faith'.[14] Catholic poets, too (including prominently 'Michael Field')[15] often chose this subject. As might be expected, R. H. Benson incorporated Mary's story into his novels. In *Come Rack! Come Rope!* the young priest Robin Audrey sees her as 'a champion for the Faith of them all, an incarnate suffering symbol, in flesh and blood, of that Religion for which he, too, was in peril'.[16] Three chapters of this book are devoted to Mary's last days at Fotheringay: young Robin visits her secretly, shrives her and gives her communion and later witnesses her execution.[17]

One can never underestimate the great change that took place in the British public's view of the Catholic martyrs of the Elizabethan period in the early twentieth century. As Bede Camm put it in 1910:

> Englishmen of all creeds have grown more sympathetic of late, as they have come to know something of the true story of that long persecution which made their Catholic fellow countrymen outlaws in their own land.[18]

Camm himself was partly responsible for the change, though it was his friend Robert Hugh Benson and other writers of the revival who were to have the greatest impact upon the general public. As one observer has put it, the novelists and historians of this period left 'a permanent mark on the popular perception of the Catholic past and helped to construct a recusant ideal and identity which remains potent'.[19]

Visions of the Future: utopian/dystopian fantasies

In the late nineteenth and early twentieth centuries there was a considerable vogue for 'time travel' novels. Though some were utopian, far more
common were pessimistic and often nightmarish visions of the future which
have become known as 'dystopias'. Prominent among these were Richard
Jefferies' *After London: or Wild England* (1885) and H. G. Wells' *The Time
Machine* (1895). They were followed in the first half of the twentieth century
by many others. These stories were produced not merely as neutral fantasies about what the future might hold. They were a highly suitable vehicle
for conveying the authors' views about the possible effects in the future of
what they considered to be dangerous trends in the present.[20] It is hardly
surprising that a number of Catholic authors should have decided to write
novels or short stories of this type, given the strength of their opinions on
the nature of modern society.

The first Catholic futuristic novel is, however, hard to categorize in these
terms. Fr. Rolfe's *Hadrian the Seventh* (1904) is neither utopian nor dystopian; nor does it take us far into the future. It is, rather, an extraordinary
study of wish-fulfilment in the immediate future, a fantasy whereby George
Arthur Rose, a thinly disguised figure of Rolfe himself who has like him
been refused for the priesthood, is transported from a life of poverty to the
Vatican where, eventually, he is elected Pope. As Pope, he sets on foot various
reforms and to that extent this work shares some characteristics of utopian
literature, in that some of the author's own views are here illustrated to the
full. They are a strange mixture of highly reactionary political and social
attitudes, Catholic anti-clericalism and some forward-looking views, such
as the need for the Papacy, imprisoned in the Vatican, once more to turn
outwards to the world, relinquishing any claim to temporal power, and to
seek accommodation with the secular power in Italy. But the main impact of
this book is caused not by these concerns, but by two very different characteristics. The first of these is its extraordinary and original style and forms
of expression, which A. J. A. Symons described as 'a feat of writing difficult
to parallel; original, witty, obviously the work of a born man of letters, full
of masterly phrases and scenes'.[21] The second striking aspect is the depiction of the hero. In him we find much of Rolfe himself: the prickliness, the
alienation from society, the thwarted vocation, the 'exasperation' with the
world, with the Church and with everything around him. But we are also
compelled, as Graham Greene has pointed out,[22] to sympathize with him
in his evident desire for goodness, for purity. In his anguished prayer in the
first scene of the novel a tortured soul longing for union with God is laid
out before us:

God, if ever you loved me, hear me, hear me. De profundis ad Te, ad Te clamavi. Don't I want to be good and clean and happy! What desire have I cherished since my boyhood save to serve in the number of your mystics? What but that have I asked of You Who made me?

Not a chance do You give me – ever – ever –

Listen! How can I serve You? How be happy, clean, or good, while You keep me so sequestered?[23]

Our sympathy for the hero remains right to the end of the novel, where Hadrian is assassinated and forgives his murderer. The final sentence of the novel is a resonant one: 'Pray for the repose of His soul. He was so tired.'[24]

Among those most impressed by *Hadrian the Seventh*, when it first came out in 1904, was Robert Hugh Benson, who wrote to Rolfe with great enthusiasm:

I hope you will allow a priest to tell you how grateful he is for *Hadrian the Seventh*. It is quite impossible to say how much pleasure it has given me in a hundred ways, nor how deeply I have been touched by it. I have read it three times, and each time the impression has grown stronger of the deep loyal faith of it, its essential cleanness and its brilliance . . . You have taught me the value of loneliness, and many other lessons.[25]

Rolfe's book influenced in various ways Benson's *Lord of the World*, which appeared in 1907. An Englishman who unexpectedly becomes Pope, and the uncanny physical likeness of that Englishman to another person, are central to both plots; and much of the description of the Holy City in Benson's novel is reminiscent of Rolfe, as is the obsession with Papal ceremonial and the distaste for modern politics of the Left.

Benson's attempts at such novels, however, come nowhere near the literary quality of Rolfe's book. They tend to be turgidly written. Nevertheless, Benson's imaginative power makes of them powerful additions to the genre. In Wellsian manner, *Lord of the World* contains an underlying message of warning about the way in which the present-day world is likely to develop, though here the theme is that of the danger of the emerging secularized society. Benson takes us to a time a hundred years hence, to the year 2007, in which Britain and the world have been taken over by what he describes as 'dogmatic secularism'.[26] Religion has been all but abolished; euthanasia has been introduced on an institutional scale; capital punishment has been abolished; socialistic policies have changed the class system. The Church had been helpless to resist all this. Protestantism, which consists of individualism and 'sentiment', has weakened religion in the face of secular forces, as has Modernism within the Catholic Church, which has undermined both the authority of the Church and the basis of belief (this novel was, of course, written in the middle of the Modernist crisis).[27] So it is, in this future world, that the Protestant Churches have gone out of existence and only a small and depleted Catholic Church, resting on authority and tradition and rejecting Modernism, stands in the way of total secularization. We see that Church gradually suffering more and more persecution.

Soon everything comes to a head in a most alarming way. The new Humanism is taking on more and more the guise of a religion. And now, at the head of it all, there comes a mysterious figure called Felsenburgh. Not only is he the spitting image of the new Pope (an English priest, formerly Father Percy Franklin); he also appears to be a grotesque parody of Christ himself, calling himself the 'Son of Man', and being worshipped by the adherents of the religion of Humanity. We gradually begin to realize that Felsenburgh is the Antichrist, the 'Lord of the World', and that the end of the world is nigh. As the persecution of the Church intensifies, there are ever clearer signs of impending doom. These are remarkably similar to the effects of climate change in our own day. The earth is becoming unbearably hotter and this is accompanied by violent changes in weather patterns, including 'earthquakes of astonishing violence, a ripple [that] had wrecked not less than twenty-five towns in America; an island or two [that] had disappeared'.[28] The novel ends with a magnificent scene in which, as the world comes to an end, the last Pope celebrates his last Mass and Benediction.

This is a sensational novel. Benson did not, however, believe that this imagined society of the future was in any way unreal. As he was later to say, he had 'attempted to sketch the kind of developments a hundred years hence which, I thought, might *reasonably be expected* if the present lines of what is called "modern thought" were only prolonged far enough.'[29] Four years after *Lord of the World*, Benson produced another fantasy of the future, *The Dawn of All* (1911). In the preface he gave his reasons for writing it. He had been assailed by comments that *Lord of the World* was 'exceedingly depressing and discouraging to optimistic Christians'. He had therefore decided to produce another picture of the future, of 'the kind of developments, about sixty years hence which, I think, *may reasonably be expected* should the opposite process begin, and ancient thought (which has stood the test of centuries, and is, in a very remarkable manner, being "rediscovered" by persons even more modern than modernists) be prolonged instead.'[30] It is significant that this more optimistic novel was written at the height of the Integrist reaction to Modernism, under Pope Pius X.

Unlike most of the 'novels of the future' in this period, this appears to have been intended as a utopia rather than a dystopia. This being so, it can hardly have been the author's intention that dystopian features should emerge in it – but Benson's vision nevertheless turns out to be strangely disturbing at times. His treatment of certain themes is oddly ambiguous, as though the certainty with which he was able to deal with negative subjects (as in *Lord of the World*) failed him when he had to deal with the possible positive outcomes of his beliefs.

The Dawn of All's voyage into the future is not a real one, but takes the form of a dream. An apostate priest, lying on his deathbed, is projected into the year 1973, where he finds that he is Monsignor Masterman, Secretary to the Cardinal of Westminster. This enables the technique of the naïve observer to be used, as this 'outsider' is able naturally to ask all sorts of questions (claiming loss of memory), and to be vouchsafed all kinds of information. What he has come to is a clerically dominated society, in which the ecclesiastics regularly make use of Latin as their spoken language. It is explained to him that for a short period, from about 1900 to 1920, it had looked as though Socialism would dominate the world.[31] But gradually people had come to realize that the truth lay with religion and with tradition. The Catholic Church became the dominant expression of this.

Masterman finds that new 'Christian' laws have been introduced, abolishing divorce, making fornication a felony and using ecclesiastical courts to deal with heresy, for which those convicted are handed over to the secular power.[32] The treatment of heresy is an issue on which Benson seems in two minds. Masterman finds that a sincere young priest, who has been unable to accept the Church's stance on 'the miraculous in religion', has been condemned to death. Masterman reacts to this with 'horror and loathing'. But the authorities and even the condemned man himself, explain to him the necessity for society to defend itself in this way, with a Catholic country having 'a perfect right to protect herself by the death penalty against those who menace her very existence as a civilized community'.[33] Masterman eventually comes to accept this.

What is one to make of this? At all events Masterman, as he returns to the present day in his hospital, becomes reconciled to the Church as a result of his experiences. As he says to the young priest who has come to give him the last rites:

> The sign of the Prophet Jonas, . . . Resurrection. That is what I have seen . . . No; I know it was a dream . . . But it is possible; the Church has the power within her. It may happen some day; or it may not. But there is no reason why it should not.[34]

One of the most amazing of the novels of the future, written in the interwar period, was John Gray's *Park* (1932), whose subtitle was 'a fantastic story'.

Its author was the remarkable priest, based in Edinburgh, whom we have seen, in his earlier existence, as a major figure of the group around Oscar Wilde in the 1890s. *Park* (published in a limited edition of 250 copies) was, like its author, idiosyncratic, clever and complicated. Clearly aimed at a small, elite audience, it is full of knowing allusions to other works and to features of the faith. Where it differs from other Catholic novels of the future is that, though it has a religious theme, it does not seem to have a discernible message.

A Catholic priest, Mungo Park, walking in the Cotswolds, suddenly finds himself in a future civilization existing in the same landscape. The first person he meets speaks to him in Latin; and he discovers that he has come to a society ruled by the Catholic Church. The debt to Benson's *Dawn of All* is obvious. Where he differs from Benson, is in the fact that this theocratic society is entirely made up of black people, many of whom are priests. Gradually he begins to realize (like Wells' hero in *The Time Machine*) that there is also another race, that had once been the white population of the country, living underground, where they have taken on rat-like characteristics.[35]

A mere enumeration of sources, however, can in no way convey the originality of this book. One of its main characteristics is a ludic series of hints and nudges to the reader, often relating to sources or to ecclesiastical in-jokes. The very name of the main character points us in part towards Gray's Scotland (and to St Mungo, or Kentigern – the protagonist also calls himself Kentigern) and in part towards Mungo Park's *Travels into the Interior of Africa* (1799), in which Park showed himself at times impressed by the civilized qualities of some of the natives. Another source, the title of which is slyly alluded to in the text, is Herman Melville's *Typee* (1846), which parallels the theme of Park's captivity among his new acquaintances and also certain details of his experiences.

Side-references slyly bring in Gray's friends and interests, as when, he compares some pictures to those of his close friend David Jones, the Catholic artist and writer: 'At the next he almost gave a cry: pure David Jones.'[36] Mungo Park's love of books, manuscripts and art clearly echoes Gray's own. Above all, the many conversations in this book are written in a terse, allusive style which is typical of Gray's quirky mind and which also reminds one, at times, of the style of Ronald Firbank.

As with the other writers of novels of the future, Gray shows us these events in an easily recognizable landscape, the Cotswolds. And, like other Catholic novelists, he dwells upon the liturgical and theological features of the faith, one of the central scenes being a celebration of Mass in the cathedral.

As in *The Dawn of All*, the whole vision of the future turns out to be a kind of dream. At the end, Park is lying by the roadside, having had some kind of blackout. He hears kind strangers discussing him (even here, a Firbankian quality is felt when one of the ladies, told by her companion that the nearest hospital is in Cirencester, corrects his pronunciation: 'Cizzeter, she corrected, having a mania of her own').[37] In hospital, he is recognized as Dr Park, who has been staying in Malmesbury. All in all, this is a fascinating and unusual book, which deserves to have a far wider readership than it at present enjoys.

One year later Evelyn Waugh was to produce the short story 'Out of Depth' (1933), which owed a great deal to *Park*. This was his first specifically Catholic work and its message is that of the continuity and indestructibility of the faith throughout the ages.[38] Much later, Waugh was to produce a remarkably unsuccessful story, 'Love among the Ruins' (1952), which owes a great deal to Aldous Huxley's *Brave New World* (but which contains very little in the way of a Catholic message). Apart from that, the genre, though continuing to flourish in secular literature, died out as a Catholic phenomenon.

The most important element in Catholic stories of the future, for us, is the insight they give us into the basic ideas and philosophies of the authors concerned.

Visions of the Supernatural: ghost stories

The attitudes towards spirituality of many French Catholics of the turn of the nineteenth and twentieth centuries have been described thus:

> A fear of Evil personified in a material spirit, the Demon, who can persecute us and pursue us everywhere, . . . a quasi-Manichaean battle between independent forces . . . . At the same time, a large part of the Catholic public took delight above all in revelations, in miracles, in tangible signs of divine or evil interventions. There was a taste for the magical and the extraordinary, a belief in the efficacy of certain rites, and interest in the exterior manifestations of mysticism, which were reduced to a series of automatic effects produced by magical formulae and incantations.[39]

These characteristics were shared by many Catholics in Britain in the same period. There are a number of examples among the writers of the English revival; and nowhere more clearly than in the stories of the supernatural written by R. H. Benson and one or two others. One sometimes gets the impression that for Benson, as for Huysmans, 'credo' could mean 'je suis crédule', and that in his works the Devil sometimes loomed larger than God.

The ghost story was very much in mode in secular literature in the early twentieth century. At Cambridge Montague R. James, Provost of King's College, composed horrifying stories which were eventually collected in the *Ghost Stories of an Antiquary* (1904). Among those influenced by him were the three Benson brothers and Shane Leslie, all of whom were in or around Cambridge in the mid-1900s (E. F. Benson and Shane Leslie both being Kingsmen).[40] All four of these men were to be well-known proponents of the ghost story. In the work of R. H. Benson (whose collection of ghost stories, *A Mirror of Shalott*, appeared in 1905), and Shane Leslie, we find a particularly Catholic slant to this genre, which is also to be found in such other Catholic exponents as 'Roger Pater', whose stories were published in the volume *Mystic Voices* (1923).[41]

Benson delighted in the ghoulish and was obsessed with ghosts. Shane Leslie describes him 'sitting in the firelight of my room at King's, unravelling a weird story about demoniacal substitution, his eyeballs staring into the flame, and his nervous fingers twitching to baptise the next undergraduate he could thrill or mystify into the fold of Rome.'[42] In such readings, 'his success was enormous', and 'his only rival was the Provost of King's, whose *Ghost Stories of an Antiquary* was being read to nervous listeners at the time.'[43]

Like his brother E. F. Benson,[44] Robert Hugh was strongly affected by spiritualism. Though E. F.'s attitude was one of detached interest in psychical phenomena, R. H., as a Catholic, took a more adverse view of the matter. In his view, spiritualism was a great and mortal danger. He did not consider it, as did many of its opponents, to be a futile and unreal fantasy; for him, spiritualist activities could be efficacious, carrying with them a very real danger of the unleashing of demonic forces into human souls. In his novel *The Necromancers* (1909) a young man who has been dabbling in spiritualism finds himself completely taken over by an evil force. There are some powerful scenes in this novel – above all the final scene of a Manichaean struggle between good and evil, in which the young man's whole being is torn apart by the being that possesses him, before it is evicted by the purity and steadfastness of a young girl who loves him. Not, however, before she has been aware that 'the Thing had come from a spiritual distance so unthinkable and immeasurable, that the very word distance meant little.'[45]

Benson's stories in *A Mirror of Shalott* (in which a series of priests recount their experiences of the supernatural) often portray a similar belief in diabolic possession. In 'Father Girdlestone's Tale' a priest is unaccountably, for no apparent reason, assailed by an evil force which affects him 'mind, body and soul'. Here, too, the climax is a Manichaean battle, in the confines of the priest's study, where he experiences 'that endless war of spirit and spirit which has been raging since Michael drove Satan from heaven – that ceaseless untiring conflict in which all that is not for God is against Him, seeking to dethrone and annihilate Him who gave it being.'[46]

The Devil plays a major part in most of these stories. He appears as an evil force within people, as in 'Father Meuron's Tale', a story of diabolic possession in the Caribbean, or a solid figure who tries to interfere in human events, as in 'Father Martin's Tale'. In this story an apparently human figure attempts to mislead a priest in order to deprive a dying woman of the last sacraments.

Benson continually contradicts the modern view of psychological disorders. They are, he claims, not a clinical aberration to be explained by physical causes, but a horrifying and truthful awareness of the terrible forces that lie beneath our conscious world and which are far more real than it is:

> The 'delusions' of the mad are not non-existent – they are glimpses, horrible or foul or fantastic, of that strange world that we take so quietly for granted, that at this moment and at every moment is perpetually about us – foaming out its waters in lust or violence or mad irresponsible blasphemy against the Most High.[47]

Dom Roger Hudleston, who wrote ghost stories under the pseudonym of 'Roger Pater', was a much gentler figure. Many of the stories in *Mystic Voices* (1923) are calm depictions of the past impinging on the present. Usually this past is that of the persecutions of the penal times. The central figure in the book is a squire-priest of recusant stock, Philip Rivers Pater. In 'The Priest's Hiding Place' and 'The Treasure of the Blue Nuns'[48] there are vivid re-enactments of clandestine masses and martyrdoms, produced either by the influence of a place where these things took place, or by an object connected with them. Such experiences of the past are not restricted to the British martyrs. In 'The Persecution Chalice' a priest relives, while celebrating mass, the experience of some French priests celebrating mass at danger to their lives, with the same chalice that he is using, during the French Revolution.[49] Another of Roger Pater's major themes, as in the stories 'De Profundis' and 'The Footsteps of the Aventine', is that of attempts by souls in Purgatory to communicate with the living in order to find ways to alleviate their suffering.[50]

Benson's influence can however be perceived in 'The Astrologer's Legacy' and 'A Porta Inferi'. In both stories spiritualism and necromancy are major themes. 'A Porta Inferi' is particularly horrible and echoes themes from *The Necromancers*. A former spiritualist, now an inmate of a psychiatric hospital, is possessed by the spirit of a long-dead murderer. In a rare moment

of escape from the being that lives within him, he begs the priest-narrator
to save him:

> 'My God! How I hate him, devil that he is; and oh, to think that I let him
> in so willingly . . . He uses me, I tell you, like a slave. My hands, my limbs,
> my brain, my will, he's got it all, all of me, at his mercy. The filthy, hateful
> devil that he is, and did it by pretending to be my friend.'

In a typically Bensonian ending, the priest combats the evil spirit that inhab-
its his friend. The spirit taunts him through his friend's mouth: '"A nice,
mean, low sort of priest's trick to play on me. Thought you'd get hold of
yer old pal, and pilot him into heaven while number one was out, did yer?
Bah!" – and he spat at me – "You dirty swine!"' By the power of God, the
priest eventually manages to remove the evil being from his friend's body
but the man, now it has gone, is dead.[51]

One question is raised: how could believing Catholics such as Benson,
Hudleston and Leslie justify creating such stories? As Shane Leslie has put
it: 'It is generally believed that among other restrictions Catholics (R. C.)
are not allowed to believe in ghosts.' Yet he goes on to say that though this
may be the popular belief, 'incidents constantly break in contrariwise', and
'Catholics, both priests and laymen, report ghosts or what are called "psychical phenomena".'[52]

Leslie's *Ghost Book* (1955), which relates supposedly true stories, was
the last gasp of the credulous attitude to such matters typical of many in
the Church of his youth. In it, he reported almost any such story that had
come his way during his long life, often at second- or third-hand. Typical
formulae are: 'I am indebted to Father Coghlin, OSB, of St Gregory's Church,
Cheltenham, for an interesting story that he heard first-hand from Father
Flint, of the Northampton Diocese'; 'One of the strangest stories that I
ever heard came from the lips of a bishop, the late Dr Lyons of Kilmore,
who referred me to the Bishop of Galway. He had heard it at the same time
when the story was told at Maynooth in 1935.'[53] Though Leslie occasionally expresses doubts about some of the stories, his other comments show
how much he is prepared to accept of even the wildest tales. For example,
he explains the fact that 'ghosts are not much heard of in Catholic countries compared with the British Isles' by the possibility that 'perhaps they are
less persistent where Masses can be easily procured for their allayance.'[54]
And he notes a number of the most typical phenomena: 'A common type
of ghost in Catholic circles is the return of the spirit of some priest anxious
that Masses should be said for himself or on the score of Masses left unsaid';
'Haunted presbyteries are common'; 'Many convents are very happily

and quietly haunted by the spirits of nuns who died in peace but are permitted to pay little visits or to finish up little tasks'.[55] No doubt through the influence of his mentor Benson, Leslie was also strongly convinced of the dangerous powers of spiritualism and of the 'evil spirits' that it could let loose.[56]

Benson, 'Pater' and Leslie, though they represent one area of turn-of-the-century Catholicism, are not however representative of their English Catholic contemporaries as a whole. G. K. Chesterton exemplifies another attitude to these things. In the 1926 volume *The Incredulity of Father Brown* Father Brown is sceptical about people's belief in supernatural phenomena, pointing out on several occasions, how unchristian such beliefs are. In 'The Oracle of the Dog' the character describes this modern trend:

> People readily swallow the untested claims of this, that or the other. It's drowning all your old rationalism and scepticism, it's coming in like a sea, and the name of it is superstition. . . . It's the first effect of not believing in God that you lose your common sense and can't see things as they are. Anything that anybody talks about, and says there's a good deal in it, extends itself indefinitely like a vista in a nightmare.[57]

In another story, Father Brown makes it clear that a character had made a mistake by deciding to tell him a supernatural story, in order to put him off the scent of the truth: 'He had the notion that because I am a clergyman I should believe anything. Many people have little notions of that kind.'[58] And, in a typical Chestertonian paradox, in yet another story he suggests that superstition is a product of materialism:

> Don't think I blame you for jumping to preternatural conclusions. The reason's very simple, really. You all swore you were hard-shelled materialists; and as a matter of fact you were all balanced on the very edge of belief – of belief in almost anything.[59]

Chesterton's comments about the 'materialistic' nature of superstition are not wide of the mark. Most turn-of-the-century Catholics, whether in France or in England, tend to have seen mysticism as being better expressed by material external manifestations than by a more intimate relationship between the earthly and the heavenly.

Amid the plethora of ghost stories that appeared in the early twentieth century, Catholic ghost stories had a place, though it was a very limited one. M. R. James voiced the criticism held by many other secular writers when he said that R. H. Benson's were 'too ecclesiastical'.[60] Yet they appealed to the

Catholic public of the time and give us some insight into the more esoteric beliefs of some of those contemporary Catholics.

The Detective Story – Chesterton's Father Brown

One of the most popular literary genres in the late nineteenth and early twentieth century was that of the detective story, as we can see not only from the cult of Conan Doyle's Sherlock Holmes, but also from the great variety of stories that appeared at that time about other idiosyncratic detectives who each echoed, if in different ways, the unusual qualities of Doyle's hero.[61] These were to be followed in the twentieth century by a whole series of similar detective-heroes – Hercule Poirot, Miss Marple, Campion, Lord Peter Wimsey, and others.

G. K. Chesterton's Father Brown stories are the only important Catholic works in this genre.[62] Published between 1911 and 1935, they had enormous success and as was seldom the case for Catholic literature, that success extended to all sections of society. Chesterton created another detective figure whose superior insights were the result of his unusual way of looking at the world – but in this case the figure was a Catholic priest. He was depicted as a most unlikely person to show worldly skills – a clumsy, dumpy, amiable little man with 'a face as round and dull as a Norfolk dumpling'.[63] This contrast was a sure-fire formula for success with the reader. These stories are at first sight merely ingenious examinations of the real world around us, seen from unusual angles. Nevertheless, throughout the series, we continually find religious messages being subtly introduced.

Of course, at the time he wrote the earliest collections Chesterton was not yet a Catholic. But, as many commentators have pointed out, even before his actual reception into the Church in 1922 Chesterton had been Catholic in all but name. And even the earliest stories contain, in their nub, lessons of specifically Catholic import. In the first collection *The Innocence of Father Brown* (1911), for example, the story 'The Queer Feet' depicts the occasion when Brown had 'averted a crime and, perhaps, saved a soul'.[64] He has rescued the extremely valuable fish knives and forks of an exclusive dining club called the Twelve True Fishers', which had been stolen. The thief, he tells them, has repented. Their reaction is uncomprehending. He explains to them:

'If you doubt the penitence as a practical fact, there are your knives and forks. You are the Twelve True Fishers, and there are all your silver fish. But He has made me a fisher of men.'

'Did you catch this man?' asked the colonel, frowning.

Father Brown looked him full in his frowning face. 'Yes', he said, 'I caught him, with an unseen hook and an invisible line which is long enough to let him wander to the ends of the world, and still to bring him back with a twitch upon the thread.'[65]

This image has influenced other Catholic writers and thinkers in England and France – most notably Evelyn Waugh in his *Brideshead Revisited*. It also appears to have been the origin for Paul Claudel's wide-ranging use of the same image in his play *Le Soulier de Satin* (1929) where, in a scene between the heroine Prouhèze and her Guardian Angel, the image of the fisherman who plays the fish is used to explain God's hold over Prouhèze, wherever she may wander in this world.[66]

The next collection, *The Wisdom of Father Brown* (1914), contained much less in the way of religious comment. In the three collections that appeared in the interwar period, after Chesterton's conversion, *The Incredulity of Father Brown* (1926), *The Secret of Father Brown* (1927) and *The Scandal of Father Brown* (1935), religious issues come fully to the fore. The stories in *The Incredulity* are mostly centred, as the title suggests, around the paradox whereby unbelievers are more credulous, in relation to the supernatural, than Christians. Those in *The Secret* are mostly to do with the theme of forgiveness and are told within the framework of a discussion in which Brown describes how he solves cases by imagining himself into the mind of the criminal. In 'The Man with Two Beards' Brown rebukes someone who said of someone else, 'Hang it all, after all, he was a convicted thief', by saying 'Yes, and only a convicted thief has ever in the world heard that assurance: "This night shalt thou be with Me in Paradise".' The man had been, Brown says, 'one of those great penitents who manage to make more out of penitence than others can make out of virtue', 'he was not whitewashed, but washed white'.[67] In another story, 'The Vanishing of Vaudrey', the villain is described as 'a man with a character which he had made out of a temperament that might also have been turned to good'.[68] Throughout these stories 'the difference between human charity and Christian charity'[69] is highlighted by the attitudes of some of the non-Christian participants.

The final collection, *The Scandal of Father Brown* (1935), ends with a story that sums up Chesterton's aims and attitudes. The plot revolves around the attempted theft of a world-famous reliquary. An apparent murder, tinged with sacrilege, takes the attention of Brown, but he gradually realizes that this was not a murder, but an elaborate hoax using an already dead body, which had been devised to cover the attempted theft of the reliquary. He saves the reliquary and it is taken to the monastery of Casterbury, where it is going to be placed in the chapel after Benediction. As Father Brown is quietly praying in the chapel, the story, and the book, end magnificently with a depiction of Catholic liturgy typical, as we shall see,[70] of so much of the literature of the English Catholic revival:

> He raised his eyes and saw through the veil of incense smoke and of twinkling lights that Benediction was drawing to an end while the procession waited. The sense of accumulated riches of time and tradition pressed past him like a crowd moving in rank after rank, through unending centuries; and high above them all, like a garland of unending flames, like the sun of our mortal midnight, the great monstrance blazed against the darkness of the vaulted shadows, as it blazed against the black enigma of the universe. For some are convinced that this enigma also is an Insoluble Problem. And others have equal certitude that it has but one solution.[71]

Thus ends the saga of Father Brown, with an affirmation of the ageless nature of Catholic worship and the value of 'time and tradition'. The role of the detective, who solves 'insoluble problems' in this life, is linked to that of the priest, who has certainty that there is 'but one solution' to the ultimate mystery which so many see as insoluble. It sums up what Chesterton has been doing in these stories; using human detective problems to give us, through the interpretations put on them by the priest-detective, insights into ultimate truths.

Chesterton's use of a popular genre was infinitely more successful than that of his fellow Catholic authors. His stories are not only outstanding works of art by any standard; they also had a wide-ranging appeal, an appeal which has lasted until our own day.

The Catholic authors of this period were on the whole more successful in the historical novel and the novel of the future, than in the novel of modern life. This was in part, in the case of Benson, because these genres, full of action, required far less in the way of convincing psychological motivation. More generally, straightforward propaganda is far more justified as part of a historical story and the whole genre of the 'novel of the future' has always been based upon a biased glimpse into the results in the future of events in the present. Indeed, we will find when looking into the political and religio-political trends in this period (in Chapters 9 and 10) that the novel of the future will be of particular use to us, encapsulating as it does so clearly the ideas of the authors.

Ghost stories and tales of the supernatural are something of an anomaly in Catholic literature. While they can be seen as an obscure reflection of some of the more extreme 'mystical' beliefs of the generation of Catholics at the turn of the century, the essentially Manichaean struggles at the centre of so many of them raise doubts about the nature of their authors' beliefs.

In the detective story Chesterton achieved the ideal that so many Catholic authors aimed at – the entertaining incorporation of Catholic messages into a secular form, in a way that appealed to a wide readership, both secular and Catholic.

Notes

1   Evelyn Waugh, *Edmund Campion*, p. 109.
2   *Westward Ho!* p. 58.
3   See Margaret Maison, *The Victorian Vision*, pp. 169–82.
4   The new biographies included T. E. Bridgett's *Life of Blessed John Fisher* (1898) and J. B. Milburn's book on the Venerable Margaret Clitheroe, *A Martyr of Old York* (1900). The 1896 reprints included Richard Simpson's 1867 biography of *Edmund Campion*.
5   These included an important reprint in 1908 of the sixteenth-century account, by Cardinal William Allen and Henry Walpole, *A Briefe Historie of the Glorious Martyrdom of Twelve Reverend Priests: Father Edmund Campion and his Companions* (1582).
6   It is true that in the late nineteenth century there had been a few novels about the Elizabethan persecution – for example, Lady Georgiana Fullerton's *Constance Sherwood* (1865), Mrs Ogden Meeker's *Fortune's Football* (1864) and Cecilia Caddell's *Wild Times* (1872), but their literary quality was poor and their impact on the general public had been slight, aimed as they were at a specifically Catholic public. Little else in the way of Catholic historical novels preceded Benson.
7   Quoted in Margaret Maison, *The Victorian Vision*, p. 158.
8   Quoted in Blanche Warre Cornish, *Memorials of Robert Hugh Benson* Vol. 1, p. 31.
9   Benson, preface to *The Queen's Tragedy*, p. 9.
10 Benson, *By What Authority?* p. 53.
11 Hilaire Belloc, letter to A. C. Benson, 1 August 1907, quoted in C. C. Martindale, *The Life of Monsignor Robert Hugh Benson*, Vol. 2, p. 45.
12 See, for example, Christopher Hollis' *The Monstrous Regiment*, pp. 114–15. Benson got most of his information about this family from Bede Camm's *Forgotten Shrines*, in which it is the first and longest chapter (the first eighty-odd pages of the book).
13 Christopher Hollis, *The Monstrous Regiment*, pp. 114–15.
14 Fr. Rolfe (Baron Corvo), *Hadrian the Seventh*, p. 182.
15 'Michael Field' was the pseudonym of Catherine Bradley and Edith Cooper
16 Benson, *Come Rack! Come Rope!* p. 189.
17 Ibid., pp. 196–216.
18 Dom Bede Camm, OSB, *Forgotten Shrines*, p. xi.
19 Dom Aidan Bellenger, OSB, introduction to Bede Camm, *Forgotten Shrines* (2004), p. vii.
20 In Jefferies' case, the predictions were the dangers of the urban society and of

the neglect of natural rural values; in Wells', the dangers of the class divisions in modern society.

21   A. J. A. Symons, *The Quest for Corvo: An Experiment in Biography*, p. 6.
22   Graham Greene, 'Frederick Rolfe: Edwardian Inferno' (1934), in *Collected Essays*, p. 172.
23   Fr. Rolfe (Baron Corvo), *Hadrian the Seventh*, p. 16.
24   Ibid., p. 401.
25   Quoted in Symons, *The Quest for Corvo*, pp. 189–90.
26   Benson, *Lord of the World*, p. 7.
27   For the Modernist crisis, see pp. 129–36.
28   Benson, *Lord of the World*, p. 194.
29   Benson, preface to *The Dawn of All*, p. 5. My italics.
30   Ibid., p. 5. My italics.
31   Ibid., p. 25.
32   Ibid., p. 34.
33   Ibid., p. 136.
34   Ibid., p. 231.
35   John Gray, *Park*, p. 62.
36   Ibid., p. 12.
37   Ibid., p. 105
38   For 'Out of Depth', see pp. 180–2.
39   Richard Griffiths, 'Huysmans et le mystère du péché', p. 5.
40   Robert Hugh Benson was at the Catholic chaplaincy 1904–5 and then curate of Our Lady and the English Martyrs, 1905–8. His brother Arthur C. was a Fellow of Magdalene from 1904 onwards. His other brother Edward Frederic had been an undergraduate at King's under M. R. James and was a frequent visitor to his old college. Shane Leslie, of a younger generation, was an undergraduate at King's at the time of R. H. Benson's 'apostolate' in Cambridge.
41   'Roger Pater' was the pseudonym of Dom Roger Hudleston.
42   Shane Leslie, *The End of a Chapter*, p. 76.
43   Shane Leslie, 'The Cambridge Apostolate', in *Memorials of Robert Hugh Benson*, p. 47.
44   Among E. F. Benson's papers one finds letters of advice (in relation to such things as spirituality, the Tarot, making predictions and the use of such themes in his novels) from a clairvoyante called Miriam Harvey (aka Madeleine) and a bundle of 'letters to Madeleine from souls in torment'. (Benson papers, Bodleian Library, 3/67 and 3/68.) E. F. Benson's ghost stories often involve spiritualism.
45   *The Necromancers*, pp. 218–35.
46   *The Mirror of Shalott*, p. 116.
47   Ibid., p. 115.
48   Roger Pater, *Mystic Voices*, pp. 31–41, 93–103.
49   Ibid., pp. 13–20.
50   Ibid., pp. 42–55, 117–28. It is interesting to note that one of the best ghost stories by R. H. Benson's non-Catholic brother, E. F. Benson, 'The Confession of Charles Linkworth' (1912), involves a murderer who has been executed without confessing his crime and who desperately tries to get in touch with someone in order to confess it now. In the end, he is absolved by a (in this case Anglican) priest.

51 Ibid., pp. 81–92.
52 Shane Leslie, *Shane Leslie's Ghost Book* (1955), p. 3.
53 Ibid., p. 62, 90, 92.
54 Ibid., p. 130.
55 Ibid., p. 57, 61.
56 Ibid., p. 64.
57 G. K. Chesterton, 'The Oracle of the Dog', in *The Incredulity of Father Brown* (Cassell, 1926: reprinted in *The Father Brown Stories*, 1947, pp. 367–8).
58 'The Dagger with Wings', in ibid., p. 420.
59 'The Miracle of Moon Crescent', in ibid., p. 385.
60 Quoted in David Rowlands, introduction to Roger Pater's *Mystic Voices*, 1923.
61 See, in particular, the various volumes devoted by Hugh Greene to 'The Rivals of Sherlock Holmes'.
62 Though some other Catholics, such as Monsignor Ronald Knox, wrote successful detective novels, these did not have any specific Catholic content and therefore have no place in a study of 'Catholic literature'.
63 Chesterton, 'The Blue Cross', in *The Innocence of Father Brown* (1911), collected in *The Father Brown Stories* (1947), p. 10.
64 'The Queer Feet', in ibid., p. 39.
65 Ibid., p. 50.
66 Claudel was an enthusiastic reader of Chesterton's Catholic apologetic works. He also read the Father Brown stories with great interest. Strangely enough, as Claudel noted in his diary, his *Soulier de Satin* was translated into English by Father John O'Connor, the priest on whom Chesterton had based the character of Father Brown (*The Satin Slipper*, translation by J. O'Connor, preface by Paul Claudel, Sheed and Ward, 1931).
67 'The Man with Two Beards', in ibid., pp. 495–7
68 'The Vanishing of Vaudrey', in ibid., p. 539.
69 'The Chief Mourner of Marne', in ibid., p. 583.
70 See pp. 106–13.
71 'The Insoluble Problem', in *The Scandal of Father Brown*, pp. 703–4

8

Liturgical Ceremonies, Tacky Aesthetics and Class Distinctions: Some Themes in the English Novel

A major concern of British Catholic novelists in this period was to depict those things that differentiated Catholicism from other forms of the Christian religion and particularly from the Anglicanism from which so many of them had come. This led to an overriding concern with the liturgy and with ceremonial. It also led to a stress on some of the things that seemed strangest to non-Catholics – for example, the 'bad taste' of popular objects of devotion. And, given the class-based nature of British society at the time, the British Catholics also took delight in pointing to the aristocratic nature of the Catholic religion, as opposed to 'middle-class' Anglicanism. All this is very far from the concerns of the Catholic novel on the other side of the Channel. Let us start, however, by examining the extent to which the British Catholic novel, up to the late thirties, did or did not follow its French counterpart.

A Major French Preoccupation: the miraculous and vicarious suffering

The French Catholic novel has been described as having had three major strands. The 'pious', or 'sentimental' novel, a sub-literature of no great value; the 'conversion novel', of which Huysmans' *En route* (1895) was the prototype, followed by other works such as Ernest Psichari's *Le Voyage du Centurion* (1915); and the most widespread form, the 'miraculous', or 'mystical novel', in which the framework of the realist novel served as a backdrop for mystical and often miraculous events. A far less prominent strand was that exemplified by some of the novels of Paul Bourget, in their examination of human dilemmas relating to faith (it was this strand, minor in France, that was to become the dominant one in Britain).

One of the major characteristics of the 'mystical novel' was a particularly literal interpretation of the mystical experience. The prayers and sufferings of certain individuals had an influence (often described in almost mechanical terms) upon the events of the novel. Above all, vicarious suffering took a central place (and was used as much as a literary technique as a religious doctrine, both in the novel and in other literature of the period, including the plays of Claudel and the poetry of Péguy). In the novels of Léon Bloy, Émile Baumann, Adolphe Retté, Paul Bourget, André Lafon and many others (and, later on, Mauriac and Bernanos), central characters could take on suffering to expiate the sins of the world, or the sins of others, and the plot could revolve around the miraculous results of that sacrifice. Other forms of miraculous intervention were similarly used to stress the importance of the spiritual life that lay behind the appearances of reality depicted by the realist novel.

What of the English Catholic novel? England certainly produced, from the mid-nineteenth century onwards, many examples of the 'pious' or 'sentimental' novel. It also produced one or two examples of well written and effective 'conversion novels', such as John Henry Newman's *Loss and Gain* (1848) and Compton Mackenzie's *The Heavenly Ladder* (1934). But what of the 'miraculous' or 'mystical' novel? Though the importance of suffering, in the Christian life, was an essential theme of the English novel, this was not on the whole linked with the miraculous, or with 'vicarious suffering', until Graham Greene embarked on his career as a Catholic novelist in the late 1930s. In its place, as we have seen, we find a number of other genres, which accord more with British concerns: historical novels dealing with the British Catholic past, novels of the future, but above all novels of contemporary life which, eschewing the miraculous, dealt with moral dilemmas which reflected the problems of Catholics living in the modern world. This latter has remained the dominant strain in English Catholic narrative prose up to the present day.

The exception to this was R. H Benson. Though his modern novels on the whole adhere to the pattern above, we at times find use of the supernatural (though in a diabolic context) in works such as the ghost stories of *A Mirror of Shalott* (1905) and the novel *The Necromancers* (1909). In one of the ghost stories, 'Monsignor Maxwell's Tale' (1905) and in the novel *A Winnowing* (1910), moreover, we find techniques similar to those of the French Catholic novel. Both contain distortions of the doctrine of vicarious suffering and show the clear influence of one of Benson's favourite French authors, J. K. Huysmans.

Benson's debt to Huysmans is shown by his acceptance of the unorthodox version of the doctrine adopted by Huysmans and the heretical priest the Abbé Boullan. Vicarious suffering, as normally interpreted, denotes suffering willingly taken on in order to expiate the sins of others. It was originally seen as being suffering for humankind as a whole, to complement the sufferings of

Christ on the Cross.[1] This was eventually extended to suffering undertaken on behalf of *an individual*, to expiate his or her sins. Huysmans's extra variation on this belief (developed under the influence of Boullan) involved the actual taking on of the *sins themselves* of others, or even the other person's *temptations*.[2] This could lead to serious aberrations, both of belief and of behaviour.[3] It is significant that amid Benson's wide reading of Huysmans's books, *Sainte Lydwine de Schiedam* (1901), in which the doctrine of 'mystical substitution' is expounded most fully, should have been his favourite.[4] In the novel *Initiation* (1913), it is true, Benson did expound, in the mouth of the hero, an entirely orthodox version of the doctrine as suffering for the sins of another,[5] but elsewhere the distorted Boullanian version comes only too obviously to the fore.

This is particularly true of 'Monsignor Maxwell's Tale', in *A Mirror of Shalott*, where Benson not only follows this version of the doctrine; but goes even further by producing someone who is prepared to *lose his faith* in order to bring someone else to God. Significantly, Benson calls this a 'contract'.[6] The contract is fulfilled and the man goes through the most terrible suffering as he is deprived of his belief. This idea of someone giving up his faith, of God withdrawing his faith from him because he has asked God to do so, is of course extremely doubtful theologically, in that it presumes that God would accept such an extraordinary arrangement. As in so much of Benson's other writings, we feel a sense of uncertainty as to theological and spiritual values and as to the meaning of the doctrines he is expounding. One is reminded of Maisie Ward's view, that there were things in the Catholic faith that Benson really did not understand. 'Swiftly instructed and swiftly ordained', she wrote, 'he had had no opportunity to acquire an all-round Catholic intellectual equipment.'[7] Add to that the fact that he seems to have read widely but indiscriminately and that he appears to have taken uncritically on board some of the most questionable attitudes and opinions of writers like Huysmans, and you have a recipe for muddled and often contradictory Christian beliefs. In many respects he was the religious version of an autodidact, reading everything, believing everything and understanding nothing – a 'Bouvard and Pécuchet' of the Christian religion.

A Winnowing (1910) also centres round a tit-for-tat arrangement typical, in some respects, of the French Catholic novel. Yet here this hardly comes under the heading of vicarious suffering, in that the heroine offers herself in order to bring back to life her husband, who has just died. This is not suffering for expiation of sin. But even if expiation, the theological basis for vicarious suffering, is not present, there is no doubt that an arrangement of a dubious kind *is* here being entered into between a human being and God and that the miraculous does play a central role in the novel.[8]

Apart from these rare examples, no other British Catholic novels of this period introduce the miraculous as part of their main plot structure (if one excepts, in the 1930s, the heavy-handed whimsicality of Bruce Marshall's *Father Malachy's Miracle* (1931), where the miraculous is used mainly for humorous effect).

Indeed, at times novelists were at pains to deny the possibility of the miraculous. In Maurice Baring's *The Coat Without Seam* (the title of which seems to promise the miraculous), the curé who possesses part of the relic which was claimed to be the seamless robe worn by Christ before the Crucifixion, takes care to stress that part of the importance of relics lies in what people believe of them, rather than what they are. This relic in fact has no miraculous effect upon the plot of the novel and merely serves as a technique for bringing together various themes within the protagonist's life. In Baring's novels, as in those of so many other British Catholics, divine intervention does not come in as part of the equation.

A Shared Preoccupation: the 'explicators'

In both the French and the English Catholic novel, there was a tendency whereby authors set out to *explain* things, whether directly or indirectly. Of course, as we have seen, Catholic authors are prone to one form or other of didacticism. Like political novelists, they want to convey a message. Otherwise they remain novelists just like others, with their political or religious *engagement*, however important it is in their lives, having no real importance in their work. A lot depends, however, on the way such concerns are incorporated. In both the English and the French Catholic novel there were certain techniques that were often used, the major of which were either the provision of an 'explicator' to convey the author's intentions, or (more clumsily) the author's own interventions for the same purpose.

There were two orders of things that authors tended to wish to *explain*. On the one hand, there was the pure didacticism of which we have seen an extreme case in Emily Agnew:[9] a desire to convey religious or historical truths, in very obvious lectures. On the other hand, there was the aim of 'explicating' the action of the novel itself, of making the reader aware of the implications of what was going on.

The openly didactic vein on theological or historical matters was, it is true, used less widely in English Catholic novels in the twentieth century than it had been in the nineteenth. R. H. Benson was, as in so many other things, an exception to this, particularly in his historical novels. The use of the authorial voice, for example, could become overwhelming in his books, as in *By What Authority?* Even when he uses the mouths of other characters for the same purposes, it is always the author's voice that we hear. And when he uses the naïve observer technique,[10] he only too often puts into the mind of that character things which he or she could not possibly have known through observation or through foreknowledge.

The other strand of 'explication', concerned with explaining the events of the novel's plot or with prescribing action to the characters, was the most widespread in the novels of the early twentieth century. Often the purveyor of such information was a priest, to whom the characters went for advice. We have already seen how, in Maurice Baring's *Daphne Adeane*, this technique was used (to the detriment of what was otherwise a far more subtle and complex novel). Similar priestly counsel is given in many other novels in this period, including Mrs Wilfrid Ward's *One Poor Scruple* and *Great Possessions* and Baring's *Cat's Cradle*. The privileged informant need not necessarily be a priest. In Benson's *A Winnowing* the heroine comes to an understanding of the meaning of what has been happening to her through a lengthy interview with the prioress of a French community of nuns to whom she has given shelter, and in his *The Sentimentalists* it is Mr Rolls, the reclusive 'mystic', who 'explains' the situation of Chris Dell and who prescribes what is to be done. In a completely different context, *The Necromancers* contains a character, Mr Cathcart, who can explain everything about necromancy and is a tower of strength in relation to the specific situation being faced.

It is now worth looking at some of the recurrent themes in the English Catholic novel – themes that replaced those in the French equivalent. We will start with one of the most insistent of these themes, the liturgy.

A British Preoccupation: the liturgy

The liturgy dominated British Catholic literature during this period to an extent that was never reached in the equivalent French Catholic literature (except in the exceptional cases of Huysmans and Claudel).[11] One is led to ask oneself what the reasons can be for its insistent presence.

For many writers, the liturgy was central to their vision of the specifically British experience of the Church. The celebration of the Mass was seen as standing for the continuity of the Catholic religion in this country, through all its vicissitudes. Above all, the emotional impact of Catholic services struck a chord with those whose own previous tradition had too often seemed to them loveless or perfunctory.

One modern critic, writing about John Gray, has declared that 'modern taste reacts against the fetishistic, nineteenth-century form his Catholicism took – Benediction, Exposition and Perpetual Adoration: the stock-in-trade of the nineties convert.'[12] This is to take far too 'modern' a view of things. For most British Catholics in Gray's time Benediction and the Exposition of the Blessed Sacrament, which had been imported into the English Church in the mid-nineteenth century, were an integral part of their devotions. Where this statement is correct, however, is in the fact that this particular aspect of Catholic worship, with its concentration on the transubstantial belief in the actual presence of Christ in the Blessed Sacrament, did have a powerful impact upon this generation of converts.

The descriptions of these services are often detailed and at times make use of technical terms that clearly show they are being reassuringly aimed at a Catholic audience (or, conversely, at a non-Catholic audience which could be suitably impressed and mystified).

The liturgy could have various functions. At its simplest, it provided a dramatic moment at a crucial point in the plot. Often this was at the end of a novel, as in Mrs Wilfrid Ward's *One Poor Scruple*, where the tortured heroine shocks the priest by her distraught appearance at Mass, or at the end of the same author's *Great Possessions*, where the repentant heroine finds peace as she participates in the adoration of the Host alongside nuns in a Chelsea convent.[13] At the end of Maurice Baring's *The Coat Without Seam*, the semi-delirious dying hero, wounded in the front line in France, is present at a celebration of the Mass in a small French village. Though he has long been estranged from the Church, the service takes him back to the events of his youth: 'When the bell rang for the Elevation, he saw the church at Vernay.' Finally, he 'mechanically' takes part in all the crucial parts of the Mass:

> The Server said the Confession, and Christopher repeated it mechanically . . . Now it was the Blessing. Christopher mechanically made the Sign of the Cross. And then came the last Gospel, and the prayers after Mass. Christopher said them, too, mechanically. He remembered his early instruction and murmured the words *ex opere operato*.[14]

In Baring's *Daphne Adeane* the liturgy is similarly used at a moment of crisis. The hero and heroine are just behind the front line in France. The Angelus rings as they pass a little church and they go in. The Rosary is being said, the five Glorious Mysteries, and they join in. They know that they are 'on the eve of what was called "a big push", the new French offensive, of which great results were expected.' After the Rosary there is Benediction and the litany of Loretto[15] in the vernacular. They join in (parts of the text being quoted at this point). As they leave the church, we hear of their forebodings about the offensive.[16]

Even in ghost stories there are detailed descriptions of the Mass and other services, often in precise detail. In Roger Pater's short story 'The Priest's Hiding Place', for example, the priest-hero hears in the night, the 'echo' of a Mass celebrated in penal times in the very room he is in, with much of the text being quoted:

> Quite distinctly, in a low clear voice, came the words, '*In nomine Patris et Filii et Spiritus Sancti, Amen. Introibo ad altare Dei*' . . . All at once there came another surprise. The unknown priest was saying the *Confiteor*, and had got to '*Sanctis Apostolis Petro et Paulo*', and in my mind I was going on to '*omnibus Sanctis*', when the voice inserted the extra words, '*beato patri nostro Benedicto*' . . . 'So you are a Benedictine monk', I thought to myself.[17]

Similarly, in the same author's 'The Persecution Chalice', full details are given of the Christmas Mass that the hero celebrates:

> Just after the Offertory, when I had washed my fingers and was bowing down for the prayer before the *Orate fratres*, I noticed a sound far away outside the monastery. It was only a momentary distraction, and I paid no real attention to it, but went on to say the Secret and the Preface. At the *Sanctus* the boy rang the bell as usual, though there was no congregation. As I commenced the Canon I heard the sound again.[18]

In these cases, the considerable and often technical detail that is given of the Tridentine Mass appears to be aimed specifically at a Catholic audience. It and the other details of Catholic services and customs given in so many of Pater's stories, appear to be an attempt to vouch for the Christian aspect of these tales of the supernatural.

In the many Catholic historical novels and particularly in those relating to the reign of Queen Elizabeth, the Mass has a very dramatic role of a specific kind to play. R. H. Benson's novels depict clandestine celebrations of the Mass in times of great danger. In *By What Authority?*, for example, we have three lengthy depictions of the Mass and in *Come Rack! Come Rope!* the interrupted celebration of the Mass in the chapel at Padley plays a crucial part in the plot. Similarly, in Benson's book on the reign of Charles II, *Oddsfish!*, clandestine Masses are an important part of the plot and the final dramatic scene depicts the secret administration of the last rites to the dying King. And a clandestine Mass celebrated in Newgate prison, by three priests who are about to be executed on the morrow, is a central scene of Mrs Ward's *Tudor Sunset*.

In certain novels, the Mass and Benediction have an even more dramatic, and more detailed, role to play. The ending of R. H. Benson's *Lord of the World* (1907) is an outstanding example of this. An earlier secular novel, widely read in its time, had had a strong influence upon it and upon other depictions. This was Ethel Lilian Voynich's *The Gadfly* (1897), which takes place in the Italy of the Risorgimento. In it the Catholic Church plays a baleful and repressive role. The hero ('The Gadfly') is a revolutionary who is also the lost natural son of Cardinal Montanelli, depicted as one of the more liberal figures among the Church's hierarchy. The climax of the novel is the Cardinal's agreement to the death of his son (who has been taken captive) in the interests of peace and order. In the final scene, the Cardinal participates in a High Mass, followed by Benediction. During it, he becomes obsessed by the images of blood in the liturgy and gradually loses his mind. During this scene, 'Tantum ergo' and 'O salutaris hostia', the two great hymns of Benediction, are quoted at length, as are other important texts referring to the Sacrament. As the Cardinal enters the chancel bearing the Host in its monstrance, he imagines that it is bleeding:

He saw their hungry eyes fixed on the sacred Body that he bore; and he knew why they bowed their heads as he passed. For the dark stream ran down the folds of his white vestments; and on the stones of the Cathedral floor his footsteps left a deep, red stain . . . And as he stood before the altar, holding aloft with blood-stained hands the torn and mangled body of his murdered love, the voices rang out in another peal of song;

> O salutaris Hostia,
> Quae coeli pandis ostium;
> Bella premunt hostilia,
> Da robur, fer, auxilium!

Finally, after violently addressing the congregation in the words of a God who, like him, has given up his Son, but who now regrets it and berates those he feels responsible, he flings down the monstrance containing the Host and voices a parody of the prayer of consecration:

'This is the body that was given for you – look at it, torn and bleeding, throbbing still with the tortured life, quivering from the bitter death-agony; take it, Christians, and eat!'

He had caught up the sun with the Host and lifted it above his head; and now flung it crashing down upon the floor.[19]

Ethel Voynich's novel was to become, in the twentieth century, required read-ing in the Soviet Union (where it sold over two and a half million copies) and later in the People's Republic of China. What is less well known, however, is that it was a best seller in every kind of circle in the years immediately following its publication and not least in Catholic circles, where its depic-tions of the liturgy appear to have outweighed the revolutionary content, no doubt because the Cardinal, and the tortures of his decision, were depicted in such a sympathetic light. A number of Catholic authors were influenced by the scene we have just described. R. H. Benson was clearly one of them, as the internal evidence of *Lord of the World* shows us.

At the end of Benson's novel the world is coming to an end. The last Pope, who with his Cardinals had been awaiting final destruction by their enemies, celebrates his last Mass, followed by Benediction, in the Holy Land where they have taken shelter. *O salutaris hostia* is sung and the humeral veil[20] is laid upon his shoulders. The world, which has been becoming hotter and hotter as the end draws nigh, is the vivid background to the ceremony:

Above the hills twenty miles away rested an enormous vault of colour . . . All was the one deep smoulder of crimson as of the glow of iron . . . Here, too was the sun, pale as the Host, set like a fragile wafer above the Mount of Transfiguration, and there, far down in the west where men had once cried upon Baal in vain, hung the sickle of the white moon . . .

> . . . *In suprema nocte coena,*
> sang the myriad voices,
> *Recumbens cum fratribus*
> *Observata lege plena*
> *Cibis in legalibus*
> *Cibum turbae duodenae*
> *Se dat suis manibus . . .*

Finally, the storm breaks, as they sing the 'Tantum ergo'. Events reach a climax, with the singing ever louder – and then come the last words of the novel, the simple, calm phrase: 'Then this world passed, and the glory of it.'[21]

Though the content, and the message, are naturally completely differ-ent from Voynich's, the technique, including the interspersing of text and Latin liturgy, is remarkably similar. Both in Voynich and in Benson, there is a pause between the Mass and Benediction, in which the central priestly figure, who has been finding difficulty during the Mass, tries to pull himself together. Benson appears to have been impressed by Voynich's revelation of the power such a liturgical scene could create as the climax of a novel and to have turned the technique to his own purposes. It makes of the last chapter of his book a fitting culmination to the theme of the triumph of the Antichrist, followed by the end of the world.

A number of these authors were concerned with expounding what the Mass signified. Often this was done by means of a comparison with the inferior worship of the Protestants and the Anglicans. Benson, in *By What Authority?* gives full explanations as to why the Mass takes the form that it does. He does this by depicting it through the eyes of a naïve observer, Isabel, a former Puritan who is attracted to Catholicism and who attends a clandestine Mass. She considers the meaning of what is going on, contrasting it with the Protestant worship she has attended, where the minister spoke loudly and distinctly to the congregation 'so that the intellect could follow the words, and assent with a hearty Amen':

> It was unlike anything she had ever imagined worship to be . . . The priest was addressing God, not man; therefore he did so in a low voice, and in a tongue, as Campion had said on the scaffold 'that they both understood'. It was comparatively unimportant whether man followed it word for word, for . . . the point of the worship lay, not in an intellectual apprehension of the words, but in a voluntary assent to and participation in the supreme act to which the words were indeed necessary but subordinate.

Behind Isabel we see Benson, for what is being produced is an apologia for the Catholic Mass. She not only observes the scene, but also *interprets it*, in a way of which she would have been incapable. Benson is, as so often, producing a didactic message in an unreal way. He ascribes to Isabel a clear picture of some of the central doctrines of the Catholic faith: the eucharistic sacrifice, transubstantiation and the sacramental role of the priesthood. She is aware that, for those around her, God is looking down and seeing the act of Calvary re-enacted:

> As He looked down well pleased into the silence and darkness of Calvary, and saw there the act accomplished by which the world was redeemed, so here (this handful of his disciples believed), He looked down into the silence and twilight of this little lobby, and saw that same mystery accomplished at the hands of one who in virtue of his participation in the priesthood of the Son of God was empowered to pronounce these heart-shaking words by which the Body that hung on Calvary, and the Blood that dripped from it there, were again spread before His eyes, under the form of bread and wine.[22]

Baring, in similarly didactic passages, is careful to create a more realistic picture of the role of the observer. In his novel C, the hero, who has recently attended a Catholic Requiem, describes in a letter to Beatrice, a Catholic, how impressed he has been. He is not Catholic, but on the basis of what Beatrice has told him and of a 'penny copy' of the Mass for the Dead that he has read, he is able to produce, rather more convincingly, a message akin to Benson's:

> You used to tell me when people criticised your services because they were in Latin and not everyone could understand and follow the words of the Mass, that it didn't matter whether they did or not; that the Mass was a Drama, and the people did not need to follow the words in their book; they could follow the action and say any prayers they liked. When you used to say this, I wondered what you meant . . . After reading the penny book, I began for the first time to have an inkling.

And C contrasts all this with Protestant ignorance:

> I seemed to begin to understand what you meant – the reason Protestants thought as they did, or, rather, received the impressions they received, when they went to Catholic services was that they had not the slightest idea what it was all about.[23]

Finally, one of the most dramatic uses to which the Liturgy is put, in the Catholic novel, is as a catalyst for conversion. Thus, in Mrs Wilfrid Ward's *Horace Blake* the hero, who, though he had been brought up as a Catholic, has for years been virulent in his attacks on religion, finally returns to his faith in a small Breton church, during Mass:

> From the first words of the Mass Horace was almost overwhelmed by the strangest, sweetest, saddest sense of familiarity. He knew it all so well – the *Confiteor*, the *Kyrie Eleison*, the *Credo*, and the warning note of the bell at the *Sanctus*. At length he came to the very central action of the Sacrifice; he bowed his soul in a heart-broken humiliation at the foot of the Cross of the Lord Who had taken upon Him the iniquities of us all.[24]

An even more dramatic scene takes place in Compton Mackenzie's *The Heavenly Ladder* (1924). At the Mass, a powerful force engulfs the hero, Mark:

> At Mass the church was filled with a sound from heaven as of a rushing mighty wind, and Mark heard above the sound Truth speaking with the

voice of a little child: 'If any man will come after Me, let him deny himself, and take up his cross daily, and follow Me. For whosoever will save his life shall lose it; but whosoever will lose his life for My sake, the same shall save it.'[25]

The Mass, Benediction, the Rosary and other aspects of the liturgy, served many purposes in English Catholic literature of this period. They provided dramatic moments, created a colourful backdrop for the action, illustrated the heroism of the days of persecution, and evoked the eternal truths of a faith lasting from century to century. Explanations of the form that the Mass took could be used to contrast it with Protestant practices. None of this, however, explains why detailed depictions of the liturgy played so much greater a part in English Catholic literature than in its French equivalent. One probable explanation is the contrast converts, from Newman onwards, felt between the 'wordy' worship of Anglicanism and the meaningful 'action' of the Mass. Added to this, some were no doubt attracted by what would shock low church or middle-of-the-road Anglicans. The Catholic Mass, in a language not 'understood by the people', and with much of it being intentionally inaudible, shocked those who believed that the clergy should speak to the intellect of their flock. And then there was the question of the nature of the Eucharistic sacrifice and those elements in the ritual of the Mass and of Benediction which revolved around the adoration of the Sacrament. In a country where 'Popery' had been for so long not just a term of abuse, but a symbol of fear, and where the atavistic reactions of the majority of the population were still affected by the historical mistrust engendered by previous ages, the Catholic liturgy stood for all that was abhorred in Catholicism. For many Anglicans 'the sacrifices of Masses' were still seen as 'blasphemous fables and dangerous deceits', and they believed that 'the Sacrament of the Lord's Supper' was not intended to be 'reserved, carried about, lifted up, or worshipped'.[26] Attacking both Roman Catholics and Anglican Ritualists, Lord John Russell had listed in 1850, among those practices that he considered to be most pernicious, 'the honour paid to saints, the claim of infallibility for the Church, the superstitious use of the sign of the cross, the muttering of the liturgy'[27] and so on. Attitudes were to remain much the same for many years to come. Depictions of the Mass and Benediction were a perfect way for those who had come from one faith to another to prove the great change that they had undergone. And for the former high churchmen among them, it was a perfect way to show their former colleagues how much more perfectly the Tridentine Mass translated the ideas of Ritualism!

A British Preoccupation: objects of devotion

Many British Catholic authors admired the liturgy not only as an arche-typal reflection of the truths of the faith, but also as an expression of beauty and magnificence. At the same time, they could also stress, as yet another example of the strangeness and 'difference' of their faith, the value of those aspects of Catholic art that were not aesthetically pleasing to the cultured eye. In this they differed greatly from most of their contemporaries in the French Catholic Revival.

It must be said that most of the French Catholic writers were artistic snobs. They ridiculed the popular religious art of their day, with its senti-mentalism and its vulgarity. The *objets d'art* sold in the little religious shops in the Place Saint-Sulpice in Paris, 'les bondieusarderies de la Place Saint-Sulpice', came in for particular opprobrium. Bloy, Baumann, Huysmans and many others described with horror the grotesque depictions of the crucified Christ and of the Sacred Heart. Huysmans, indeed, was convinced that 'the terrible appetite for ugliness that at present dishonours the Church'[28] had something supernatural, even Satanic, about it.

During the Catholic Revival in Britain, attitudes were on the whole quite different. Woodman, it is true, commenting on the prevalence of such 'tat' in British Catholic literature and experience, suggests that British Catholics could be divided into those for whom it had a 'populist appeal', and the 'clever, artistic and cultured', who (like the French authors) must often have been offended by it, but who (in a kind of 'inverted snobbery') tried to get the best of both worlds by accepting popular art for the people, while retaining themselves 'a strong sense of the Catholic high-art tradition'.[29] This is, however, to underestimate the importance of tawdry Catholic art even for the most sophisticated writers in this country, and the virtues they ascribed to it.

A man such as Rolfe could, of course, ape the French attitude when he referred scathingly to the 'tawdry insolence'[30] of most of the Catholic churches that he had attended. But in this, as in many other things, Rolfe was out of step with other British Catholic writers. Far more typical was Maurice Baring, whose heroine Beatrice Fitzclare, in the novel *C*, describes how the spiritual experience of the Mass can be felt as much in a village church as in a grand cathedral. Such churches may be filled with 'the cheapest coloured statuettes of St Joseph and the Sacred Heart and sham stained-glass made of coloured paper, and images of Our Lady like penny dolls dressed in tinsel', but these things are valid, because the Divine is indescribable in human terms, so that a child's picture may, in its simplicity, be a *better* rep-resentation than great art:

All these things help, I assure you; they don't hinder, because, don't you see, where the object represented is Divine and indescribable in human terms and by human means, the image is none the worse for being childish. After all, the best picture by the greatest artist in the world of something like the Crucifixion, is just as *inadequate* as a child's picture, and a child's picture is often more satisfactory, not as *art*, but as an image of the Divine, where the beauty is beyond human reach; the more frankly unpretentious and naïve the attempt at presentation the better; it becomes then a symbol.[31]

Often, in order to stress the virtuous and specifically Catholic nature of this unsophisticated art, the device of a naïve outsider was used. A good example is found in Mrs Wilfrid Ward's *One Poor Scruple*, where the author stresses the aristocratic credentials of such art. Here the aesthete Mark Fieldes attends Benediction in the private chapel in the house of the recusant Riversdale family:

It took some moments before Fieldes realised its ugliness . . . The chancel was small and square. Its corners were fitted with pilasters of imitation marble, and the door that opened from it into the sacristy had heavy supports and cross beams of the same salmon and green-tinted material . . . The Roman altar was of yellow marble, and on it stood tall gold candlesticks, of that kind of Parisian Gothic so common in French churches. Above the altar was an apse, filed by an enormous transparency, representing the resurrection, and . . . a cunningly disguised gas jet, now lighted, showed up the singularly unfortunate colours of this representation . . . He was half fascinated by the curious hideousness of the whole effect.[32]

Here the point is made even more clearly by the fact that the naïve observer is a Paterian aesthete who has been superficially attracted to religion by his love of beauty. By the end of the novel, the emptiness of Fieldes' approach to religion will have been made clear to us. Already, a contrast is being presented between him and the 'unworldly, God-fearing, country-loving Englishmen',[33] those recusants whose simple uncomplicated faith was reflected in the appurtenances of their religion. Indeed, even as he sits in the chapel Fieldes is aware that, despite its hideousness, he gained there 'a certain sense of its being a consecrated atmosphere into which he had been admitted. To whatever this atmosphere was to be attributed, he had always recognised it in Catholic churches.'[34]

The word 'tawdry' recurs again and again in English Catholic novels of this period, usually used approvingly, particularly in connection with the practices of the more aristocratic figures. Plaster statues of St Joseph play a particularly important part. In Benson's *The Sentimentalists* the priest Richard Yolland is characterized, from the start, by the objects surrounding him in his room, including 'plaster statues of Joseph and Mary'.[35] Later in the novel, he places letters he has written in front of 'the little plaster statue of God's mother', 'the little tawdry image', asking for guidance before he sends them off. Later still, when things seem to be going better, he goes into church to give thanks, 'kneeling under the low smoky roof, staring up and smiling towards the gilt tabernacle that shone tawdrily splendid in the gloom'.[36]

This concentration on the value of the ugly and tawdry was peculiar to British Catholicism and very different not only from the attitudes of French Catholicism, but also – more importantly to British Catholics – those of Anglicanism. Writing to his Anglican father at the time of his conversion, Gerard Manley Hopkins drew a contrast between the two religions:

> I am surprised you shd say fancy and aesthetic tastes have led me to my present state of mind; these wd be better satisfied in the Church of England, for bad taste is always meeting one in the accessories of Catholicism.[37]

English Catholic writers found ugliness, tawdriness, to be in no way contrary the worship of God, but on the contrary its sincere expression. Such tawdry art could also be a sign of the contrast between the convert's faith and the views of the uncomprehending masses surrounding him.

A British Preoccupation: class

British Catholic authors were obsessed with class. In part, no doubt, this was because Britain was a far more class-conscious society than France; but it also had much to do with the history of the Catholic Church in this island. The middle-class converts sat uneasily between the aristocratic romanticism of the old recusant families and the down-to-earth vulgarity, as they saw it, of the working-class Catholic majority. In the event, the glamour of the former won the day and, despite the numerical predominance of working-class Catholics, it was the upper classes and above all the recusants who formed the subject of predilection for the writers of the Catholic Revival. This can, of course, be seen as an example of the 'Catholic chic' identified by Thomas Woodman.[38] But, though a concern for what was 'smart' did enter into many of these authors' concerns, there was more to it than that. Recusancy represented the heroic days of the Catholic faith in this country and also the continuity of that faith over the centuries of deprivation and persecution.

Catholic historical novels had done much to raise awareness of the landed families who hosted the visiting priests in the times of persecution, at peril to their lives. As a spin-off from this, a further literature was devoted to fêting the scions of the same families in modern times. Dom Bede Camm, OSB, was typical of this trend. In his book *Forgotten Shrines: An Account of Some Old Catholic Halls and Families in England and of Relics and Memorials of the English Martyrs* (1910) he introduced his readers to some of the great houses inhabited by the recusant families, not only recounting the great events that had taken place in them, but also showing how they had remained in the possession of later generations of the same families, who shared in the same glamour.

Recusant families were not only envied for their history of fidelity to Rome; they were also admired, socially, for their distance from modern middle-class attitudes. Inevitably, the descriptions of them tended to be coloured by these romantic concerns. This is why it is perhaps best to start with a more balanced description by someone who was not a convert and was herself a scion of a recusant family: Josephine Mary Ward (Mrs Wilfrid Ward), who was descended through her mother, Lady Victoria Howard, daughter of the 14th Duke of Norfolk, from one of the most prominent Catholic families in the land. In *One Poor Scruple* she describes, as we have seen, the recusant Riversdale family. Two Riversdales had been martyred in the sixteenth century, and in the seventeenth 'the family had gone through all the ups and downs, all the hopes and disappointments that befell Catholics in England.' After the departure of James II 'the darkness thickened, and the Riversdales and many other Catholics with them, became as those who had no hope in the world.' With the repeal of the penal laws, the position had gradually become better. History had left its mark, however, on the later generations:

Catholics had, to a great extent, won their position socially and in the professions, and were on good terms with their immediate neighbours. Their traditions and their way of life, however, bore many traces of their past history. The persecuted had come, in many cases, to idealise the enforced seclusion and inaction of penal days. Politics was too dangerous, and the army and navy soul-imperilling professions – in which moreover Catholics were long debarred from the higher grades. A curious, hardly expressed tradition regarded idleness even in the younger sons as both virtuous and aristocratic. This was partly due no doubt to the fact that in the last century trade, which was then looked upon as a shop-keeping sort of occupation, was almost the only way in which a Catholic could expect to make a fortune.[39]

Yet most of these people were 'men of blameless honour, of warm affections, unworldly, God-fearing, country-loving Englishmen'.[40] This family stands, in this novel, for decent, traditional, rural Catholicism, in contrast with the 'fast' life of fashionable London society. Old George Riversdale is typical of those recusant landowners who, in Bernard Bergonzi's words, 'fulfil[led] impeccably the duties of country gentlemen and landowners, and otherwise devote[d] themselves to field sports or purely private pursuits.' He and his family 'preserve all the decencies of a rural order, and inherited forms of piety and regular religious observance.'[41] George Riversdale is described by Mrs Ward as 'a strong man, strong in will, large in affections, just in personal judgments; a fox-hunter who made an hour's meditation every morning, and a powerful landlord who carried soup to bedridden old women.'[42]

A similar picture is painted by other Catholic authors and in particular R. H. Benson, who in *By What Authority?* depicts a sixteenth-century counterpart, Sir Nicholas Maxwell, who 'fingered his cross-bow or the reins of his horse all day, and his beads in the evening', a combination of activities which was epitomized by the contents of his room, 'with the tapestry of the hawking scene and the stiff herons and ladies on horseback on one side, and the little shelf of devotional books on the other.'[43] And Father Gerard, the clandestine aristocratic priest in Mrs Ward's *Tudor Sunset*, conforms to the same pattern, with 'such carelessness in [his] whole rich attire as marked the country sportsman.'[44] Similar descriptions, but of present-day Catholic country aristocrats, abound in early twentieth-century Catholic fiction.

This ideal of a squirearchical society, devoted to country sports and pursuits, and at the same time continuing over the ages to practise the true Faith, constituted a large part of the ethos of the new Catholic public schools, Stonyhurst (1794), Ampleforth (1802), Downside (1814) and Beaumont (1861), which were run by a series of sportsmen/monks/priests/schoolmasters. Indeed, the list of attributes which a historian of Beaumont has recently ascribed to the ethos of that Jesuit school prominently contains the following: 'character formation . . . athleticism . . . gentry aspirations . . . intimacy with aristocracy and royalty'.[45] It was an old boy of Beaumont, Monsignor Alfred Gilbey, who during his time as Catholic chaplain in Cambridge University (1932–65) epitomized the old traditions, and who combined the country pursuit of beagling with Jacobite loyalties, the frequenting of the drawing-rooms of the old recusant families and a powerful personal devotion.

The romanticism of the old recusant families and houses fills British Catholic literature. The hero of Roger Pater's short stories, *Mystic Voices* (1923), for example, is a priest who is also a squire, whose family, living in the old manor house of Stanton Rivers, had 'kept to the old religion all through the penal times'.[46] One of his ancestors was a Catholic martyr, and a number of these ghost stories relate to the recusant past of this and other houses. The Astons in Maurice Baring's *A Triangle* (1923) are described by one of the Protestant characters as gentry 'who have always been Papists', and who have always lived in a fine old house called Sandbridge.[47] And Mr Rolls, in R. H. Benson's *The Sentimentalists* (1906), is reputed to have even greater recusant quality, in that one of his ancestors was 'a kind of *aide-de-camp* to Mary Stuart',[48] and he lives in an Elizabethan moated manor house that has been in his family for centuries and which contains an old chapel.[49] (One can see here, as in Benson's other novels, the strong influence of Dom Bede Camm, who had a 'special liking for moated manor houses'.)[50]

Not all Catholic writers in this period were, of course, enamoured of the contemporary recusant families. 'Oxford' converts such as W. G. Ward could be scathing about their intellectual shortcomings. And Rolfe, too, had a violent aversion to them. In his view, the Penal Laws had deprived them of 'that culture which contact with a wider world alone can give' and had 'rendered the Catholic aborigines corporeally effete and intellectually inferior to the rest of the nation'.[51] But then, there were very few categories of people whom Rolfe did not abhor and his ripest insults were usually reserved for his fellow Catholics. More serious objections to recusant society included its attitude towards more recent converts. Maurice Baring's hero 'C' describes, with mixed feelings, the reactions of a grand Catholic lady when she hears that someone has just been converted:

> She gave a slight sniff, just as old men do, just as my uncles do when they hear that a *nouveau riche* has been elected to their favourite club. That is what I mean, they treat it as a *club*, a hereditary, aristocratic club into the bargain.[52]

Nevertheless, the predominant impression one gets from Catholic literature up to 1940 is one of a delight, on the part of the many converts, in the aristocratic aspects of the old religion. This was an admiration not just for those recusant families who had lasted the years, but for the upper classes as a whole, and a desire to associate oneself with them by way of religion. Often this admiration was directed at the houses in which they lived. In Benson's *The Sentimentalists*, for example, we soon find that the priest-hero Dick Yolland's father, though a convert, is a 'Catholic country gentleman' who lives in a fine Georgian house which stands 'in a lake of gravel, flanked by shrubberies'. Inside is a large hall, 'stone-flagged and classically adorned, with a tiger skin or two, some mahogany furniture, and an array of buffalo horns.' Soon after Dick and his guest arrive, 'the opulent sound of a gong' calls them to lunch. Dick turns to his guest: 'Will you shoot after lunch?' he says. 'There are plenty of guns.'[53]

In the books of Maurice Baring, too, we find a similar romanticism of grand country houses, some of which have been converted to accommodate a Catholic who has married into the family, or a convert. In particular the romanticism of the private chapel with the 'little flame of the sanctuary lamp',[54] as evoked by Mrs Ward in the Riversdale household, is described in almost identical terms by Baring and others. In Baring's *Daphne Adeane* Daphne's husband (who is not a Catholic) has allowed her to create a chapel within their house. The memory of Daphne, who has died before the novel begins, lingers around this chapel, which has by Mr Adeane's orders been left just as it was before her death:

> We went down the passage . . . to that room at the end of the corridor which you remember. We walked in. It was just the same, except the little lamp was not lit. There were flowers round the two statues . . . Curiously enough, this was the only room in the house that did not feel empty. Here I could imagine that she might really walk in and kneel down, as I so often saw her do, at that little rail, or sit in that chair and open one of those books, or tell her beads.[55]

It was not just houses that betrayed the social attitudes of these authors. Consciously or unconsciously, they constantly gave evidence of their own social presumptions. Benson, for example, constantly makes us aware of the virtues of 'breeding': 'Dick has plenty of breeding . . . He'll stiffen into the most proper rigidity when the crisis arrives. I suppose it's the result of breeding';[56] 'These three passions were held down by that slender thing which we call breeding'.[57] In Benson's novels, even the use of simile and metaphor can reveal contempt for the lower orders, as in the phrase used to describe a row of houses, in *The Sentimentalists*:

> Tall house-fronts rose against the sky on either side, set with square windows, suggestive of nothing but conventionality and a terrible kind of social pride, as of a retired tradesman striving to conceal his past.[58]

It was not just middle-class authors who took such attitudes. The aristocratic Mrs Wilfrid Ward, in her novel *Tudor Sunset*, felt able to deliver a fine put down to the Royal Family. One of her characters, who has just been in the presence of Mrs Ward's ancestor Lady Arundel, describes her as 'his ideal of a Mater Dolorosa and a great English lady', and draws a slighting comparison with Queen Elizabeth: 'The Queen might be, *was*, he believed, a great woman . . . But Anne Boleyn's daughter was not precisely a lady'.[59]

Baring is even more *insouciant*. He shows an unconscious belief that his readers must be Etonians like himself, when he uses the arcane language of Eton in his novels, with no explanation, as in the following:

> The house boasted of no member . . . of the Victory, and of no member of Pop . . . He took Upper Fourth on arrival, which was another shock to Forsyth's and to Lady Hengrave, as they had confidently expected him to take Remove. [. . .] Bentham was a Colleger . . . C. was up in the Lent half to D. D. Keanes . . . Calmady was a dry-bob.[60]

Eton played a large part, too, in the psyches of 'the two Monsignors', R. H. Benson and Ronald Knox (1888–1957), who also had in common the fact that they were sons of Anglican bishops (in Benson's case the Archbishop of Canterbury), were both prolific authors and both had as their flock (though in different eras) the undergraduates of one of the ancient universities (Knox as Catholic chaplain to Oxford and Benson in a more peripheral role in Cambridge). As Knox put it, 'the sentiment we feel towards Eton and the sentiment we feel towards the Church have something of a causal connection.'[61] Both Benson and Knox gathered around them young men from public schools and from the old families. Both of them cultivated 'ardent friendships' on the pattern of their school experiences. And, while both of them were clearly men of prayer and of undoubted personal piety, their outside appearance could sometimes be that of socialites. The atmosphere of the Oxford chaplaincy in Knox's time was brilliantly captured in Graham Greene's review of Evelyn Waugh's biography of him. Knox, he said, 'had his apostolate in a region which I have always found uninteresting and even at moments repellent', and he knew that world 'to the last drain of the glass of dry sherry'. This was summed up, for Greene, by Knox's obituary of Father John Talbot, of the Oratory. Talbot, wrote Knox, 'was always there when you wanted him', particularly if 'you marked yourself out as the sort of young man one meets in John Talbot's room'. His 'characteristic clientèle . . . were in great measure the young men of fashion who are commonly reproached with shunning clerical society.'[62]

The link between Catholicism and smart society was not restricted to the universities, of course. It extended from the country gentry to the smart salons of Mayfair and Belgravia. After the Second World War, as we shall see, working-class and lower middle-class Catholicism were to come into their own in Catholic literature. Yet again, however, in a completely different context, this proved to be an example of the obsession with class that underlies English Catholic literature and which mirrors the same obsession in British life in general.

This survey of some of the underlying themes and concerns of the English Catholic novel before 1940 has, perhaps, already made the reader aware of the origins of some of the characteristics that we will find in the works of Greene and Waugh and of some of their successors. At the same time there were, of course, great differences. This we will be examining in later chapters.

Notes

1   This was based on an interpretation of Col. 1.24: 'It makes me happy to be suffering for you now, and in my own body to make up all the hardships that still have to be undergone by Christ for the sake of his body, the Church' – a quotation frequently used by Huysmans in his published works and which he underlined in his personal copy of the Bible. (See Gaël Prigent, *Huysmans et la Bible: Intertexte et iconographie scripturaires dans l'oeuvre*, pp. 189, 327, 330, 436, 442, 526, 555, 561).

2   It is true that this reflects, in some respects, aberrations that had already emerged in previous centuries. In the early seventeenth century, for example, Father Surin, who had been sent as confessor to the possessed nuns of Loudun, had been prepared to take on their 'possession' himself. See Jean-Joseph Surin, *Correspondance* (ed. Michel de Certeau).

3   See Richard Griffiths, 'Huysmans et le mystère du péché' (1999).

4   Father Martindale tells us that Benson 'was devoted' to this book and recounts a story of a friend of Benson's 'who professed herself "disgusted" by it'. Benson insisted on buying the book from her, 'as she was unworthy to possess what she could not appreciate'. (C. C. Martindale, SJ, *The Life of Monsignor Robert Hugh Benson*, Vol. 2, p. 364).

5   Benson, *Initiation*, p. 258.

6   'It was of the very essence of his contract that he should suffer severely' ('Monsignor Maxwell's Tale', in *A Mirror of Shalott*, p. 35).

7   Maisie Ward, *Insurrection versus Resurrection*, p. 153.

8   It is worth noting that this theme is taken up by Graham Greene in *The End of the Affair* and in *The Potting Shed*.

9   See p. 25.

10 As in *By What Authority?*

11 The liturgy dominated Huysmans's post-conversion novels. This was in part based on an enthusiasm for the beauty of the services he attended and in part on nostalgia for the spirituality of the Middle Ages. Apart from occasional uses of the liturgy in, for example, Henry Bordeaux's novels, there is nothing, in French literature, like the all-pervasive invasion by it that one finds in English Catholic literature. Paul Claudel, in his plays used the liturgy occasionally in an effective structural role through the mingling of liturgical and dramatic effects. But these writers were something of an anomaly, in this respect, among the other writers of the French Catholic revival.

12 Philip Healy, afterword to John Gray, *Park: A Fantastic Story* (1984), p. 126.

13 Mrs Wilfrid Ward, *Great Possessions*, p. 292.

14 Maurice Baring, *The Coat Without Seam*, pp. 301–2. The phrase '*ex opere operato*' alludes the doctrine of the objective operation of the sacraments, independent of the subjective attitudes of either the minister or the recipient, grace being conferred so long as the conditions of the institution are fulfilled. The doctrine of *ex opere operato* was approved at the Council of Trent.

15 A Litany which consists of a series of invocations of the Blessed Virgin Mary under various titles, for example, 'Mother of Divine Grace', 'Consoler of the afflicted', 'Queen of Angels', each followed with the words: 'Pray for us'. Often used at Benediction.

16 Maurice Baring, *Daphne Adeane*, pp. 251–2.

17 Roger Pater, *Mystic Voices*, pp. 35–6. The Confiteor is the form of confession of sins used at the start of the Mass, and confession was made, in Pater's day, to God, the BVM, St Michael, St John the Baptist, St Peter, St Paul, 'and all the saints'. An order such as the Benedictines would add the name of their founder to the list of saints. Since 1969 the confession has been made to God and those present and prayers are asked of the BVM, the angels and saints without reference to individual saints.

18 Ibid., p. 17. The *Orate, fratres* is the sentence addressed to the people, at Mass, immediately after the Offertory, asking the prayers of the people before the Prayer of Consecration. The 'Secret' was a prayer said silently by the priest, after the offering of the bread and the wine. The 'Canon' is the prayer of consecration, from the Sanctus onwards.

19 Ethel Lilian Voynich, *The Gadfly*, p. 327, 331.

20 The humeral veil is a silk shawl laid round the shoulders, serving to cover the hands when they are holding sacred things. At High Mass the subdeacon used to hold the paten with it. At Benediction it is worn by the celebrant, as he picks up the monstrance containing the Host.

21 R. H. Benson, *Lord of the World*, pp. 221–3.

22 R. H. Benson, *By What Authority?* p. 174.

23 Maurice Baring, *C*, pp. 635–6.

24 Mrs Wilfrid Ward, *Horace Blake*, pp. 118–19.

25 Compton Mackenzie, *The Heavenly Ladder*, p. 353.

26 Articles 28 and 31 of the Thirty-Nine Articles of the Anglican Church, first published in 1562.

27 Lord John Russell, letter to the Bishop of Durham, *The Times*, 7 November 1850. Quoted in Edward Norman, *Anti-Catholicism in Victorian England*, p. 160.

28 J. K. Huysmans, *La Cathédrale* (Paris, 1898), p. 8.

29 Woodman, *Faithful Fictions*, p. 70.

30 Fr. Rolfe (Baron Corvo), *Hadrian the Seventh*, p. 48.

31 Maurice Baring, *C*, p. 518.

32 Mrs Wilfrid Ward, *One Poor Scruple*, p. 121.

33 Ibid., p. 97.

34 Ibid., p. 121.

35 R. H. Benson, *The Sentimentalists*, p. 1.

36 Ibid., pp. 70–3, 75.
37 Gerard Manley Hopkins, letter to his father, 16/17 October 1866 (Hopkins, *Poetry and Prose*, 1998, p. 130).
38 Thomas Woodman, *Faithful Fictions*, pp. 61–77.
39 Mrs Wilfrid Ward, *One Poor Scruple*, pp. 41–3.
40 Ibid., p. 97.
41 Bernard Bergonzi, introduction to *One Poor Scruple*, 1985, pp. vii–viii.
42 Mrs Ward, *One Poor Scruple*, p. 44.
43 R. H. Benson, *By What Authority?* p. 79.
44 Mrs Wilfrid Ward, *Tudor Sunset*, p. 185.
45 B. R. Caparrini, 'A Catholic public school in the making: Beaumont College during the Rectorate of the reverend Joseph M. Bampton, SJ'.
46 'Roger Pater' (Dom Roger Hudleston, OSB), *Mystic Voices*, p. 3.
47 Maurice Baring, *A Triangle*, pp. 31–4.
48 R. H. Benson, *The Sentimentalists*, p. 95.
49 Ibid., pp. 130–3.
50 Dom Aidan Bellenger, OSB, introduction to 2004 edition of Camm's *Forgotten Shrines*, p. viii.
51 Fr. Rolfe (Baron Corvo), *Hadrian the Seventh*, p. 184.
52 Maurice Baring, C, p. 544.
53 R. H. Benson, *The Sentimentalists*, pp. 18–19.
54 Mrs Wilfrid Ward, *One Poor Scruple*, p. 131.
55 Maurice Baring, *Daphne Adeane*, p. 138. See similar descriptions on pp. 146–7, p. 199.
56 Benson, *The Conventionalists*, p. 291.
57 Ibid., p. 314.
58 Benson, *The Sentimentalists*, p. 142.
59 Mrs Wilfrid Ward, *Tudor Sunset*, p. 184.
60 Baring, C, pp. 62–83.
61 Quoted in Evelyn Waugh, *Ronald Knox*, p. 53.
62 Graham Greene, 'The Oxford Chaplain' (1959), in *Collected Essays*, pp. 376–9.

Some Religious and Political Attitudes in the Period up to 1940

9

Authority and Heresy

Authority

Converts from Anglicanism in the late nineteenth and early twentieth century were above all attracted by the certainty and authority of the Catholic Church's teachings and its decisions. This seemed a safe anchor amidst all the uncertainties they had felt until this time. They tended to contrast this with what they regarded as the free-for-all of Anglicanism. R. H Benson was typical of such people. In *Lord of the World*, which takes place in 2007, one of the Catholic characters comments on the fact that widespread secularization had been caused by Protestant lack of authority in religion, and that 'men do recognise at last that a supernatural religion involves an absolute authority and that Private Judgment in matters of faith is nothing else than the beginning of disintegration'.[1]

In his *Confessions of a Convert*, Benson describes his visit to an 'eminent dignitary' of the Church of England, at the time when he was contemplating conversion to Rome:

> Here was one of [The Church of England's] chief rulers assuming, almost as an axiom, that I must accept only those dogmas that individually happened to recommend themselves to my reason or my temperament. Tacitly, then, he allowed no authoritative power on the part of the Church to demand an intellectual submission . . . Or, if this seem too strong, it may be said that the prelate in question at any rate denied the existence anywhere on earth of an authority capable of proposing the truths of Revelation in an authoritative manner, and hence, indirectly evacuated Revelation of any claim to demand man's submission.[2]

When he was an Anglican priest, Benson had felt that 'I was an official of a church that did not seem to know her own mind even on matters directly connected with the salvation of the soul.' When he looked around him for a clear statement, 'I did not find it'. Gradually, he came to see 'the absolute need of a living authority'.[3]

That question of authority was central, as its title suggests, to Benson's historical novel *By What Authority?* In it the Protestant Anthony Norris gradually becomes aware of its importance:

> Was there or was there not an authority on earth capable of declaring to him the Revelation of God? For the first time he was beginning to feel a logical and spiritual necessity for an infallible external judge in matters of faith; and that the Catholic Church was the only system that professed to supply it.[4]

Benson's attitudes were typical of many of his contemporaries and successors. Maurice Baring's characters, for example, continually come back to this question. Beatrice, in *C*, declares that she accepts the 'dogmas guaranteed by the authority to whose mast I have nailed my flag',[5] and in *Daphne Adeane* Fanny, coming to ask the advice of Father Rendall, does so because he has 'the authority of the Church' behind him and because she wants 'the authoritative view on this matter, not that of the Scribes'.[6] This same theme, 'not as the Scribes', is taken up again by the hero C in the novel of that name. Attracted to Catholicism, but not yet convinced, he writes to the Catholic Beatrice:

> If I could believe in anything, I think I should believe in your Church. I feel it is a solid fact, a reality, something different from all the others (. . . 'Authority*, not as the Scribes').[7]

Such attitudes were not confined to converts, however. Hilaire Belloc, a Catholic by upbringing, was one of the most strident advocates of the Church's primacy in this matter. For him, there was never any doubt or questioning:

> All men accept authority. The difference between different groups lies in the type of authority which they accept. The Catholic has arrived at the conviction . . . that there has been a Divine revelation . . . [The doctrines of the Catholic Church] form a consistent whole, which is not only the sole full guide to right living in this world, but the sole just group of affirmations upon the nature of things. To take up that position is to be a Catholic. To doubt it or deny it is to oppose Catholicism.

Having accepted 'the authoritative Divine character in the Church', Belloc goes on, one must subject to it 'one's own less perfect experience and less perfect power',[8] and obey it in all things, even if one's reason tells one otherwise. Such obedience must be absolute. The Catholic 'will accept established doctrine and prefer it to any possible conclusions of his own limited experience, judgment and powers.'[9]

Events later in the twentieth century were to shake the foundations of the belief of a number of such people. For the moment, however, and particularly in the pontificate of Pius X, with its hard-line response to any questioning of traditional Catholic belief, many British Catholics remained similar to their contemporaries of the French Catholic revival, in their intransigent attitude to any challenge to the Church's authority. Yet such attitudes were by no means universal in this country, perhaps because of the British attitude of questioning that had originally led many of these converts to leave the Church in which they had been brought up. Modernism was never the crucial issue in British cultural circles that it had been for the French, reactions to it being far less uniform.

Modernism

> I saw the tomb of St Dominic at Bologna. I have a deep veneration for him. He saved Europe in one of its half-dozen crises by squashing the filthy Albigenses.[10]

Hilaire Belloc's belligerent attitude to heresy, as expressed here, was typical of the French background from which he came. It might almost have been Léon Bloy speaking, or Paul Claudel.[11] While there were a good number of British Catholics who shared these views, there was nevertheless a wide spectrum of attitudes among the Catholic intelligentsia in this country towards what the Church defined as heresy. This became particularly clear at the time of the Modernist crisis, in the first decade of the twentieth century.

Modernism was a term invented, by their opponents, to describe a number of widely differing Catholic writers and thinkers, whose only common feature was the aim of bringing the tradition of Catholic belief more into line with modern thought. These tendencies, which had emerged in the late nineteenth century, were most vigorous in France. One of the main strands, later associated with the priest Alfred Loisy, was concerned with a modern approach to Biblical exegesis. Such an approach to the Biblical texts was believed by traditionalists, however, to deny divine inspiration. Many of these new approaches, which appeared radical at the time, are now an accepted part of Biblical scholarship. The Abbé Duchesne exemplified a new approach to Church history. In the field of philosophy men such as Blondel, Le Roy and Laberthonnière tried to bring Catholic belief more into line with what they considered to be acceptable to the mind of modern man; they glossed over the idea of transcendental revelation and attempted to show that the proof of transcendental truth was immanent in man himself. All these trends, together with the parallel (and associated) political and social concerns of liberal and social Catholicism, were essentially a questioning of tradition and a desire for open debate. But in the first decade of the twentieth century the Church was not ready for such departures.

Under Pope Leo XIII (1878–1903) these tendencies had, on the whole, been tolerated. His successor Pius X (1903–14) took a much harder line and in 1907 Modernism was officially condemned in the encyclical *Pascendi*. Many of the Modernist clergy were excommunicated and by 1910 an anti-Modernist oath had been imposed on all priests suspected of such attitudes. Loisy, who had already had to abandon his priestly functions, was excommunicated in 1908 and soon left the Church. In Britain, the two foremost Modernists were the Jesuit Father George Tyrrell (1861–1909) and Baron Friedrich von Hügel (1852–1925), a half-Austrian, half-Scottish lay theologian who in his writings was much influenced by Blondel. Von Hügel escaped formal condemnation by the Church. Tyrrell, who showed strong immanentist tendencies in his writings, had had problems with the authorities well before the papal condemnation and left the Society of Jesus in 1906. On the appearance of *Pascendi* in 1907, he wrote two letters of protest to *The Times*.[12] He was excommunicated. Unlike Loisy and a number of other Modernists, he never left the Catholic Church. When he died two years later, at the age of 48, at the house of a Catholic friend Maud Petre, he received Extreme Unction. He was, however, refused Catholic burial. His funeral in the parish graveyard at Storrington was attended by Miss Petre, Baron von Hügel and a number of other friends. The French priest, the Abbé Henri Bremond, said prayers at the graveside. For this Bremond was suspended by the Bishop of Southwark from saying Mass and Miss Petre was excommunicated locally by the same bishop.

Given their emphasis on authority, one would expect most English Catholic writers of the early twentieth century to have been fervent opponents of Modernism, particularly after the papal condemnation in 1907.[13] Indeed, the presence of two prominent Modernists in Britain might have led one to presume that the whole matter might be very central to their interests. It is striking, however, how little space (except, predictably, in the writings of R. H. Benson) this crisis occupied in the English Catholic literature of the period. The authors opposed to it did, however, express their views in private conversations and correspondence. G. K. Chesterton, for example, compared Father Tyrrell's expulsion from the Church to someone belonging to the National Liberal Club and then making speeches incompatible with

Liberal principles, thus meriting expulsion;[14] and in a private letter Belloc commended Pope Pius X's 'noble' remarks in his encyclical *Pascendi*, because he had 'gently hinted' that the Modernists 'can't think – which is true'.[15]

In R. H. Benson's novels we find a visceral anti-Modernism expressed, particularly in *Lord of the World* and *The Dawn of All*. The former was published in the year of the encyclical *Pascendi*, when Modernism was uppermost in the minds of many Catholics. In it, the triumph of secularism and the decline of the Church are ascribed largely to 'the Exodus of the Intellectuals', the climax of 'the whole conflict that began with the rise of Modernism at the beginning of the century'.[16] *The Dawn of All*, on the other hand, written in 1911 (when Pius X's repressive regime was policing the Church),[17] depicts a future world in which the Church is all-powerful, 'that short-lived movement called Modernism'[18] having been driven out. The time-traveller from the early twentieth century is depicted as naïvely taking the received non-Catholic wisdom of his own time about Pius X's reactionary policies and as being put right by his twenty-first century informant. Typically, France is at the forefront of Benson's concerns:

> 'The Church is re-established [in France], and is practically supreme. That is traceable entirely to Pius X's policy.'
> 'Pius X! Why –'
> 'Yes, Monsignor?'
> 'I know all about that. But I thought Pius X simply ruined everything.'
> 'So they said at the time. His policy was to draw the lines tight and to make no concessions. He drove out every half-hearted Catholic by his regulations, and the result was a small but extraordinarily pure body. The result has been that the country was re-evangelized, and has become almost a land of saints.'[19]

Benson stands somewhat on his own, however, nowhere else did anti-Modernism loom so large in English Catholic literature. A number of Catholic writers showed considerable ambivalence towards the English Modernists. Father Tyrrell was a far more attractive figure than his French contemporaries and had had a considerable following among the Catholic intelligentsia before the climax of the modernist crisis. And Tyrrell was a saintly, devout man, devoted to his faith and to his God, who, unlike Loisy, remained a Catholic even when deprived of the sacraments. Contemporary newspapers reported great popular sympathy in Britain for Father Tyrrell at the time of his excommunication.[20]

English sympathy for Modernism, even among the most obedient Catholics, was sometimes stronger than that. This becomes particularly clear when we look at a novel published in 1906, the year before the *Pascendi*, by Mrs Wilfrid Ward. Her husband Wilfrid had considerable sympathy for the Modernists at this time, making the pages of the *Dublin Review* available to them, as well as to a variety of more traditional Catholic thinkers. He was, however, also a Catholic obedient to authority, which was to cause him considerable mental anguish in years to come. He was a moderate man, fearful of the relish for conflict that was only too common in the Modernists he admired. These complex attitudes were shared by his wife, and her novel reflects them closely.

Out of Due Time (1906), depicts a group of intellectual Catholics striving to persuade the Church to accede to their wish to bring the Church's attitudes into line with the thought of the time. In their view, the best way to oppose contemporary secular philosophies was to take those philosophies over and incorporate their findings into Catholic doctrine. Near the end of the novel, the movement's principles are condemned by the Papacy.

The depiction of these issues is sympathetic. The narration is in the first person and much of it (apart from some quoted letters from a central character, the Catholic journalist and thinker George Sutcliffe) comes to us through the eyes of a young girl, who has been enthused and attracted by the philosopher Count Paul d'Etranges, his sister Marcelle and Sutcliffe (based in part on Mrs Ward's husband Wilfrid). Their aspirations seem justified, part of the ongoing progress of knowledge and doctrine. Their most violent opponents seem narrow and vindictive. Eventually, we are forced to realize that the issues are more complex. We gradually see that Paul is headstrong, impatient of opposition and unaware of the need for restraint and diplomacy. We are also made aware of the various forces at work within the system at Rome, where there is much sympathy for the reformers, but an awareness of the need for gradual movement over time. The voice of sense, the *raisonneur*, is George Sutcliffe. At one point, he explains how, by placing the historical approach to Biblical scholarship in direct opposition to the view of the Scriptures as 'inspired', Paul has forced the hand of the Church:

> D'Etranges is too impatient, he pushes things too far. To say 'not inspired in matters of history' is to go too far, and to ignore theology and tradition. Had he said, not 'literally true', his case would have been far stronger. No one now believes (for example) in the literal truth of Joshua's account of the sun standing still, yet we do not say that the account is *not* inspired. Father Pianciani, a hundred years ago, told us that the account in Genesis of the seven days' creation meant seven visions of the writer, yet we don't say the account is *not* inspired. The account is inspired, though some passages are to be *interpreted* as allegories, and others as the mere record of

things as they appeared to the science of pre-scientific days. The message is inspired, but it reaches us through the medium of men of the same nature as ourselves; the integrity of the message is guaranteed, *not* the infallibility of the human medium on matters extraneous to the message.[21]

The condemnation is therefore seen as inevitable, given Paul's character and tactics. He insists on a decision from Rome on his propositions, even when the Roman officials are trying to persuade him of the inevitable outcome of such a move. After the condemnation Paul, like Loisy, leaves the Church. The succinct ending to the novel shows that his sister thereafter lived a life of charity and suffering and that at her death Paul was reconciled to the Church, accepting its decisions.

This novel, while showing the need for the Church's authority to be upheld, nevertheless expresses considerable sympathy and understanding for the Modernist philosophy. The essential message is that mutual understanding was needed between the two sides. The Church changes over time, what is unacceptable can eventually become acceptable and it is for the Church to decide when that time has come. It is perhaps significant that the epigraph to the novel is an equivocal quotation from the Italian Modernist Antonio Foggazzaro, whose famous novel *Il Santo* had appeared in 1905. The quotation can be interpreted as summarizing the balance Mrs Ward was trying to achieve between modernity and authority: 'La modernità è buona ma l'eterno è migliore' (modernity is good but the eternal is better).

One can imagine how Mrs Ward felt, one year after publishing the novel, when she saw the wholesale condemnation of all 'Modernist' tendencies by Pope Pius X, followed over the next seven years by the Integrist persecution of all who acceded to such views, in any measure.[22] What is clear, however, is that she and her husband unhesitatingly bowed to the Church's demands. Wilfrid no longer printed articles by challenging thinkers in the *Review* and gave a public warning against 'unchastened and irresponsible speculation',[23] believing that it was the duty of every Catholic writer to obey 'Supreme Authority'. Privately, however, he noted that 'while the Papal condemnation might have been necessary, the handling of the crisis on the human side was both clumsy and cruel', and that the Pope had been too 'narrow'.[24]

In the period before the 1907 condemnation, a number of other British Catholic writers had shown a certain amount of sympathy for the Modernist standpoint. John Gray, for example, showed much interest in the question of modern Biblical scholarship and Loisy was often mentioned in his correspondence with Raffalovich. Gray's attitudes to the new Biblical criticism were equivocal, but by no means condemnatory. In 1902 he was confident enough of the eventual acceptance of the principles of the new criticism, to write that 'it is consoling to think that the operation of submitting the scriptures to the historical method is passing so peaceably.' Nevertheless, even then he was aware of the dangers of Loisy's dogged refusal to compromise and felt that if 'there had to be a certain number of "morts et blessés"' Loisy would be among them.[25]

Pascendi changed people's attitudes considerably, as we have seen with the Wards. For some, it was the occasion for a return to dogged acceptance of authority. For others, it led to considerable anguish. Among the latter were Gray and Raffalovich's two friends who wrote under the pseudonym of 'Michael Field' (Katherine Harris and Edith Cooper, known as 'Michael' and 'Henry'). Writing to Gray in November 1907, 'Michael', while regretting the tone of Tyrrell's letters to *The Times*, nevertheless declared 'I maintain my right to criticise the encyclical letter'. She had been told that the Church was 'the home of freedom', and yet if she bought and read the replies of the Modernists in their own defence, 'I incur (officially) mortal sin – and may be excluded from the Sacraments of the Church'. Sturdily, she declared that she would nevertheless continue to read them (comparing in the process the Pope's forces to those of the Armada, against which even English Catholics had fought):

> But English Michael will read his Times attentively every morning. (Not all the Pope's horses nor all the Pope's men will keep him from the Times!!! And large extracts will surely be given from the defence. English Catholics fought for freedom against the Armada, and surely they will have to do this again.)

'Henry', her more retiring companion, was, she said, suffering worse than her: 'She suffers as a man when tight cords are drawn across his brain'. Their local priests were, she said, 'very narrow'. Finally, she implored Gray for help and advice:

> I do feel that any day the most terrible of deprivations might be mine. Do give me help. I wish you had told me of this letter [*Pascendi*]. *How does it affect you?* And how about the Church being the home of freedom?[26]

The anguish of 'Michael Field' shows that not all the authors of the Catholic Revival toed the Church's line in relation to Modernism; and the harsh treatment accorded to Tyrrell had aroused much sympathy even in those who were opposed to his views. Raffalovich (who had known Tyrrell for some years, but was less sympathetic than Gray to his ideas) magnanimously offered him financial assistance when he was expelled from the Church. A number of English Catholic authors in this period privately expressed sympathy for Tyrrell.

After this period of crisis Modernism receded as an issue; and by 1913 R. H. Benson, in his *Confessions of a Convert*, found himself able to pronounce that the Catholic Church, one and indivisible, never had any internal dissension of importance:

> There is no 'seething discontent', so far as I am aware, within the walls of the Church. Certainly I continually am hearing of it, but always from non-Catholics. There is no intellectual revolt on the part of the stronger minds of the Roman communion that I have ever heard of – except from non-Catholics. . . . Of course occasionally a little revolt breaks out, as it will break out in every human society; of course self-willed persons . . . will occasionally dissociate themselves from Catholic life, or, worse still, attempt to remain Catholic in name while wholly un-Catholic in spirit. But what I mean to deny is that these incidents even approximate to tendencies – still less that, as tendencies, they are in the faintest degree characteristic of Catholicism – or that the astonishing calm on the surface of the Church is, as a matter of fact, undermined by fierce internal struggles. It is simply not true.[27]

When Modernism was mentioned in English Catholic writings, from now on, this tended to be in terms of a battle that was over. In 1917, for example, Father Martindale, SJ, dismissively wrote: 'No one now takes that old-fashioned phenomenon known as "Modernism" as a conceivable variation of Catholicism.'[28] And the rejection of Modernism was to remain, almost as a matter of course, the keynote of British Catholic ideas in a wide variety of contexts right up to the late 1930s, as can clearly be seen in Maisie Ward's 1937 statement about her father's attitudes at the time of the Modernist crisis: 'Wilfrid realised then, *as we all must today*, that the old truth, the essential truth, Revealed Truth was in peril and that the first task of the Church's rulers was to preserve it'.[29] And she felt how difficult it must now be for a Modernist like Maud Petre 'to re-state the Modernist faith when the Catholic conviction has proved so well founded'.[30] Another example of entrenched anti-Modernist attitudes in the 1930s was the 1934 review in the *Catholic Times* of Alec Vidler's groundbreaking book *The Modernist Movement in the Roman Church*:

> The encyclical 'Pascendi' brought the Modernist movement to an end. It is dead, let it be buried. This attempt at exhumation, even on a plea of history, is not worth the attention of Catholics.[31]

Why, however, did Modernism remain, even at the height of the crisis, comparatively absent from English Catholic literature written by traditionalists? Might it have been that British believers in the Church's authority considered the whole thing to be unworthy of consideration, or to be a specifically French problem? Might others have shared the 'British' sense of injustice, when viewing the specific case of Tyrrell, and therefore have left the matter alone? Or may it just have been that, with Protestantism and Anglicanism on their doorstep, such writers preferred to see the Catholic Church as one and indivisible and to ignore phenomena that detracted from that unity in face of the outside world?

Anglicanism and Protestantism

'English Catholics are just Protestants, protesting against Protestantism.' D. H. Lawrence's statement has a certain amount of truth in it. It was above all Anglicanism that obsessed the English Catholic writers, however. In large part that obsession was experienced by converts from Anglicanism. As we have seen, the best way to stress the importance of the Church's authority was to use the contrast with Anglican fudge; the best way to pinpoint Catholic values was to mock conventional Anglican presumptions; and the best way to praise Catholic worship was to evoke the shortcomings of its Anglican counterpart, obsessed as it was with conveying 'meaning'. Much of the satirical writing on the subject gives the impression that Anglicanism was seen more as an object for scorn, than a positive danger. Only occasionally (as in Benson's two novels of the future, or in some of Belloc's essays) do warnings emerge of the results for Christendom as a whole, if the laxity of Anglican values were to become contagious.

One might, of course, have expected Catholics to have some fellow-feeling with the Anglo-Catholic wing of the Anglican Church, from which so many of the converts came. However, the predominant feeling seems to have been that Anglo-Catholicism was even more of a 'fudge' than the rest of the Established Church. The Anglo-Catholics were seen as people who had had a glimpse of the truth, but who had then failed to follow that perception through to its logical conclusion. As Belloc wrote in an open letter 'To an Anglo-Catholic friend', amid the daily insults that Catholics received in Protestant countries the sole sympathetic voice was that of the Anglo-Catholics. And yet Belloc finds himself more in sympathy with sceptics than with anyone who, believing so much of what Belloc does, fails nevertheless to see the 'sole solution of our riddles and therefore the salvation of mankind: the only House.' He poses a fundamental question: 'How can the Universal Authority be national?' and asks how people who believe in the necessity for a universal Church, can fail to see that there is and can be, only one: 'There is a city full, as are all cities, of halt and maimed, blind and evil and the rest; but it is the City of God. There are not two such Cities on earth. There is One.'[32]

For every serious treatment of the question of Anglicanism in the literature of this period, there are myriad examples of contemptuous humour at its expense, from the depiction of self-satisfied clergymen in Benson's novels to Baring's hilarious description of the heroine's two Anglican aunts – one evangelical, the other Anglo-Catholic – in *Cat's Cradle* (1925). The ignorance of non-thinking, purely superficial Christians is also pilloried. In Antonia White's *Frost in May* (1933), for example, the heroine's mother, visiting her at her Catholic school, twitters her incomprehension of what she sees.[33]

Whether by serious criticism, warning of dangers, or humour at its expense, middle-of-the road Anglicanism was the main form of non-Catholic Christianity that was criticized in English Catholic literature. What should have been regarded as a far more serious heresy, extreme Protestantism, seems on the whole to have got away with it lightly (except in the historical context of Benson's *By What Authority?*, in which Puritanism at one stage becomes the target).

There was, of course, one area of the United Kingdom where extreme Protestantism had not only flourished but been a dominant political force: Scotland. Woodman has pointed out how virulent the attacks on Calvinism were, by Scottish authors such as Compton Mackenzie (1883–1972), Fionn MacColla (1906–75) and George Mackay Brown (1921–96).[34] The very different histories of the two countries explain the virulence of much of this writing. Again and again, the historical facts are mulled over. Compton Mackenzie, writing in 1936, compared the victory of the Reformation in Scotland as having been achieved in a similar manner to the Bolshevik Revolution.[35] In his view, the collection of 'traitors and murderers', the 'blackest villains that ever defiled the pages of history', who had been responsible for expelling Mary Queen of Scots to her captivity and death, were the very same people who had 'consolidated the work of the Reformation in Scotland'.[36] Mackenzie's view of the future, on the other hand, was one of hope for the destruction of Protestantism and the triumph of Catholicism throughout the world:

The rapidity with which Protestantism all over the world and in all its myriad manifestations is now crumbling away into a negligible emotional convention, from which perhaps within less than a century it will have become a heap of inconspicuous ashes, is evidence enough by itself of the validity of that tremendous promise made to Peter by his Saviour.[37]

George Mackay Brown, the Orkney poet, and Fionn MacColla (Thomas MacDonald), mingled this message with an idealized vision of a pre-Reformation Scotland. Mackay Brown depicted the people of the Orkneys as having seen their daily labours as 'a divine image for their strivings heavenwards'. Though they were poor people, he said, they 'were yet lords and princes with heavenly treasures lying thick about them', and 'these beliefs gave them gaiety and confidence.' And then came the Reformation. 'It is almost impossible, at a distance of four centuries, to estimate the catastrophe that Calvinism brought to Orkney (and to the rest of Scotland)'. They were deprived of their sacraments, their altars and their images. 'Black preachers solemnly impressed on them that their strivings towards the consummation of heaven would avail them nothing, since either their salvation or their damnation was sealed before the beginning of the world . . . Innocence gave place to a dark, brooding awareness.' For Mackay Brown, all the ills of the present day Orkneys were traceable to these events:

> The Orcadians have always been a religious people, and it is more than possible that religion gone sour has contributed to the striking incidence of mental trouble in the islands over the last few centuries.[38]

There is no equivalent, in the Catholic literature of England and Wales, for the anguish expressed by these Scottish authors. South of the border, the target was above all Anglicanism and attitudes to this were expressed either in arguments as to the superiority of the Catholic outlook, or in mockery for Anglicanism's shortcomings.

The concern with central authority was something new in English Catholicism. In the centuries before the nineteenth, contact between the English Catholics and Rome had at best been tenuous. By the nineteenth century, however, ultramontanism had become more and more the dominant strain in Catholicism throughout Europe and the old attempts at national autonomy, such as Gallicanism, had gone into decline. With the influx of Roman attitudes at the time of the restoration of the English hierarchy, ultramontanism predominated here, reinforced by the attitudes of the newly-converted 'Oxford' products, many of whom were 'more papal than the Pope'. The cult of authority was central to the new English Catholicism. Unlike in France, this did not always translate itself into outright rejection of what appeared to challenge that authority. The mixed feelings that we have observed in English Catholics, at the time of the Modernist crisis, bears this out; a secular sense of 'fair play' appears to have entered into many people's reactions. Once Rome had spoken, however, almost everyone toed the line and for the next two generations attitudes to change were as immutable in Britain as in the Church at large. Only in the period after the Second World War did some English Catholic writers begin to exhibit that freedom in thought that was to infuse, for a short time, the Church itself.

Notes

1   R. H. Benson, *Lord of the World*, p. 8.
2   Benson, *Confessions of a Convert*, pp. 88–9.
3   Ibid., p. 58.
4   Benson, *By What Authority?* p. 165.
5   Baring, C, p. 515.
6   Baring, *Daphne Adeane*, p. 292.
7   Baring, C, p. 636.
8   Belloc, 'The Catholic Church and the Modern State', in *Essays of a Catholic*, pp. 52–3.
9   Ibid., p. 54.
10 Belloc, letter to J. S. Phillimore, 3 March 1922, in *Letters from Hilaire Belloc*, p. 118.
11 Claudel famously said: 'I have had to fight, all my life, against error, and I have had to react with the utmost violence, with the greatest brutality, against it' (*Mémoires improvisés*, Paris, 1954, p. 223). Bloy's view was that 'one must never give anything away to the enemy, anything, anything, ANYTHING'. Letter to Bernaert, 5 October 1899; quoted in Joseph Bollery, *Léon Bloy* (Paris, 1947) Vol. 3, p. 302.
12 *The Times*, 30 September and 1 October 1907.
13 Of the writers of the French Catholic revival, I have written: 'One could hardly expect a literary movement so grounded in the concept of authority to do anything but condemn them [the Modernists] in its turn'. (*The Reactionary Revolution*, p. 26). The British experience, however, shows just how possible other attitudes were.
14 Quoted in Joseph Pearce, *Wisdom and Innocence: A Life of G. K. Chesterton*, p. 169.
15 Belloc, letter to Miss Hamilton, quoted in Speaight, *The Life of Hilaire Belloc*, pp. 250–1.
16 Benson, *Lord of the World*, p. 6.
17 See Émile Poulat, *Intégrisme et Catholicisme intégral: Un réseau secret international antimoderniste: La 'Sapinière' (1909–1921)*.
18 Benson, *The Dawn of All*, p. 27.
19 Ibid., p. 36.
20 See *New York Times*, 3 November 1907.
21 Mrs Wilfrid Ward, *Out of Due Time*, pp. 265–6.
22 For a depiction of the Church's tactics in these years, see Poulat, *Intégrisme et Catholicisme Intégral*.
23 Quoted in Paschal Scotti, *Out of Due Time: Wilfrid Ward and the Dublin Review*, p. 76.

24 Speaight, *The Life of Hilaire Belloc*, p. 251.

25 Gray, letter to Raffalovich, 13 October 1902, quoted in Brocard Sewell, *In the Dorian Mode: A Life of John Gray 1866–1934*, p. 111.

26 'Michael Field', letter to Father John Gray, 5 November [1907], quoted in Sewell, *In the Dorian Mode*, p. 120.

27 Benson, *Confessions of a Convert*, pp. 110–11.

28 C. C. Martindale, SJ, *The Life of Monsignor Robert Hugh Benson*, Vol. 2, p. 83.

29 Maisie Ward, *Insurrection versus Resurrection*, p. 232. My italics.

30 Ibid., p. 297.

31 *Catholic Times*, 19 October 1934.

32 Belloc, 'A Letter to an Anglo-Catholic Friend', in *Essays of a Catholic*, pp. 111–14.

33 Antonia White, *Frost in May*, pp. 87–8.

34 Woodman, *Faithful Fictions*, pp. 559–60.

35 Compton Mackenzie, *Catholicism and Scotland*, p. 72.

36 Ibid., p. 85.

37 Ibid., pp. 72–3.

38 George Mackay Brown, 'The Broken Heraldry'.

10
Modern Crusaders: Catholicism and Politics, 1900–1940

France and Britain

The writers of the French Catholic revival showed a strong interest in politics, mainly of the Right. This was largely due to the conflict between Church and State which dogged French politics throughout the Third Republic; but it also reflected an intransigent strain within these writers' religious philosophy. At the start of the British revival, fewer writers showed a major interest in secular politics, perhaps because the controversies into which they entered tended to be more religious than political. There were, however, a small number of writers who expressed strong political views. These were often of an extreme Right-wing nature and most of them gave evidence of a major influence of the French Right and later of the European Right in general. What were the salient characteristics of this French Right, which was to be so influential?

One has, of course, to distinguish between different kinds of Right. In France there had been a number of varying strands, of which the most straightforward was that of the traditional Catholic Right: strongly opposed to the modern world, to the Republic, to liberalism, to democracy, to socialism – a series of attitudes mainly defined by their negative qualities. These intransigent Catholic thinkers took the opposite standpoint from the tenets of liberal republicanism: for liberty, they substituted discipline and order (together with a 'Caesarist' longing for dictatorial government); for equality, they substituted the need for hierarchy; for fraternity, they substituted charity.[1] They had an obsession with the modern world, which they saw as responsible for most of the evils around them. As they looked back with nostalgia to a more perfect world, which in fact had never existed, they contrasted the virtues of a rural agrarian society, in which everyone had known their place and where religion had been the basis of the community, with the evils created by the industrial society: class divisions, unrest, disorder, poverty, neglect, atheism. It was but a short step to an attack on the international

141

capital that had created this situation. And it was a yet-shorter step, in the atmosphere created by the writings of Édouard Drumont in the 1880s, to an association between the powers of capitalism and the Jews. Anti-Semitism became a leading feature of the French Catholic Right, coupled with a fear of and aversion for Freemasonry, which was seen as the occult power behind the French Republican political establishment.

Against this background another, more radical form of Right-wing politics emerged, part of a European phenomenon which has been characterized as 'the revolutionary Right' or 'the radical Right'.[2] In contrast to the conservatism of mainstream Catholic reaction, these people, in varied ways, produced radical policies that often vied with the Left on its own ground. Their anticapitalism was far from the nostalgic vision we have seen; it was grounded in positive doctrines for change, looking to a re-ordering of society rather than a simple return to the past. This new style of Right-wing tendency has rightly been seen as a kind of 'pre-fascism'. Among the major figures involved in the period before the First World War (though in widely differing ways) were Maurice Barrès, Georges Sorel and of course Charles Maurras,[3] whose popular movement *Action Française* was, from the 1890s to the 1940s, pre-eminent in the practical politics of the French Right and was to be widely influential outside France.

Rolfe and Benson

When we look at the few British Catholic writers who showed a strong interest in secular politics in the first decade of the twentieth century, two come immediately to mind as having been strongly influenced by the traditional French Catholic Right – that irrepressible duo, Fr. Rolfe and Robert Hugh Benson. In their works expressions of visceral hatred for the forces of the modern world predominated. Though the expression of their views was sometimes caricaturally violent, there is no mistaking the seriousness with which these authors viewed the state of the modern world – nor can one miss the French positions from which they started. In *Hadrian the Seventh* (1904), Rolfe's Pope issues, as one of his first proclamations, a condemnation of the doctrine of Equality: 'It proclaimed the dogma of Equality as scientifically, historically and obviously false and impracticable: as a diabolical delusion for the ruin of souls.'[4] This novel contains a strange mixture of actual facts from contemporary politics (mainly French) and apparently consequential events in the imaginary future in which the hero is living. In the process Rolfe lumps together politics and politicians of widely differing types, incidentally revealing his complete ignorance of politics of the Left. A good example is the passage in which, starting from contemporary events (the Radical Prime Minister Combes' anticlerical regime of 1902–5, in which Combes was supported by the Socialist leader Jean Jaurès; the War Minister General André's post-Dreyfus purging of Catholics from the French Army; and the Navy Minister Camille Pelletan's unionization of the Navy and defence of ordinary sailors against their officers), Rolfe moves into an imaginary, extremely dangerous future in which Jaurès (characterized as an 'anarchist'!) has, thanks to the governmental actions which have weakened the armed forces, been able to subject France to a new revolution reminiscent of the 1871 Commune:

[He] was reading from the *Times* of the outbreak of revolution in France, where General André's army-reforms of 1902, and the blatant scandalous venality of Combes and Pelletan . . . had thrown the military power into the hands of Jaurès and his anarchists, revived the Commune, and broken off diplomatic relations with the Powers.[5]

When Rolfe turns to British politics, his 'great wealth of lack of knowledge'[6] about the Left is equally obvious, but so is his hatred of it. When his Pope is assailed by members of 'that aggregation of intellectually purblind and covetous dullards, who formed the socialistic sect of the King of England's subjects',[7] they are described as the 'Liblab Fellowship' (a clear misunderstanding of the nature of the moderate British parliamentary alliance of that name). The caricatural depiction of these misfits leaves us in no doubt as to Rolfe's view of socialists.

Benson's treatment of such matters in *Lord of the World* (1907) was less of a caricature, but equally fearful of the potential of the Left. Like Rolfe, Benson started with contemporary events in France. He chose to ascribe power over the future events he was describing to a figure who is now almost forgotten, but who loomed large in the gallery of hate-figures of the time – Gustave Hervé, the extreme Left anti-militarist who for a short time was a major force in French Socialism in the first decade of the century. His career, in real life, was thereafter a chequered one: at the outbreak of the First World War he reversed his position, becoming a fervent patriot and militarist; in the interwar period he moved rapidly to the radical Right, becoming a proponent of Fascism; and in the Second World War his was the first collaborationist newspaper to reappear in Paris after the defeat. Benson's assessment of Hervé's future career was therefore entirely faulty; but there is no doubting his conviction of the dangers facing 'civilization' from the various forces of the Left, including that greatest of all French Catholic bugbears, Freemasonry:

'In England our party [Catholicism] was first seriously alarmed at the Labour Parliament of 1917. That showed us how deeply Hervéism had impregnated the whole social atmosphere. There had been Socialists before, but none like Gustave Hervé in his old age – at least none of the same power . . . After the fall of the French Church at the beginning of the century and the massacres of 1914, the bourgeoisie settled down to organise itself; and that extraordinary movement began in earnest, pushed through by the middle classes, with no patriotism, no class distinctions, practically no army. Of course, Freemasonry directed it all . . . [In England], in 1917 the Labour party gathered up the reins, and Communism really began.'[8]

In Benson's other novel of the future, *The Dawn of All* (1910), we find a society that has rejected Socialism and its works and reinstated the Church, so that it is now based on the Catholic virtues of hierarchy, discipline and authority. Here again, France is taken as a prime example of the changes that have taken place. A monarchy (in the Orleans line) has been re-established there and the country has been re-evangelized, becoming 'almost a land of saints'.[9]

Belloc and Chesterton, and a Younger Generation of Catholic Thinkers

While Rolfe and Benson may seem to stand at an extreme, they were not alone in their views. With Hilaire Belloc (1870–1953) we find someone whose very upbringing had been imbued with the principles of the French Right. The son of a French father (who died young) and an English mother, Belloc was educated in England, but also spent much time at the family home just outside Paris, where the patriotic extremist Paul Déroulède was a neighbour and a family friend.[10] Belloc joined Déroulède's *Ligue des Patriotes* when he was a young man and was a keen admirer of Maurras and his Action Française movement throughout his life. He read the newspaper *L'Action Française* regularly,[11] and maintained contact with several of the movement's most prominent members. Henri Massis, one of the most virulent of Action Française publicists, became a good friend.[12] It is significant that when Belloc visited his old regiment in the front line in France in January 1940, he was accompanied by Massis.[13]

Belloc's time in the French Army during his national service in 1891–2 imbued him with a very populist form of anti-Semitism. Throughout the rest of his life he referred, in conversation, to Jews as 'Yids'. It was hardly surprising that, from 1898 onwards, he should have held strongly anti-Dreyfusard views. For the rest of his life he continued to echo the most extravagant claims of the anti-Dreyfusard press, asserting that 'ninety-nine Frenchmen out of a hundred' shared his view and that the agitation for a retrial had been dictated by a small Jewish minority who were in control of the money-power.[14] After his initial certainty as to Dreyfus' guilt, he did later claim to have 'no certain conclusion in the matter'. However, like Maurras, he believed that even if Dreyfus had been innocent, the interests of the Nation and of the Army meant that his guilt should have continued to be maintained. As late as 1932, he was to berate English Catholics for having 'during the whole of the Dreyfus struggle . . . sided with the filth of Zola and the anti-Catholic Freemasons'.[15] It is true to say that among the British public in general, including British Catholics, Belloc's views on the Dreyfus Affair were grossly untypical.

Belloc's anti-Semitism was, however, not merely an expression of popular prejudice and of truculent bad taste. His attitude to the Jews was grounded in a hatred of capitalism typical of certain parts of the extreme French Right. And though, like many anti-Semites, he claimed to have 'many Jewish friends' and though, in sections of what he called his 'admirable Yid book', *The Jews* (1922), he dissected in what at times appears a dispassionate manner the dangers of excessive anti-Semitism, the main tenor of that book (as contemporary reviewers perceived) was strongly anti-Semitic. From its start, Belloc stressed that 'the continued presence of the Jewish nation intermixed with other nations alien to it present a permanent problem of the gravest character', and that 'the wholly different culture, tradition, race and religion of Europe make Europe a permanent antagonist to Israel'. There were, in his view, two ways 'of reducing or accommodating the strain produced by the presence of an alien body within any organism . . . The first is by elimination of what is alien. The second is by its segregation. There is no other way'.[16] Like so many European anti-Semites of this particular type, however, Belloc was in the 1930s to react strongly against Nazi persecution of the Jews, the kind of activity of which he had deplored the future possibility in his book.

In most other respects, Belloc was an idiosyncratic radical, ill at ease during his short spell as a Liberal member (1906–10) in the House of Commons. The British imperialistic expansion of which the Boer War was such a conspicuous example was abhorrent to him. His cynical view was that British imperialism was a crooked scheme directed by Jewish financiers. In his four savage political novels, which were written between 1904 and 1910 starting with *Emmanuel Burden*, a central figure was the Jewish financier I. Z. Barnett, whose tentacles reached into every area of the national life and who finally ended up as the Duke of Battersea. Robert Speaight rightly compares Belloc's depiction of him to 'some savage anti-Semitic caricature of Forain's illustrating some diatribe of Drumont's.'[17] This fictional character stands for the Oppenheims, the Beits, the Wernhers, those speculators and investors in the mines of the Transvaal for the preservation of whose commercial interests the South African War, in Belloc's view, had been fought.

Belloc's views were not only negative, however. His anticapitalism led to him developing, with his friend G. K. Chesterton, a new political doctrine entitled 'Distributism'. Like many of the political and economic doctrines of the radical 'pre-fascist' Right, this movement claimed a central ground between capitalism and socialism, a 'third way' which could, at first sight, appear to have much in common with the Left. Distributism owed much to the theories of the French economist Frédéric Le Play, which harked back to an ideal vision of the virtues of medieval society, in which all classes had worked together, with employers and employed joining in mutually helpful guilds, rather than in the warfare of trade unionism; it owed a great deal, too, to Pope Leo XIII's encyclical *Rerum Novarum* (1891), which while deploring the evils of capitalism, its injustices and its enslavement of the poor, nevertheless was as heavily critical of socialism as of capitalism. Significantly, Le Play and *Rerum Novarum* were also prime influences on the social policy of *Action Française* and above all on the writings of the Action Française theorist René de la Tour du Pin. Distributism appears to have owed to *Rerum Novarum* its stress on the importance of property as the lynchpin of social equality and to Le Play its stress on the protective qualities of 'a charter and a guild' on the medieval model.

Many in Britain in this period had attempted to find alternatives to capitalism, from Major Douglas and his Social Credit movement to the theorists of 'guild socialism', from Arthur Kitson to the members of the British People's Party. While some of the theories, and some of the people involved, appear to have been innocuous, there was nevertheless a tendency for anti-Semitism to creep into such movements, with 'the Jew', being held responsible for all the ills of capitalism and 'Usury' often being a convenient epithet with which to describe the Jewish influence, without being openly anti-Semitic.[18] Distributism was no exception to this, as might have been expected with Belloc as one of its leading figures. It is hardly surprising that the corporate theories of Italian Fascism, which could appear so close to those of Distributism, should have led to considerable admiration, among Distributists, for Mussolini's movement.

G. K. Chesterton, Belloc's friend and collaborator, was a far more complex figure, who never fitted neatly into any pigeon-hole. He was a strange mixture of libertarianism and desire for authority, of anti-imperialism and xenophobic 'Englishry', whose support for the 'little man' against the encroachments of the modern capitalist world at times verged on anarchism.

He had instincts of both Right and Left and his views were usually expressed in a series of paradoxical statements which, though often effective, could also tend to muddy issues. His exuberant embracing of the Catholic Faith was at one with his crusading instincts in the area of practical politics.

This attractive figure had his darker side. One wonders how much that side developed under the influence of Belloc, for Chesterton shared many of Belloc's attitudes in relation to the Jews. Much of his verse on their subject contains the same spirit of false jocularity that characterized Belloc's most vulgar efforts (and which has led some commentators to excuse Chesterton by suggesting that 'It is clear that such verses may cause offence, but it is equally clear that they were not intended to do so'[19] – despite the fact that the experience of the last century has shown that such 'jocularity' can be a dangerous starting-point for anti-Semitic activity of a far more serious kind.). Chesterton's hatred of capitalists led him, like Belloc, to a mistrust of Jews whom he felt were at the centre of the system. This is seen most clearly in his interventions, together with his brother Cecil Chesterton and Hilaire Belloc, in the Marconi scandal of 1912–13, in which a number of cabinet ministers were accused of insider dealing in Marconi shares prior to a Government contract. Among those vilified by Chesterton and Belloc's *The Eye Witness* were the Jewish figures Sir Rufus Isaacs, Attorney General (and later Lord Chancellor as Lord Reading); his brother Godfrey Isaacs, Managing Director of the English Marconi Company; and Herbert Samuel, the Postmaster General (though of course Lloyd George was implicated as well). The anti-Semitism of the attacks in *The Eye Witness* was virulent and for years thereafter, particularly in *The Eye Witness'* successor *G. K's Weekly*, G. K. Chesterton was continually to hark back to the affair, while launching new and equally personal attacks upon Jewish industrialists such as Sir Alfred Mond.[20] Like Belloc, however, Chesterton was to react strongly against Nazi persecution of the Jews. As he put it in 1937:

> In our early days Hilaire Belloc and myself were accused of being uncom-promising anti-Semites. Today, although I still think there is a Jewish problem, I am appalled by the Hitlerite atrocities.[21]

One must not over-exaggerate the importance of Belloc's and Chesterton's anti-Semitism, which was very much of its time. Beside it, they held a number of views as to the nature of capitalism and the Catholic response to the social question, which were to be of lasting influence.

By the interwar period, a new generation of Catholic Right-wingers was emerging. Many of them occupied important positions in the journalistic world and it appeared to many Catholics that a new intelligentsia was in place, that could hold its own against any comers. Prominent among these people were Douglas Woodruff (1897–1978), who was on the editorial staff of *The Times* from 1926 to 1938 and then editor of *The Tablet* from 1936 onwards; Douglas Jerrold (1893–1964), who was editor of *The English Review* at a crucial stage, 1931–6; Sir Charles Petrie, Bt (1895–1977), who wrote extensively for a wide variety of journals; Christopher Hollis (1902–77), writer of many books and articles, who later became a Conservative MP; Michael de la Bédoyère (1900–73), editor of the *Catholic Herald* from 1934 onwards; and Bernard Wall (1908–74), 'a key figure in Catholic intellectual circles during the 1930s',[22] founder and editor of *The Colosseum*.

Some of these figures, such as Jerrold and Petrie, could be classified as 'high Tories'; others, like La Bédoyère and Wall, saw themselves as social reformers, though (particularly in the case of Wall, a disciple of Belloc's) very much in the Distributist mould. Some, like La Bédoyère, found themselves, in religious matters, opposed to the conservative stance of the contemporary Church. Nevertheless, they had a great deal in common politically and the political situation of the 1930s was to show them to be particularly vulnerable to foreign influences from the Right.

The Fascist Temptation

By the late 1920s there had been considerable enthusiasm for Italian Fascism throughout Europe and nowhere more so than in Catholic circles. Ignoring the fact that Fascism on the Italian model had been in its origins a secular movement, hostile to the Church, foreign observers tended to take the Lateran Pacts of 1929 (which had essentially been an attempt at a pragmatic solution to Italian Church-State relations) as a sign that this dictatorship was based on Christian principles.

Fascism appealed particularly to the Right-leaning facet of Catholic political thought that we have been examining. Belloc, in particular, regarded Mussolini from the early 1920s onwards 'with a besotted admiration which was undiminished until his death'.[23] (Chesterton, however, detached as always, viewed Fascism with a much more cautious eye). But there is no denying the attraction felt generally in establishment circles throughout Britain for the new dictator,[24] and Catholics were at this stage merely one group among many.

One of the first British Catholic writers to see this Italian movement as a model for British politics (and not just something suitable for Italians) was James Strachey Barnes, who after the First World War went to live in Italy, claiming that that country epitomized his two great beliefs: 'my faith in standards of universal value and my worship of the Holy Spirit, Lord and

Giver of Life'. Here he experienced the 'first stirring revolutionary years of Fascism'.[25] Having become a member of the Italian Fascist Party and 'a friend of the most constructive statesman of this age, Benito Mussolini',[26] he wrote a thesis on *The Universal Aspects of Fascism*, which was published in 1928. Later, in 1931, he produced a slim volume for the Home University Library entitled *Fascism*. He also wrote innumerable articles on the subject, in British and foreign journals. The popularity of his writings is shown by the fact that both his books went into further editions. On his visits to England, he was fêted by many prominent Catholics.

Barnes's works show his thinking to have been very much in the tradition of Belloc and Chesterton. Like them, he wanted a fairer distribution of wealth, social peace and the downfall of the international financier. Fascism, for him, meant a return to the Catholic Middle Ages and was an attack on 'the ideas to which the Renaissance gave birth and which have dominated the world for several centuries'.[27] It stood for 'a sense of moral purpose' rather than any specific political tendency, whether of Left or Right. Italy, said Barnes, had been in a terrible state, but Mussolini's moral power had filled the Italian people with moral strength. Britain, which was in a similar state, required a similar solution.

By the early 1930s, a number of politically aware Catholic writers and journalists in Britain were similarly writing of the need to imitate this model of government (the economic crisis having led many to believe that democracy was doomed). Prominent among them were a group based around the journal *The English Review*, of which publisher Douglas Jerrold was editor from 1931 onwards and the historian Sir Charles Petrie a regular contributor.

Sir Charles Petrie was an Irish baronet who in 1931 had produced a book entitled *Mussolini* (published by Jerrold at Eyre and Spottiswoode). His admiration for Mussolini, whom he saw as 'the greatest figure of the present age, and perhaps one of the most notable of all time',[28] was to last into the post-war period.[29] For Petrie the two main achievements of Fascism were the corporate state and the solving of the Vatican problem (despite his realism as to the Fascist motives for reconciliation).

Jerrold's standpoint was that of the Right-wing anti-capitalist tradition. He believed that 'the only serious attack on the capitalist tradition today comes from the Right . . . Only in the Catholic press, inspired by the tradition of Chesterton and Belloc, which is carried on today by McNair Wilson, Christopher Hollis, Douglas Woodruff and Count Michael de la Bédoyère . . . are bankers attacked, foreigners treated as our equals in integrity and intelligence, or the cause of liberty sustained'.[30] The reasons for his attraction to Fascism are shown clearly by his descriptions, couched in the rhetoric of revolutionary reaction, of the best kind of politics as being 'neither Right nor Left', and opposed both to the capitalists and to organized labour:

> Between the minority of greedy financiers who wanted to continue the Edwardian gamble in men's lives and the mass of the new Trades unionists and bureaucratic planners who wanted to plant themselves securely on the taxpayer's back under the plea of public service, lay the majority of the nation.[31]

For this reason he was an enthusiast for the corporate State, which alone could 'combine democracy with efficiency', making sure that no particular class or interest could secure advantage, whether by political pressure on the State, or by a 'banker's ramp', or by a 'general strike'.[32] His novel *Storm over Europe* (1930), though set in a fictional Ruritanian-style state called Cisalpania, served as a vehicle for thinly disguised Right-wing propaganda; it makes tedious reading – a contrast to Jerrold's often trenchant journalism.

Throughout the 1930s there was to be a strong element of support for 'Mediterranean fascism' among British Catholics, who indiscriminately placed Mussolini, Salazar and Franco in the same category. To Jerrold, Petrie and Belloc one can add other prominent Catholic writers such as Bernard Wall, 'an ardent defender of Mussolini's political behaviour',[33] and Christopher Hollis, whose *Italy in Africa* justified much of Italy's 'mission' in Abyssinia.

Nazism, however, presented a completely different problem for most of these people. Admirers of Mussolini such as Jerrold, Petrie and Belloc recoiled at the 'barbarism' of Nazi methods and beliefs. Jerrold attacked Nazi anti-Semitism while continuing in his support for Mussolini.[34] Petrie saw Italian-style Fascism as standing 'for the family, for religion, and for discipline', whereas Nazism, 'the old Prussianism in a new form', applied eugenic tests to the relations of the sexes, was trying to make religion a department of state and preferred emotionalism to self-control.[35] Belloc, still besotted by Mussolini, felt that the chance for Britain to ally itself with Italy to keep Germany in check had been lost, mainly through the folly of Eden, who had opposed Mussolini's venture in Abyssinia. Belloc deplored the Munich settlement of 1938, feeling that it had 'played into the hands of the "Prussians"'.

Of course, just as there was considerable enthusiasm for Nazism in the general British public, so there were bound to be Catholic elements that shared in that feeling. Andrew Sharf, in his *The British Press and Jews under Nazi Rule*, singles out La Bédoyère's *Catholic Herald* as one of the foremost journals that tried to excuse Nazi anti-Semitism 'with the not infrequent comment that Jews had done, and were doing, as much and worse to the Christian population of the Soviet Union'.[36] For a number of people, Catholic or non-Catholic, fear and hatred for the 'godless' Soviet Union appears to have outweighed, at this point, most other considerations and they were therefore seduced by the picture of Hitler as the West's armour against Bolshevism.

Nevertheless, the main reaction to Nazi Germany of most of the Catholic writers who were attracted to Mediterranean fascism appears to have been negative.

One must beware of making generalizations about Catholic attitudes to Fascism. As in France, there were a good number of Catholics who opposed it root and branch. It remains true, nevertheless, that the 'Catholic' Fascist regimes in Spain and Portugal, and 'Catholic' Fascist movements outside government such as Belgian Rexism and the Action Française movement in France, had a fatal attraction for a number of British Catholics. Such views have been brilliantly evoked in the words of a character in Bernard Bergonzi's post-war novel *The Roman Persuasion* (1981):

I do believe that what's going on in Italy at the present time is an immensely exciting and promising transformation of society. I think it offers more hope for humanity than our bogus democracy, or the destructive nonsense of the class war, particularly in the ideal of the corporate state. That is, to bring all classes and groups together for the common good, in an order based on natural law and Catholic social teaching . . . The Fascists are . . . following Catholic tradition in returning to the ideal of an integrated, harmonious society.[37]

Such views did not on the whole extend to support for Sir Oswald Mosley's British Union of Fascists, which had a comparatively small number of Catholic members.

It was the Spanish Civil War, however, which was to create the largest amount of Catholic support for a 'Fascist' regime.

The Spanish Civil War

One of the main planks in Nationalist propaganda during the Spanish Civil War was the image of a 'crusade' against those who wished to destroy the Church. Accounts of Republican atrocities against priests, nuns and churches led many Catholics in other countries, including Britain, to believe implicitly in this propaganda and to mobilize help for the Franco side. This view was reinforced by the Spanish hierarchy's letter 'to the bishops of the whole world', supporting Franco's claims.

In Britain, support for Franco extended from the Catholic aristocracy to the working class Catholics of the inner cities. Prominent among Catholic publicists for the cause was Douglas Jerrold, who served on the committee of the thriving association the Friends of National Spain. Jerrold had flown a plane to the Canary Islands (with his friend Hugh Pollard), in order to take Franco and General Mola to Morocco to start the rebellion. In his book *Georgian Adventure* he described this adventure in a tone of youthful derring-do. Jerrold, who declared that the volunteers who went to Spain to fight on the Republican side in the International Brigade were fighting in 'a cause repugnant to the consciences not only of the whole Catholic population of the Empire, but, as I believe, to the great majority of English Christians of all denominations', wrote indefatigably on Spain (including many letters to *The Times*). The same line was taken by Sir Charles Petrie, Arnold Lunn, Father Francis Woodlock, SJ, Bernard Wall, Michael de la Bédoyère and many other prominent Catholics.

Two distinguished Catholics, General Sir Walter Maxwell-Scott and Colonel Rupert Dawson, played a prominent part in the flourishing Scottish branch of the Friends of National Spain. A resolution proposed by Dawson at a crowded meeting in Perth, which was carried by an overwhelming majority, shows that the Association's concerns were conspicuously religious. It expressed sympathy with the Spanish Christians, who were 'suffering such prolonged martyrdom',[38] called for the 'forces of anarchy, tyranny and Communism' to be crushed and hoped for 'an early triumph for unity, order, liberty and religious freedom'.

The Cardinal Archbishop of Westminster formed a Spanish committee, which included Lord Fitzalan of Derwent and Lord Howard of Penrith, to consider ways humanitarian help could be given to the Nationalist side. Evelyn Waugh's future sister-in-law, Gabriel Herbert, was typical of the young Catholics who supported its aims; she became an ambulance driver for Franco's troops. In Waugh's diary entry for 25 September 1936 we see just how much he, too, was involved in the doings of the Archbishop's committee:

> Drove to London with Mary. Lunched with Gabriel who is off to Spain to relieve insurgents . . . Went to meeting at Westminster of Archbishop's Spanish Association. Committee was appointed of Lord Fitzalan, Lord Howard of Penrith etc. Gabriel read report of her talk with Duchess of Laguna. I moved for her to be sent out to advise best means distribution.[39]

While much of this support for Franco came from upper-class and upper-middle class Right-wing Catholics, one must forget neither the considerable pro-Franco feeling that was to be found in the Catholic working class, nor the fact that the Labour Party was affected thereby. The Jewish historian Henry Srebrnik has described the domination of the East End Labour Party by Irish Catholics, many of them supporters of Franco's 'crusade', and 'more concerned with combating Communism than with stopping Fascism'. This meant that many Stepney Jews, 'thoroughly disillusioned by the official Labour Party representation', which failed to express their deep feelings against Fascism and Nazism, turned instead to the Communist Party.[40]

George Orwell assessed public opinion in 1944: 'Outside its own ranks, the Catholic Church is almost universally regarded as pro-Fascist, both objectively and subjectively'.[41]In this chapter, we have seen some of the things that may have given rise to this prejudice on the part of the public. By 1944 Germany, Italy, Spain, Portugal, Hungary, were all regarded as 'fascist' countries, without any distinction being made, as in the 1930s, between the various regimes. This meant that public ignorance now tended to equate the pro-Italian and pro-Franco tendency, which had been so strong among prominent Catholics during that period, with pro-Nazism (which had not been part of the make-up of most of these people).

Even at the time, a good number of Catholics had taken a less favourable line than this in relation to Mussolini and Franco – but there is no denying that an enthusiasm for Mediterranean Fascism was very common in Catholic circles in the 1930s. Support for Franco was, of course, immediately explicable by the myth of the 'crusade' against godless Communism, coupled with the picture of the war as a direct conflict between good and evil, which appealed to the visceral anti-Bolshevism of much of the British Right. But what of the support for Italian Fascism? When we look closely at what was written about it, it becomes clear that the anti-capitalist strain in much British Catholic thinking from Belloc and Chesterton onwards had made its mark and that the Corporate State appeared to many to be an Italian example, in a Catholic country, of the principles of *Rerum Novarum* and – closer to home – Distributism.

The 'Radical Right' and its influence on Belloc and Chesterton was the strongest strain in British Catholic political thought in the early twentieth century, rather than the more straightforward Catholic tradition which was summed up in the attitudes of men like Benson (even though the latter tradition was well represented in the ranks of ordinary Catholics). And one should not think (in the fascism-fixated way typical of our time) that that influence always led in wrong directions. The legacy of Belloc and Chesterton lives on in much Catholic social thinking, from the post-war period to the present day.

Notes

1 Paul Bourget suggested in his novel *L'Étape* (Paris, 1902), p. 394, that the national motto should be changed from 'Liberté, Égalité, Fraternité' to 'Discipline, Hiérarchie, Charité'. Vichy France, of course, changed it to 'Travail, Famille, Patrie'.

2 For a brilliant exposition of this tendency, see Zeev Sternhell, *La Droite révolutionnaire: les origines francaises du fascisme, 1885–1914*.

3 While none of these three was a practising Catholic, Barrès and Maurras used Catholicism for their own ends. Barrès saw it as an essential ingredient of 'Frenchness'; Maurras saw it as a force for order and tradition (and his Action Française movement was above all dependent on Catholic support).

4 Rolfe, *Hadrian the Seventh*, p. 178.

5 Ibid., pp. 55–6.

6 A phrase used by a Welsh miner to describe the attitude of the National Coal Board to the Welsh situation during the Coal Strike of 1984. (Philip Weekes, *A Great Wealth of Lack of Knowledge* Cardiff: BBC, 1990)

7 Rolfe, *Hadrian the Seventh*, p. 176.

8 Benson, *Lord of the World*, pp. 4–5.

9 Benson, *The Dawn of All*, p. 36.

10 See Speaight, *The Life of Hilaire Belloc*, pp. 31–2.

11 Eugen Weber, *L'Action Française*, p. 526.

12 Henri Massis, in conversation with the present writer in the 1960s, described Belloc, whom he had known well, as 'un vrai croisé dans la lignée de Maurras' (a true crusader in Maurras' lineage).

13 A. N. Wilson, *Hilaire Belloc: A Biography*, p. 372.

14 Speaight, *The Life of Hilary Belloc*, p. 97.

15 Belloc, letter to Mrs Reginald Balfour, 19 March 1932 (quoted in Speaight, *The Life of Hilary Belloc*, p. 385).

16 Belloc, *The Jews*, p. 43.

17 Speaight, *The Life of Hilary Belloc*, p. 184.

18 The writings of Major Douglas himself contain much anti-Semitic material, as do those of that ardent monetarist the 12th Duke of Bedford.

19 Pearce, *Wisdom and Innocence: A Life of G. K. Chesterton*, p. 445.

20 See *G. K.'s Weekly*, passim, in the 1920s.

21 *Sunday Times*, 18 August 1937, quoted in Pearce, *Wisdom and Innocence*, p. 450.

22 Frederick Hale, 'Moral Certitude and Moral Ambiguity in Bernard Bergonzi's *The Roman Persuasion*', pp. 95–108.

23 A. N. Wilson, *Hilary Belloc*, p. 264.

24 See Griffiths, *Fellow Travellers of the Right* (London: Constable, 1980), pp. 13–58.

25 J. S. Barnes, *Half a Life Left*, 1937, p. 12.

26 Barnes, *Half a Life Left*, p. 16.

27 Ibid., p. 324.

28 Sir Charles Petrie, *Lords of the Inland Sea*, 1937, p. x.

29 The present writer met Sir Charles Petrie in the mid-1970s, when he reiterated his overwhelming admiration for Mussolini as a politician and statesman.

30 Jerrold, *Georgian Adventure*, 1937, pp. 313–14.
31 Ibid., p. 332.
32 Jerrold, 'The Corporate State in England', *Everyman*, 13 October 1933.
33 Hale, 'Moral Certitude and Moral Ambiguity in Bernard Bergonzi's *The Roman Persuasion*'.
34 See, for example, Jerrold, 'Current Comments', *English Review*, July 1933, September 1933, March 1935.
35 Sir Charles Petrie, 'Fascism and the Nazis', *Saturday Review*, 20 May 1933.
36 Andrew Sharf, *The British Press and Jews under Nazi Rule*, p. 19.
37 Bernard Bergonzi, *The Roman Persuasion*, 1981, pp. 55–6.
38 This concentration on 'martyrdom' was a Catholic concern shared by French Catholics such as Paul Claudel, who wrote a famous poem dedicated to 'The Spanish Martyrs'.
39 Evelyn Waugh, *Diaries*.
40 Henry Felix Srebrnik, *London Jews and British Communism, 1933–1945*, pp. 32–4.
41 George Orwell, 'As I Please', *Tribune*, 24 March 1944.

Three Outstanding Figures

11

Graham Greene: A Pivotal Figure

Graham Greene (1904–91) is generally regarded as one of the greatest English novelists of the twentieth century. His writing would deserve, in any general history of the novel, a full examination. For the purposes of this study, however, we will be looking mainly at how his Catholicism was reflected (or otherwise) in his novels. These ways changed dramatically during the course of his career, partly because of changes in his own belief and partly because of literary abandonment of some techniques in favour of others.

Greene (like his hero François Mauriac) did not like the term 'Catholic novelist', preferring to describe himself as a 'Catholic who happens to write novels'. When we look at the novels of the period 1938–51, however, we find that they clearly deal with Catholic themes and use Catholic techniques. And his later novels, while eschewing such obvious characteristics and often questioning traditional Catholic values, nevertheless continue to deal with the same underlying issues.

Greene's picture of the world is a very bleak one – and his major concerns, throughout his career, were with the tangled jungle of human motivation, with 'guilt and innocence, loyalty and treachery, hopelessly confused in the world of appearances'.[1] These concerns take us to a variety of areas of human conflict, from gangland Brighton to Mexico, from Indo-China to Haiti. At other times, we visit areas of decay and futility, such as the 'white man's grave' in West Africa, or areas where efforts are being made to make some sense of the purpose of suffering, such as a central African leper colony. Against these backgrounds, human beings dance their solemn dance of futility, suffering, despair. Only at rare moments do we get some sense of hope – for it to be dashed from our lips before it is drunk. Yet, Greene at times seems to tell us, there may possibly be some point to it all, in the human capacity for compassion.

Greene's means of communicating these ideas changed drastically over the years. In some of his early Catholic novels, he made much use (unusually for an English novelist) of the paraphernalia associated with the mystical

159

approach taken in the French Catholic novel – the complicated patterns of mystical cause and effect, the central role of the miraculous, the importance of signs, the rigid adherence to forms. Within this format, however, one could already sense an impatience, tempered with cynicism. And soon he emerged from this phase, into a freer, less overtly 'Catholic' approach, in which the same underlying issues were more subtly explored. Greene's trajectory took him from the preoccupations of the first generation of English Catholic novelists to those of some of the post-war generation. He is a pivotal figure in the history of the Catholic novel in Britain.

Greene's Early Thrillers

Though Greene converted to Catholicism in 1926, his novels from that time appear, on the surface, unconnected to religion. They were 'thrillers', a genre for which he had a predilection from his childhood reading of Weyman, Henty and Buchan. Yet even an ordinary thriller can contain religious overtones. As Greene himself wrote: 'Murder, if you are going to take it seriously at all, is a religious subject'.[2]

Greene's earliest thrillers, published between 1929 and 1931, were failures and it is not hard to see why. Greene had aimed to vie with the great 'literary' authors of his time. As he himself was later to say, his concern with style and with following the literary fashions of the time, such as 'point of view' and similar literary techniques, had meant that he failed to be 'aware of simpler problems', and to see that a novel 'was not made with words but with movement, action, character'.[3] From now on the relations between author and reader, in his novels, were to bypass many of the new conventions of the twentieth-century novel and return to a simpler, more traditional novelistic method. *Stamboul Train* (1932) was the first novel in his new style. Its plot may appear over-complicated and at times *invraisemblable*, but it moves at a cracking pace and was a great popular success.

In 1932 Greene read François Mauriac's novel *Le Noeud de vipères* (which had just been published), which had a profound and lasting effect upon him. For him, Mauriac was not just a writer who managed to convey religious truth through the depiction of the real, modern world, but also, in purely literary terms, a novelist who had reacted against the 'dogmatically "pure" novel' of the 'tradition founded by Flaubert', and had reclaimed 'the traditional and essential right of a novelist, to comment, to express his views'. At the same time, Mauriac's characters had 'the solidity and importance of men with souls to save or lose', as opposed to the characters created by E. M. Forster and Virginia Woolf, whom Greene described as wandering 'like cardboard symbols through a world that was paper-thin'.[4]

Greene's novels of the mid-1930s contained very little in the way of explicit religious content. Yet with *A Gun for Sale* (1936) he explored, in an apparently non-Christian context, some of the themes that were to be central to his Catholic novels: above all, the problem of the artificiality of normal 'conventional' distinctions between good and evil. Superficially, the story follows the prototype of John Buchan's *The Thirty-Nine Steps*, with the hero, Raven, perpetually one step ahead of those who are pursuing him. But this 'hero' is not an upstanding gentleman, but a cold-blooded murderer for hire. After assassinating the Czech War Minister, he has been double-crossed by being paid in stolen notes. The police are after him because of this. He sets out to find those responsible, for vengeance. As the novel progresses, we begin to realize the powerful capitalist forces behind the murder. The ultimate irony is that we feel, by the end of the novel, a great deal of sympathy for Raven, whose background has produced an apparently thoughtless killer who, obscurely, is nevertheless able to distinguish good and evil. In a conversation with Anne (the detective Mather's fiancée, whom he has taken prisoner), Raven reveals this perception, but also his helplessness to do other than he does. Speaking to this girl, he feels he is unburdening himself to someone he can trust and that he might become a better man. However, this glimmer of hope soon passes. When, later, he is told by the villain Davis, who had hired him, that the girl is the detective's fiancée and that she has betrayed him, he despairs once more. He shoots Davis:

> Raven shot him. With despair and deliberation he shot his last chance of escape, plugged two bullets in where one would do, as if he were shooting the whole world in the person of stout moaning bleeding Mr Davis. And so he was. For a man's world is his life and he was shooting that: his mother's suicide, the lonely years in the home, the race-course gangs, Kite's death, and the old man's and the woman's. There was no other way: he had tried the way of confession, and it had failed him for the usual reason. There was no one outside your own brain whom you could trust: not a doctor, not a priest, not a woman.[5]

Pinkie, the hero of *Brighton Rock* (1938) owed much to Raven; but in the later novel a new concentration upon specifically Catholic themes had entered Greene's work and Pinkie's role is seen in a completely different light.

Catholic Influences

In Greene's novels of the period 1938–51, it is as though we have entered a completely different world, in which specific Catholic concerns figure centrally. We find, moreover, a concentration on those techniques of the French Catholic novel that had been most absent (with rare exceptions) from the English Catholic literature that had preceded them. How do we explain this?

Mauriac was almost certainly the main conduit through which these techniques and concerns were channelled into Greene's work. Yet those who know François Mauriac mainly through his three great middle-period novels (*Le Désert de l'amour*, 1925; *Thérèse Desqueyroux*, 1927; *Destins*, 1928) will be surprised to hear that. For in those novels Mauriac had decided to abandon the techniques of the traditional French Catholic novel (of which he had been a practitioner up to that time), as they were in his view incompatible with the ambiguity that was demanded of the modern novel. He saw the artificial logic of the traditional Catholic novel as being in conflict with 'the indeterminism and the mystery of life',[6] and had now decided to produce novels in which there was no overtly religious content, but which contained an implicit lesson about the state of mankind without God. 'It will be', he wrote, 'doing a Catholic act, to show the absence of Catholicism and the consequences to which that leads; merely by presenting characters who are entirely lacking in religious life, one reveals the great void within souls.'[7] In this new style he produced what many consider to be his three greatest works.

Towards the end of the 1920s, however, having been violently attacked by the Catholic literary world because of his failure to speak explicitly of religion, Mauriac returned, with *Ce qui était perdu* (1930), to the full gamut of supernatural and explicitly religious effects of his first period, together with a return to the unambiguous intervention of the author.[8] *Le Noeud de vipères* (1932), which so impressed Greene, was a product of this period, though, written as it is in the first person, it is more circumspect in its approach than *Ce qui était perdu*. There were thereafter a number of other Mauriac novels of the 1930s which not only spoke with the authorial voice, but were also strongly dependent on evocation of the supernatural.

Mauriac was not the only conduit, however, through which these literary influences came to bear upon Greene. Greene had read widely in French literature and among Mauriac's predecessors he had shown a particular interest in Léon Bloy and Charles Péguy, both of whom dealt, in differing idiosyncratic ways, with the themes of vicarious suffering and of the special role of the sinner in God's plan for the world. There are, for example, epigraphs from Bloy and Péguy to *The End of the Affair* and *The Heart of the Matter*, both of which evoke major themes of the French Catholic revival, and Péguy is specifically referred to (though not by name) in the conversation between Rose and the priest at the end of *Brighton Rock*. Hidden references to Péguy occur in many other places, too (as for example the evocation, in the last pages of *The Comedians*, of the theory of 'mystique' and 'politique' from Péguy's 1910 essay *Notre jeunesse*).[9]

Greene's four main 'Catholic novels' differ greatly from each other both in theme and in setting; but they and a play like *The Potting Shed* (1957) also have a great deal in common, including what Rose Macaulay was to describe as the 'magic solutions', with everything depending on whether one says 'Lord, Lord, before the right altars'.[10] Strangely enough, Macaulay's description fits the traditional French Catholic novel far better than it does Greene, in whose writings these easy solutions are at times complicated by uncertainty and irony and where the moral imperatives are, despite the 'rules' in which the characters believe, seldom clear.

The fact nevertheless remains that we continually find, in these novels of Greene's, elements of the 'cut-and-dried' approach to mysticism that was typical of the French Catholic revival. In *Brighton Rock* and *The Heart of the Matter*, for example, we find, in very different forms, the Maistrian theme of the closeness of the sinner and the saint, as stated in the epigraph from Péguy to the latter book: 'Le pécheur est au coeur même de la chrétienté . . . Nul n'est aussi compétent que le pécheur en matière de chrétienté. Nul, si ce n'est le saint.' François Mauriac had used the same theme centrally in a novel written only two years before *Brighton Rock* (*Les Anges noirs*, 1936) and a comparison of these two novels will help us to appreciate just how complex Greene's approach already was, when placed alongside that of Mauriac.

Les Anges noirs and *Brighton Rock*: Mauriac and Greene

This belief in the close relationship between the saint and the sinner stemmed, in French Catholic literature, from the writings of Joseph de Maistre, who in his *Éclaircissement sur les sacrifices* characterized sin and virtue as both being 'sacred'.[11] This is of a completely different order from the orthodox Catholic belief in the presence of virtue within even the most recalcitrant of sinners and in the eternal possibility of redemption (as voiced, for example, by the heroine of Mrs Ward's *Horace Blake* and by Chesterton's Father Brown). It has another, more precise dimension, suggesting a mystical relationship between saint and sinner that is stronger than anything in those who exist between these two poles. It is evoked vividly in the scene in *Les Anges noirs* where the priest Alain Forcas writes to the sinner Gabriel Gradère, who has given him a written account of all his diabolical crimes. Forcas explains to Gradère that it is the experience of sin that has taught him to recognize the supernatural, which cannot be perceived by the ordinary people around him:

Just realise the grace that you have been vouchsafed; just think that most
pious souls live and die in holiness, but knowing of the supernatural only
what their faith has revealed to them. But you, Sir! If he exists, that Enemy
of God and men, everything else exists as well.[12]

Note, here, the personification of the Devil, so typical of Mauriac in this
period.

The title itself of *Les Anges noirs* gives us the same message. Gabriel
Gradère, the main character, is a fallen angel like Satan himself. From the
very beginning of the novel, he is described as having been dedicated to the
Devil since his youth and having committed terrible crimes. He lives under
the impression that there is Someone there, directing his actions. In his
interior monologues, this maleficent presence seems to speak to him, as, for
example, when he has just composed a letter to the young priest:

> Gabriel Gradère went to lie down on the divan . . . 'Why are you writ-
> ing', he said to himself. 'What can this little priest do for you? Moreover
> I forbid you to see him. I forbid you to get to know him. I forbid you to
> mix him up in our secrets!'[13]

Face to face with this devil-driven sinner we have the young priest Alain
Forcas, a being predestined to suffering and grace. When Alain receives the
letter in which Gradère confides to him the story of his sins, he feels pity for
this 'poor soul' and meditates on the close link between sin and grace:

> Those who seem dedicated to evil were perhaps chosen before all the oth-
> ers, and the depth of their fall shows what a betrayed vocation would have
> been capable of. The blessed could not exist if they had not possessed the
> power to damn themselves; and perhaps the only ones who are damned
> are those who could have become saints.[14]

There are strong parallels between Gradère and the priest, both of whom
are capable of extreme good and extreme evil. 'We belong to the same spe-
cies, says Gradère, 'nothing separates us.'[15] Towards the end of the novel,
Gradère looks at the sleeping Alain and recognizes himself in him:

> He felt a strange, powerful feeling – the illusion that it was he, this young
> priest in the armchair, and that he had been, in another life, this stocky
> young man dressed in black, whose face was so worn. In another life, or
> in the mind of Someone? . . . 'And he, he could have been me'.[16]

Gradère and Alain are both aware that they have been 'chosen' in the mind of God ('Someone' – though as in the works of Léon Bloy, 'Someone' ['Quelqu'un'] with a capital letter can mean either God or the Devil).[17] Those who have been chosen *know*. Afterwards, it is a question of personal choice as to which direction they go. The rest of humanity is unaware, does not *know* or understand, has no choice. The other characters in this novel belong to 'the race of those deaf souls who will never be able to perceive any response from God'.[18] In the end Gradère, for whom Alain has offered his own suffering in order to save him, is converted; but in the process Alain himself has suffered doubts. All this shows once more the close link between 'sacred' sin and sanctity.

Mauriac's novel uses all the obvious, cut-and-dried techniques of the traditional French Catholic novel, battering home its message, which is underlined by techniques which Malcolm Scott has described as typical of him: 'moralising comments and abrupt switches from character's to narrator's angle.'[19] The plot, and particularly the ending, is far too 'satisfactory', in that there is no questioning of these ultimate truths, and the vicarious suffering of one character (Alain) is seen to be entirely efficacious in the salvation of the other (Gradère), with no reason for any doubt as to its efficacy. It is highly probable that Greene, with his new-found enthusiasm for Mauriac, read this new novel of his on publication. Even so, given the obvious weaknesses of Mauriac's novel, it is surprising that its theme should appear, only two years later, in Greene's *Brighton Rock*. What is abundantly clear, however, is that Greene eschews the certainties of Mauriac's treatment of the theme and gives us a far richer yet indeterminate view of what has been going on.

At first sight *Brighton Rock* (1938) appears to have a great deal in common with *A Gun for Sale*. But there is an enormous difference. The gangster Pinkie's role is not explained, like Raven's, merely by social concerns – upbringing, deprivation – though those do clearly play their part in his makeup. On a different plane, he represents a bout in the eternal battle between Good and Evil.

Even before the religious drama is tackled directly, a series of allusions serve, as with Mauriac's Gradère, to suggest the young gang-leader Pinkie's diabolical nature. Above all, the description of his eyes:

> From behind he looked younger than he was in his dark thin ready-made suit a little too big for him at the hips, but when you met him face to face he looked older. The slatey eyes were touched with the annihilating eternity from which he had come and to which he went.[20]

With typical Greenian irony, Pinkie's telephone number is 666, the number of the Beast in the Apocalypse.[21]

The drama at the centre of the novel is played out in the relationship between Pinkie and the young waitress, Rose. Pinkie has been forced to get to know her, because she has knowledge that could destroy the gang's carefully organized alibi for the murder they have committed. At their first meeting Pinkie and Rose find that they are both Catholics:

'You a Roman?' the Boy asked.
'Yes', Rose said.
'I'm one, too', the Boy said . . . 'Why, I was in a choir once', the Boy confided and suddenly he began to sing softly in his spoilt boy's voice: 'Agnus dei qui tollis peccata mundi, dona nobis pacem'. In his voice a whole lost world moved – the lighted corner below the organ, the smell of incense and laundered surplices, and the music.

Rose asks him if, despite the fact that he no longer goes to church, he still believes it's true:

'Of course it's true', the Boy said. 'What else could there be?' he went scornfully on. 'Why', he said, it's the only thing that fits. These atheists, they don't know nothing. Of course there's Hell. Flames and damnation. [. . .] torments'.
'And Heaven too', Rose said with anxiety, while the rain fell interminably on.
'Oh, maybe', the Boy said, 'maybe'.[22]

Facing these two young people we have Ida, who had spent part of Hale's (the man murdered by the gang) last day with him and who now, filled with a desire to find out what had happened to him, pursues them. She is obsessed by ignorant, worldly concepts of 'Right' and 'Wrong', which Greene contrasts with the Catholic concepts of 'Good' and 'Evil'. Ida stands as one of a long line of uncomprehending figures, in the English Catholic novel from R. H. Benson onwards, who judge by the standards of this world, as opposed to those of God. When Ida confronts the terrified Rose, trying to get her to give up her lover to the police, two distinct philosophies face each other:

'You're young. You don't know things like I do.'
'There's things *you* don't know.' She brooded darkly by the bed, while the woman argued on: a God wept in a garden and cried out upon a cross . . .

'I know something you don't. [said Ida] I know the difference between Right and Wrong. They didn't teach you *that* at school.'

Rose didn't answer; the woman was quite right: the two words meant nothing to her. Their taste was extinguished by stronger foods – Good and Evil. The woman could tell her nothing she didn't know about these – she knew by tests as clear as mathematics that Pinkie was evil – what did it matter in that case whether he was right or wrong?[23]

It is in part thanks to this intruder that Pinkie, who had thought he was using the young girl solely to protect himself, begins to feel a strange affinity with her. She comes, like him, from Brighton's slums. Even if he represents evil and she good, they each complement the other. At one point Pinkie finds her in her room, being intimidated by Ida:

It was Nelson Place and Manor Street which stood there in the servant's bedroom . . . He was aware that she belonged to his life, like a room or a chair: she was something that completed him . . . What was most evil in him needed her: it couldn't get along without goodness . . . She was good, he'd discovered that, and he was damned: they were made for each other.

Ida tells him to go and to leave Rose alone:

'You leave her alone', the woman said. 'I know all about you.' It was as if she were in a strange country: the typical Englishwoman abroad. She hadn't even got a phrase book. She was as far from either of them as she was from Hell – or Heaven. Good or evil lived in the same country, spoke the same language, came together like old friends, feeling the same completion, touching hands beside the iron bedstead.[24]

To make sure of Rose's silence, Pinkie marries her. Because of their age, they have to have a civil marriage. Both feel that they have just committed a mortal sin. But Rose loves Pinkie so much that she accepts damnation. Looking at people going to church, 'she didn't envy them and she didn't despise them: they had their salvation and she had Pinkie and damnation.' She asks herself what she can have done to be so happy: 'She'd committed a sin? that was the answer: she was having her cake in this world, not in the next, and she didn't care.'[25]

Pinkie, watched more and more by the police, decides that he will never be in safety while Rose is alive and plans to get rid of her by persuading her to take part in a suicide pact, in which he will cheat and stay alive. Rose, aware that suicide is a mortal sin, nevertheless feels her solidarity with Pinkie to be more important: 'He was going to damn himself, but she was going to show them that they couldn't damn him without damning her too. There was nothing he could do, she wouldn't do: she felt capable of sharing any murder . . . She wouldn't let him go into that darkness alone.'[26]

But it is Pinkie who dies and she who remains alive. And unlike Mauriac's heroes, Pinkie has undergone no transformation, but has remained as he is, while Rose has not in fact understood anything that has been going on. In the last scene of the novel everything comes once more into question. Here, as he was later to do in *The Heart of the Matter*, Greene uses the stock technique of the summing-up of events by a priest; but in this case he subverts it. The priest to whom Rose goes for confession appears capable, up to a point, of unravelling God's intentions. He can talk (prompted by Rose's wish to be damned like Pinkie) about Péguy's solidarity with the damned. He can talk convincingly, too, about 'the . . . appalling . . . strangeness of the mercy of God', which, as we know from his memoirs, Greene saw as central to the understanding of this and other novels.[27] And his exposition of the Maistrian relationship between good and evil is exemplary, even if couched, as all his statements, in hesitant terms:

> 'Corruptio optimi est pessima . . . I mean – a Catholic is more capable of evil than anyone. I think perhaps – because we believe in Him – we are more in touch with the devil than other people.

As he goes on, however, we find that all this leads merely to his customary words of consolation during a confession, which are 'mechanical':

> 'But we must hope', he said mechanically, 'hope and pray.'[28]

And then it is that the priest's well-meaning advice goes completely off the rails. He assures her that if Pinkie loved her, that shows that there was some good in him. If she gives birth to a child, she must make him a saint, to pray for his father. Rose goes out, full of hope for the future. And in a traditional Catholic novel, that would have been the message for the reader as well, conveyed by a priest as spokesman for the author. But this is the point at which Greene reserves for us his bitterest irony. Pinkie had made a record for Rose, in a soundproof stall, when she had asked him to record a message for her. It was at a moment when he had to be careful of her and pretend to be loving, but she had annoyed him. It was a message full of hatred: 'God damn you, you little bitch, why can't you go back home for ever and let me be?'[29] He had known, at the time, that she did not have a gramophone on which to play the record. Now, after his death, she decides to borrow a gramophone to listen to it. As the novel ends, she is going trustingly to do so:

> There was something to be salvaged from that house and room, something else they wouldn't be able to get over – his voice speaking a message to her: if there was a child, speaking to the child. 'If he loved you', the priest had said, 'that shows . . .' She walked rapidly in the thin June sunlight towards the worst horror of all.

The comparison of *Les Anges noirs* and *Brighton Rock* shows us just what a new voice Greene brought to the techniques of the French Catholic novel: a voice of doubt, questioning, and irony, as opposed to the certainty and belief in efficacious means that led ineluctably to salvation or damnation. All this, as in Greene's other novels, takes place in a world singularly empty of hope. The crooked lawyer Prewitt's quoting of Marlowe's Mephistopheles from *Doctor Faustus* sums it all up: 'Why, this is Hell, nor are we out of it.'[30]

Vicarious Suffering and 'Vicarious Damnation': a misinterpretation of Péguy

The theme which above all sums up this period of Greene's writing is that of vicarious suffering, which had been so central to the French Catholic novel. At times, however, Greene's version of it becomes an extremely doubtful one.

In *The Power and the Glory* this problem makes its first real appearance – though it has been adumbrated in Rose's beliefs and in the priest's words at the end of *Brighton Rock*. The whisky priest has fathered a child and when he, as a fugitive, visits the village in which she lives, he is 'appalled by her maturity'. He realizes just how vicious her upbringing is almost certain to make her, with 'the whole wide world coming round the child to ruin her', and he makes a promise to God of his own suffering, if only He will save her: 'He prayed silently, "O God, give me any kind of death – without contrition, in a state of sin – only save this child".'[31] Shortly afterwards, he tries to explain to the child how much he loves her: 'I would give my life, that's nothing, my soul . . .'

At the end of the novel, the whisky priest, awaiting death, is deprived of the last sacraments. He tries to confess to God directly, without intermediary. He thinks of his child, and says: 'Oh God, help her. Damn me, I deserve it, but let her live for ever'.[32] At dawn, he is executed without having been shriven.

In this novel, the theme of vicarious suffering is not rounded off satisfactorily, as it would have been in a traditional Catholic novel, with the effect of all this upon the child being clearly delineated. What we have is the priest's *belief* that his suffering can be efficacious, together with the neatness of the way in which events conspire to fulfil his half of the bargain. We are therefore bound to believe in the *possibility* of the child being saved. This theme of what Robert Hugh Benson called a 'contract' with God[33] occurs again and again in Greene's works; and here it involves a preparedness by the whisky priest to give up salvation itself for his child. He believes that he has sacrificed his soul by depriving himself of making his last confession – though Greene brings us, the readers, to feel that despite his apparent personal unworthiness (his drunkenness, his relations with women, his fear), he *must*, through his readiness to take up the burden of a priest despite dangers and through his ignominious end, be acceptable to God. In other words, *pace* Rose Macaulay, it is *not* just a question of saying 'Lord, Lord, before the right altars'.

Nevertheless, we have here something similar to the Bensonian deformation of the doctrine of vicarious suffering in 'Monsignor Maxwell's tale', whereby one's own damnation or loss of faith can be offered for the good of someone else. In Greene, however, this theme appears to stem, not from Huysmans, but from a misunderstanding of Péguy's attitude with regard to damnation. This is expressed fairly clearly by the priest in *Brighton Rock*:

> There was a man, a Frenchman . . . He was a good man, a holy man, and he lived in sin all through his life, because he couldn't bear the idea that any soul should suffer damnation . . . This man decided that if any soul was going to be damned, he would be damned too. He never took the sacraments, he never married his wife in church. I don't know, my child, but some people think he was – well, a saint. I think he died in what we are told is mortal sin.[34]

This idea recurs again and again in Greene's writings: that Péguy was, as Greene put it, prepared to 'risk damnation himself in order to save another soul'.[35] Yet on what was it based?

In the 1897, 'socialist', version of Péguy's *Jeanne d'Arc*, the young Joan of Arc is so appalled by the fate of the damned that (in true socialist style) she declares her solidarity with them and her preparedness to be damned alongside them. What Greene and one or two other commentators have however missed, is that her companion, Madame Gervaise, immediately tells her that this is blasphemous and that the real nature of the doctrine of vicarious suffering is that 'we are blessed when God, in his infinite mercy, is prepared to accept *our works, our prayers and our sufferings* in order to save a soul.'[36]

At the end of this scene Joan, despite her horror at the idea that God could be responsible for eternal damnation, accepts what Madame Gervaise has been saying: 'O God, I know that Madame Gervaise is right'.[37] This scene is repeated in Péguy's 1910 'Catholic' *Mystère de la Charité de Jeanne d'Arc*, with Madame Gervaise declaring once more the true nature of vicarious suffering and specifically excluding from it 'infernal suffering'.[38]

Some commentators, having misread this scene, have taken certain events in Péguy's life (Péguy's decision not to have a church marriage and his consequent deprivation of the sacraments) and interpreted them on the basis of that reading. The events concerned, however, appear to have another, far more likely, explanation. When Péguy was converted, his wife (an anti-clerical agnostic of firm principles) refused to take part in a religious marriage, or for their sons to be baptised. In this she was supported by her family, which had been staunchly anti-clerical for generations. Péguy was therefore excluded from the sacraments as long as this situation lasted. But he loved and respected his wife and refused to force anything on her (even if he had been able to). This sacrifice was a very human one and completely unrelated to 'vicarious damnation'. Indeed, Péguy's view of the sacraments seems to exclude such a theory. In conversation with his friend Lotte, in very anti-clerical mood, he declared prayer to be superior to the sacraments, as the latter were 'controlled' by the priests, while the former was 'at our disposal'. This view of the sacraments hardly conforms with the view that deprivation of them was a way of 'taking on damnation'. It is interesting to note, too, that in all the 694 pages of Pie Duployé's monumental and exhaustive study of Péguy's religious beliefs,[39] there is no mention of what we might call 'vicarious damnation'.

Yet this belief was very important to Greene and recurs in a number of other works. In *The Heart of the Matter*, for example, Scobie prays as he takes the bread at the Mass, when in a state of sin, for those individuals he is attached to by pity: 'O God, I offer up my damnation to you. Take it. Use it for them'; and the taste of the bread on his tongue is 'the pale papery taste of an eternal sentence.'[40] And his final suicide, a mortal sin, is undertaken as a result of his pity for others.

In *The Potting Shed* (1957) this takes an even more extreme form. In this play James Callifer, the younger son of a committed atheist family, cannot understand why he has always been treated by the family as a pariah. It appears to have something to do with a potting shed in the garden, which everyone avoids and where it is whispered by the servants that something terrible once happened. It also has something to do with his uncle, Father William Callifer, a Catholic priest. James can remember nothing that had happened to him before the age of fourteen. Eventually he discovers from the widow of the gardener that he, at fourteen, had hanged himself in the potting shed and that the gardener had thought he was dead and had left him with his uncle Father Callifer while he went for help. James now goes to see his uncle, whom he has not seen for years. In his dismal presbytery the old priest is living an appalling, drunken life, just managing to fulfil his daily tasks as a priest, but without faith or hope. Gradually, as they talk, the scene in the potting shed comes back to him. The priest describes finding his nephew dead there:

Callifer	I'd have given my life for you – but what could I do? I could only pray. I suppose I offered something in return. Something I valued – not spirits then. I really thought I loved God in those days. I said, 'Let him live, God. I love him. Let him live. I will give you anything if you will let him live.' But what had I got to give him? I was a poor man. I said, 'Take away what I love most. Take . . . take . . . [*He can't remember*]
James	'Take away my faith, but let him live'?
Callifer	Did you hear me?
James	Yes. You were speaking a long way off and I came towards you through a cave of darkness. I didn't want to come. I struggled not to come. But something pushed me to you.
Callifer	Something?
James	Or somebody.[41]

We are left to presume that the priest's dreadful state has been caused because, as he says, 'He answered my prayer, didn't he?' This depiction of a bargain in which God is apparently prepared to deprive a human being of his faith, verges on the heretical. Evelyn Waugh appears to have realized this when he attended the first performance of *The Potting Shed*. With mocking but surface politeness, he wrote to Greene, 'I am not theologian enough to understand the theological basis. I wish you would write it as a novel explaining more fully to simple people like me.' More straightforwardly, he wrote to his wife Laura, 'The play is great nonsense theologically and will puzzle people needlessly.'[42]

The 'Reporter' becomes a 'Leader-Writer': *The End of the Affair*

The End of the Affair is based on a bargain with God of a different kind. The heroine, Sarah, has promised God that if her lover, who appears to have been killed in a bombing raid, is brought back to life, she will give him up for ever. After Sarah's death, there are various miraculous healings that cannot easily be explained except by divine intervention. The story is told through the eyes of the lover Bendrix, who believes that she has left him for another man and hires a private detective to find out – only to discover, when he finally reads her diary, that his rival has been God. The first-person narration, by a man who is not a believing Catholic, strangely enough ends by making us more convinced of what the author wishes to tell us, than a straightforward omniscient narrator would (much as the same technique works in Mauriac's *Noeud de vipères*). Conor Cruise O'Brien's view is persuasive – that the essential weakness of this novel is 'the ingenuity that produced the strange devices . . . with their accumulation of "proofs" planted there by their creator, like fossils in Brighton rock'.[43]

In its straightforward treatment of the miraculous, *The End of the Affair* differs from Greene's other 'Catholic' novels, where the paraphernalia of the French Catholic novel is so often subverted and where certainty is never achieved. It is the most extreme example, in Greene's writings, despite its being written in the first person, of the authorial direction and interpretation of the action that is so typical of the French Catholic novel. As Conor Cruise O'Brien put it, basing himself on the journalist Fowler's distinction, in *The Quiet American*, between reporters and leader-writers ('I am a reporter . . . God exists only for leader-writers'), Greene had in this novel given up being a reporter and had become a leader-writer.[44]

The Later Novels

Greene's publishers Heinemann announced, 'with ill-suppressed elation', in mid-1955 that religion was to play 'little or no part' in a new series of his novels, of which *The Quiet American* (1955) was to be the first. Yet, as Conor Cruise O'Brien pointed out in a perspicacious review of that novel, the subject of his novels had not changed at all, 'only the method'. In the reporter Fowler's dry, unsentimental depiction of a tragedy played out in the context of the Indo-China War (no sense of a 'leader-writer' here) we see how innocence and well-meaning virtues can, in this world, bring destruction. And yet, as O'Brien points out, it could not be true to say that religion 'plays little or no part' in a novel which ends with this sentence: 'Everything had gone right with me since he had died but how I wished there existed someone to whom I could say that I was sorry'.[45]

There is no doubt that with this novel Greene puzzled many of his Catholic public. A character in David Lodge's *How Far Can You Go?* (1980) typifies their reactions. For him, 'the credibility of the Catholic faith was underwritten . . . by the existence of distinguished literary converts like Graham Greene and Evelyn Waugh, so any sign of their having Doubts was unsettling.' He found *The Quiet American* 'morally and theologically confused – there was not the same stark contrast between the Church and the secular world that you got in the earlier novels.'[46] Yet such readers failed to see that this new phase of Greene's novelistic existence, which he entered from the mid-50s onwards, was to create a new kind of Catholic novel.

Gone were the trappings of the traditional 'Catholic novel', whether on the French or the English model. In their place came a new, spare type of novel, in which the miraculous and the mystical had no place, but where people grappled with the same problems that had beset his characters throughout. The author often took on a new *persona*, that of a hyper-observant first-person narrator who, like the author himself, was fascinated by the *minutiae* of the human behaviour around him. One has only to look at the opening pages of many of his short stories to see this – or the first thirty pages or so of his novel *The Comedians* (1966), in which characters who are to be central to the action gradually emerge, as they co-exist on a ship heading for Haiti. Among them is the apparently insignificant small-time crook and conman Jones, who eventually becomes central to the story, dying for others – but for what belief? In a revealing passage towards the end of the novel, the narrator muses on what made Jones tick:

> I wondered whether perhaps in all his devious life he had been engaged on a secret and hopeless love-affair with virtue, watching virtue from a distance, perhaps, like a child doing wrong in order to attract the attention of virtue.[47]

The narrator of *The Comedians* is a lapsed Catholic who seems detached from everything and who has 'felt myself not merely incapable of love . . . but even of guilt'. He has been described as a 'prêtre manqué' and the communist Dr Magiot sees in him a man who, like him, has had a faith. He implores him, in his last letter, not to abandon all faith, for 'there is always an alternative to the faith we lose. Or is it the same faith under another mask?'[48] We are reminded of the lieutenant in *The Power and the Glory*; purity of faith is possible in many guises.

In the novels of this period we are made aware that virtue and compassion are not purely Christian virtues and that the Christian answers are only too often answering the wrong questions – questions that have not been put. As Bernard Bergonzi has put it, Greene's novels at this stage reflected a new spirit that had been prominent in Catholic theological developments in this period, which stressed 'that all good things come from God, that nature and grace are interdependent, and that there is a virtual and implicit Christianity as well as a doctrinally informed and committed Christianity.'[49] This comes out most clearly in *A Burnt-Out Case* (1961), which takes place in a religious leper colony in Africa. The hero, Querry, is a former leading Catholic architect who has lost his faith. His is an arid life, empty of belief and of purpose, which is compared to that of those lepers who, cured of the virulent disease, are nevertheless 'burnt-out cases' whose limbs no longer have life in them. As the novel proceeds, he seems to re-find a capacity for compassion. Because of this, a stupid priest takes him to be a saint. In contrast, the atheist Dr Colin's view is that he has been cured through learning to serve other people. The final discussion between the Fathers serving the leper colony and Dr Colin leaves unresolved the question of whether Querry has refound his faith or not. In one sense, for Greene the question is by now irrelevant.

To his friend Evelyn Waugh, who wrote to him, of *A Burnt-Out Case*, that 'I don't think you can blame people who read the book as a recantation of faith',[50] Greene replied by pointing out that he had been dealing with fictional characters and that Querry was in no way himself:

> Must a Catholic be forbidden to paint the portrait of a lapsed Catholic? . . . I suggest that if you read the book again you will find in the dialogue between the doctor and Querry at the end the suggestion that Querry's lack of faith was a very superficial one – far more superficial than the doctor's atheism. If people are so impetuous as to regard this book as a recantation of faith, I cannot help it. Perhaps they will be surprised to see me at Mass.[51]

What he had intended to do in this book, said Greene in another letter, was to 'give expression to various states of belief and unbelief.'[52] It is important to realize that for Greene, as for many other Christians of the second half of the twentieth century, doubt and faith were the two sides of the same coin; the one could not exist without the other. In conversation with John Cornwell in 1989, 'we talked about doubt', wrote Cornwell, 'which he seemed to regard an admirable virtue rather than an imperfection'. He insisted that 'It is *human* to doubt' and contrasted doubt with infallibility, 'praising Gorbachev for his rejection of Communist dogma, comparing him with John XXIII.'[53] On the same basis, he had a profound mistrust of John Paul II: 'I don't think this Pope has doubt. I don't think he doubts his own infallibility.'[54]

For Greene, Catholic questions and Catholic answers were now less important than the way in which people reacted to the world around them. Catholic questions continued, however, to need to be posed, because they *were* posed in real life. As a number of critics, from Conor Cruise O'Brien to David Lodge,[55] have pointed out, 'pity', or 'compassion', is central to Greene's moral structure for the world. Even in the earlier works, it was that 'pity' that had governed, for example, Scobie's actions in *The Heart of the Matter* and which had been in that book so hamstrung by the firm precepts of the Catholicism of the day. At the end of *The Heart of the Matter*, speaking with Scobie's widow, the priest, Father Rank (who had been so lacking in help or advice to Scobie earlier in the novel) finally, with an unexpected lucidity, gets to the heart of the conflict between rules and compassion:

> 'The Church says . . .'
>   'I know the Church says. The Church knows all the rules. But it doesn't know what goes on in a single human heart. [. . .] It may seem an odd thing to say – when a man's as wrong as he was – but I think from what I saw of him, that he really loved God.'[56]

The Greene of the 1950s and 1960s was to have, in his attitudes to the conventional teachings of the Church, much in common with a number of the new generation of Catholic writers that arose in the post-war period. His politics were, like theirs, more of the Left than of the Right. But above all, he had come to a view that certain human virtues were not necessarily based on theological rules, but on human reactions and needs. The rigidity of much of the Church's attitudes to the modern world was seen by him as irrelevant. Like many of his younger contemporaries, after longing for some relaxation of the Church's attitudes, he found cause for hope in the advent of Pope John XXIII and then in the Second Vatican Council. Earlier, when he had consulted Father John Talbot of the Oratory about a moral dilemma facing him when he thought he had epilepsy (should he get married? And if so, should he use contraception?), Talbot had played it 'by the rules':

> There was only one hard answer he could possibly give ('the Church knows all the rules', as Father Rank said), while the meter of the taxi ticked away the repetitions of our fruitless argument. It was the Rock of Peter I was aware of in our long drive, and though it repulsed me, I couldn't help admiring its unyielding façade.[57]

This was, Greene says, 'before John Roncalli was elected Pope'. Nowadays (1971) 'how differently he would have answered my question, telling me, I have no doubt, to follow my conscience.' We shall find other Catholic writers sharing that same sense of a new dawn at that time. How grievously they were to be disappointed!

Greene stands as a rock at the centre of the Catholic literature of his time. The development of his career spans a change from the baroque traditions of the 'Catholic novel' to a new literature of freedom, ambiguity and allusiveness, coupled with moral awareness. In this he was to be followed by a number of Catholic novelists of the post-war period.

Notes

1 Conor Cruise O'Brien, *Maria Cross*, p. 249.
2 Greene, *The Pleasure Dome: Collected Film Criticism 1935–40* (Oxford: Oxford University Press, 1980), p. 192. Quoted in Brian Diemert, *Graham Greene's Thrillers and the 1930s*, p. 63.
3 Greene, *A Sort of Life*, p. 199.
4 Greene, 'François Mauriac' (1945), in *Collected Essays*, pp. 115–21.
5 Ibid., p. 172.
6 François Mauriac, *Le Roman*, 1928. (Pléiade, 2, p. 765).
7 Frédéric Lefèvre, 'Une heure avec M. François Mauriac', *Les Nouvelles littéraires*, 26 May 1923.
8 For a study of these developments in the work of Mauriac, see Griffiths *Le Singe de Dieu: François Mauriac entre le 'roman catholique' et la littérature contemporaine, 1913–1930*.
9 Greene, *The Comedians*, p. 311.
10 Rose Macaulay, letter to Father John Johnson, 13 November 1951, in *Letters to a Friend* (1951), pp. 218–19.
11 Joseph de Maistre, *Les Soirées de Saint-Pétersbourg*, pp. 337–429. For the impact of this theory on the Catholic novel, see Richard Griffiths, 'Le sacré et le dé-sacré dans le roman catholique', pp. 57–68.
12 Mauriac, *Les Anges noirs* (1936), p. 328.
13 Ibid., p. 244.
14 Ibid., p. 316.
15 Ibid., p. 1040.
16 Ibid., p. 355.
17 See Griffiths, 'Quelqu'un qui ne sentait pas bon fit son entrée'.
18 *Les Anges noirs*, p. 362.
19 Malcolm Scott, *The Struggle for the Soul of the French Novel*, p. 190.
20 Greene, *Brighton Rock*, 1938 (Penguin edition, 1971), p. 21.
21 Ibid., p. 48.
22 Ibid., p. 52.
23 Ibid., p. 199.
24 Ibid., pp. 126–7.
25 Ibid., pp. 194–5.
26 Ibid., p. 228.
27 '"The appalling strangeness of the mercy of God" – a mystery that was to be the subject of three more of my novels.' (*Ways of Escape*, p. 60).
28 Greene, *Brighton Rock*, pp. 245–7.

29 Greene, *Brighton Rock*, p. 177.
30 Ibid., p. 210.
31 Greene, *The Power and the Glory*, pp. 81–2.
32 Ibid., p. 207.
33 See 'Monsignor Maxwell's Tale', p. 35.
34 Greene, *Brighton Rock*, p. 246.
35 Greene, 'Man Made Angry' (1939), in *Collected Essays*, p. 132.
36 Péguy, *Jeanne d'Arc*, 1897, Act II (*Oeuvres poétiques complètes*, NRF Gallimard Pléiade, 1960, p. 36. My italics.
37 Ibid., p. 40.
38 Péguy, *Mystère de la Charité de Jeanne d'Arc*, 1910 (*Oeuvres poétiques complètes*, NRF Gallimard Pléiade, 1960, p. 424)
39 Pie Duployé, OP, *La Religion de Péguy*, 1965. In the course of several conversations in the late 1960s, Duployé confirmed the present writer in his view that Greene had completely misunderstood Péguy's attitude upon this matter.
40 Greene, *The Heart of the Matter*, p. 225.
41 Greene, *The Potting Shed*, p. 75.
42 Waugh, letter to Greene, 6 February 1958; letter to Laura Waugh, 6 February 1958, in *The Letters of Evelyn Waugh*, pp. 501–2.
43 O'Brien, *Maria Cross*, p. 250. O'Brien clearly does not realize what 'Brighton rock' is. His simile would run better as: 'like the lettering in Brighton rock'.
44 O'Brien, review of *The Quiet American* in *New Statesman and Nation*, 10 December 1955 (reprinted in *Maria Cross*, ed. cit., pp. 249–51.
45 Ibid.
46 Lodge, *How Far Can You Go?*, p. 41.
47 Ibid., p. 290.
48 Greene, *The Comedians*, p. 312.
49 Bergonzi, 'The Decline and Fall of the Catholic Novel', in *The Myth of Modernism and Twentieth Century Literature*, p. 177.
50 Letter from Waugh to Greene, 5 January 1961, in *The Letters of Evelyn Waugh*, p. 559.
51 Letter from Greene to Waugh, 6 January 1961, in *A Life in Letters*, p. 253.
52 Letter from Greene to Waugh, 4 January 1961, in ibid., p. 252.
53 John Cornwell, 'A Catholic to the Last', in *Articles of Faith: The Collected Tablet Journalism of Graham Greene*, p. 151.
54 'Why I am still a Catholic', ibid., p. 138.
55 See O'Brien, 'Graham Greene: The Anatomy of Pity', in *Maria Cross*, pp. 57–86; Lodge, 'Graham Greene', in *The Novelist at the Crossroads*, pp. 87–118.
56 Greene, *The Heart of the Matter*, p. 272.
57 Greene, *A Sort of Life*, pp. 189–90.

12
Evelyn Waugh: The Culmination of a Tradition

Evelyn Waugh (1903–66) presents something of a contrast with Graham Greene. Greene stands as a turning-point in twentieth-century Catholic literature, looking back to what had preceded him, but also looking forwards, as his career progressed, in new directions which, though some have seen them as an abandonment of the Catholic novel, were in fact a restructuring of it in new and vital ways. Waugh, on the other hand, represents the culmination of a tradition, its finest flowering – but his work is essentially a dead-end. This is in no way to denigrate his achievement. *Brideshead Revisited* is one of the masterpieces of the Catholic novel. It remains, however, firmly fixed within the tradition of the English Catholic novel that had preceded it, while at the same time giving it a new and more complex life.

The richness of the literary experience that we gain from Waugh's Catholic writings is in part enhanced by those elements from his earlier, highly successful, secular novels, which he carried forward into them.

Waugh before *Brideshead Revisited*

Waugh's earliest novels, *Decline and Fall* (1928) and *Vile Bodies* (1930) were books of social satire, depicting the frivolous and cynical behaviour of the post-war generation of English high society. The style is brittle, with the conversations, in particular, moving at a fast pace and brilliantly capturing the mood. The world that is depicted is as brittle as the style. Morals have no place in it, drugs replace reality, and tragedy and death are depicted as frivolously as the mad round of parties, 'all that succession and repetition of massed humanity'[1] which was summed up in the title *Vile Bodies*.

These novels gave readers a sense of sharing in a smart world that was full of excitement. The books consisted above all of close observation enhanced by skilful exaggeration. Waugh himself, in the 1920s, had led 'an intense social life, at first among the those of his old circle who were still in Oxford, and later among the Bright Young People.' He has been described, however, as having been 'on the fringe rather than at the centre of this world'.[2] His own attitude to it, as gleaned from his diaries, appears to have been mixed: on the one hand, admiration of it and enjoyment of its *chic*; on the other, a detachment from it, possibly caused by the personal melancholia which was to be a constant in Waugh's life. For the moment, this was to come out in his writings not in the form of moral criticism, but as a kind of despairing cynicism. In *Decline and Fall* vice continually wins and virtue and innocence are continually duped; by *Vile Bodies* vice and virtue no longer have any meaning.

Waugh was received into the Catholic Church in September 1930. At first, this does not seem to have affected his writing. His next novel, *Black Mischief* (1932), though set in Africa, continues the caricatured view of contemporary society that was to be found in its predecessors. It may have seemed that Waugh's conversion had not made any change to his writing. In the following year, however, he produced a short story which dealt with a specifically Catholic theme, 'Out of Depth' (1933). This is the sole explicitly Catholic piece of fiction by Waugh in the years before *Brideshead Revisited* and will repay some attention.

The first thing to note is that the story, a fantasy of the future, is clearly derivative. Some critics have pointed out that the story has much in common with R. H. Benson's *The Dawn of All* (1911) but a far closer source is John Gray's *Park* (1932), which had appeared merely a year before it.[3] *Park* itself had owed much to *The Dawn of All*, but various important features of the plot of 'Out of Depth' link it specifically to *Park* rather than to Benson's book – particularly the fact that the new, future Catholic society that is depicted is ruled by a black ecclesiastical hierarchy and that the indigenous white population has declined into barbarity. One can only presume that Waugh had read one of the small number of copies of *Park* printed in the limited edition. How he came to know it, we cannot tell (though of course Gray and Raffalovich attracted to their Edinburgh salon many major literary figures from England, one of whom may have brought the novel to Waugh's attention).

Waugh's story, though set from the start in the superficial London society familiar to us from his novels has, despite the apparent flippancy of its tone, a serious, simple message underlying it. An American expatriate called Rip van Winkle meets a magician at a party of Lady Metroland's. In an aside, we gather that Rip has been brought up as a Catholic. At the end of the evening, he and Alastair Trumpington accompany the magician to his house, where he reveals that he has chosen them, 'because you are the most ignorant men I ever met', to undertake two journeys into time for him, in order to 'recover the garnered wisdom which the ages of reason have wasted.'

Trumpington is to go back to the time of Ethelred the Unready. Rip is to go five hundred years into the future. As they leave the magician's house, their car is involved in an accident.

We now accompany Rip into the future. He finds himself in a London where a herd of sheep is grazing near Piccadilly Circus, beside a reedy pool. Great flats of mud, submerged at high water, stretch across the Strand.[4] There Rip finds a cluster of huts, inhabited by savages who are 'fair-skinned and fair-haired, but shaggy', and who speak 'in the sing-song tones of an unlettered race who depend on oral tradition for the preservation of their lore . . . Their words seemed familiar but unintelligible.' Among the words he can make out are 'white' and 'black boss'. These are the descendants of the twentieth-century English. Soon they are visited by a boat manned by black men, who barter trinkets with them. A black anthropologist comes to study Rip. We discover that this dominant black race is Catholic. A black Dominican friar arrives, heading a 'Mission' to the natives and suddenly Rip knows that 'out of strangeness, there had come into being something familiar: a shape in chaos.' Mass is being celebrated:

> Something was being done that Rip knew; something that twenty-five centuries had not altered; of his own childhood which survived the age of the world. In a log-built church at the coast town he was squatting among a native congregation . . . all round him dishevelled white men were staring ahead with vague, uncomprehending eyes, to the end of the room where two candles burned. The priest turned towards them his bland, black face.
>
> 'Ite, missa est'.

Rip now wakes up in hospital. A priest is by his bed. Later, he asks the priest how he came to be there. He replies that he had in fact been brought to see Sir Alastair: 'He isn't a Catholic, but he seems to have had some kind of dream while he was unconscious that made him want to see a priest.' So Alastair, in the Middle Ages and Rip, in the future, have found the same thing: the Catholic faith continuing throughout history. *This* is the 'garnered wisdom which the ages of reason have wasted', which the magician had sent them to recover.

Like other Catholic writers of tales of the future, Waugh clearly has an axe to grind. His message is typical of his beliefs and attitudes throughout the rest of his career. It stresses the continuity of the Catholic faith throughout the ages and its indestructibility even amid the most violent changes in society and the world. This continuity is, for Waugh as for his predecessors of the Catholic revival, indissolubly linked with the survival of specific forms of worship (however mistaken his view of the history of those forms of worship may be).[5]

'Out of Depth' stands, however, at this stage of Waugh's career, as an isolated example of a work containing a specific Christian message. The novels he produced after his conversion appeared at first sight to remain as secular in content as those that had preceded them. He did produce a major religious work, but this was non-fictional: his biography of *Edmund Campion* (1935), written in honour of the rebuilding of Campion Hall, Oxford, the Jesuit hall of the University. This is the most vivid of all the biographies of the Catholic martyrs that had been written over the years, in large part because Waugh brought a novelist's eye to the many remarkable contrasts in Campion's life, from the royally favoured Oxford scholar to the clandestine priest and then, after pursuit and betrayal, to the martyr. He was clearly fascinated by the characters both of Queen Elizabeth and of Campion himself. The whole book is lively, and alive.

It would be wrong, however, to classify all the novels of this period as mere continuation of what had gone before. *A Handful of Dust* (1934) contains no overt Christian theme, but it does contain a new element of seriousness. Its hero, Tony Last, is living what appears to be a highly idyllic existence with his wife and child at his ugly ancestral home Hetton Abbey, to which he is devoted. Soon, however, Tony's wife Brenda's affair with the unsuitable social climber John Beaver reveals the gap between this idyll and the appalling, amoral London society in which Beaver and Brenda move (which gives full rein for Waugh's satirical skills). Their cruel and heartless treatment of Tony and his acceptance of it, even to the extent of agreeing to act as 'guilty party' in their divorce, are a pattern only finally broken when Tony, realizing Brenda's grasping determination to double-deal on the divorce settlement, which will now force him to sell his ancestral home, rebels and refuses to play ball. His ideal of a chivalrous world of tradition has been destroyed: 'A whole Gothic world had come to grief . . . there was now no armour glittering through the forest glades, no embroidered feet on the green sward; the cream and dappled unicorns had fled . . .' His decision is adamant: he refuses the divorce and decides to go away for six months, after which, if she wishes it, he will divorce Brenda without settlements of any kind.

The story ends, as do so many of Waugh's, with a cruel twist. Usually, that twist is to do with death. Here, it is a living death. Tony has been persuaded by an explorer to go in search of a lost city in South America and ends up wandering deliriously through the jungle, on the verge of death. He staggers into the domain of Mr Todd, a strange and sinister figure whose enthusiasm for Dickens' works leads him to keep Tony captive so that he can read to him. Tony gradually realizes that he will never escape. In London Brenda, penniless and deserted by Beaver, is informed by Tony's solicitors that in the absence of a will the estate will go to Tony's distant cousins.

This novel had originally stemmed from its penultimate chapter ('Du Côté de Chez Todd'), a version of which had previously appeared as a short story in its own right, 'The Man who liked Dickens' (1933).[6] Waugh later explained that the main body of the eventual novel had been written in order to lead up to this climax:

> After the short story was written and published, the idea kept working in my mind. I wanted to discover how the prisoner got there, and eventually the thing grew into a study of the other sort of savages at home and the civilized man's helpless plight among them.[7]

For the first time in Waugh's work, we here have heavy criticism of those scions of 'modern life' who figured so centrally in his previous novels. The hero, though like previous heroes a hapless figure caught up in a world he does not understand, is also a defender of traditional values, a trusting and civilized man amid savages. The tale is a moral if bleak one; its harsh conclusion contains no hint of forgiveness.[8]

Echoes of this contrast between tradition and the modern world are found in Waugh's later novels. Though *A Handful of Dust* holds no mention of Catholicism, we can already see, in embryo, what Waugh was going to be like when he eventually launched into the genre of the Catholic novel.

Before he did so, however, he was to publish two other novels. *Scoop* (1938), a farcical novel about journalism, reverts to the style initiated by *Decline and Fall*. Any seriousness found in *A Handful of Dust* has here disappeared. The adventures of William Boot, plucked in error from his country estate and sent to report on a war in an African country, are accompanied by an array of larger-than-life characters, two of whom (the megalomaniac newspaper proprietor Lord Copper and Julia Stitch, the powerful society lady whose web of influence extends into the highest political and social circles) will recur in later novels. *Scoop* was, straightforwardly, a comic novel, as was its successor, written after the outbreak of war, *Put Out More Flags* (1942). These novels seemed to mark a resurgence of the old Waugh. Only a few years later, however, he was to surprise the literary world with a work of serious Catholic intent.

Brideshead Revisited

Brideshead Revisited was first published in 1945. In the preface to the revised edition of 1960, Waugh described its theme as being 'the operation of divine grace on a group of diverse but closely connected characters.'[9] Unlike so many other Catholic novels, however, this one does not assail the reader 'up front' with an obvious message and the theme only gradually emerges during the course of the novel. Indeed, so subtly is it introduced that many people, enjoying the novel for other reasons, have failed to realize how Christian a work it is. When Waugh went to Hollywood in 1947 to discuss a film version of the novel, he noted that the writer who would be adapting it for the screen '[saw] it purely as a love story' and that none of those involved saw 'the theological implication'.[10]

But the inveterate reader of Catholic novels has to beware of another kind of mistaken judgement. Because certain stock themes that had characterized the English Catholic novel up to this time play a large part in this one, it is all too easy to succumb to the temptation of taking a view of Waugh, as Catholic author, which is just as faulty, in another direction, as that of the American scriptwriter had been.

The most obvious of the Catholic themes is that of the aristocracy and of grand houses. We see them through the eyes of an apparently naïve observer, Charles Ryder, the middle-class undergraduate admitted into the household at Brideshead by his friendship with the son, Sebastian. Brideshead is not a recusant house; but it is very much a Catholic house, marked, as were those of Mrs Ward, Benson, Baring and others, by the chapel in which the sanctuary lamp is burning. As in Baring's *Daphne Adeane*, the chapel has been created by a husband for his Catholic wife; it is also, within both novels, a source of nostalgia. The eventual extinction of the sanctuary lamp marks in both novels a sense of loss (though in *Brideshead*, of course, it is eventually lit once more).

Another such theme is that of the 'bad taste' of the chapel's decoration, the tawdry bad taste that was so prized by British Catholics. Interestingly, what the narrator Ryder sees as such bad taste is a style that is nowadays much admired – the arts and crafts design of the late nineteenth century – though Ryder's description would make even the most hardened arts-and-crafts aficionado flinch.[11] The theme of Catholic 'tat' is continued, too, in the descriptions of Nanny Hawkins' room, with its oleograph of the Sacred Heart mingled with the mementoes of the Flyte children and the volume of Burke's Peerage, and in the grander room of Lady Marchmain herself, with a plaster St Joseph alongside posthumous miniatures of her three soldier brothers.[12] These parallels are meaningful. Nanny Hawkins has appeared at first sight to be the natural successor of the various retired nannies and nurses who inhabited the rooms of William Boot's mansion Boot Magna Hall, in *Scoop*. Though she, like them, is accepted as an integral part of the life of this aristocratic family, she is also a snobbish working-class admirer of the doings of the household and stands for a particularly naïve adherence to the faith. Both of these characteristics are in their way distorted reflections of the values of Lady Marchmain and her son Brideshead. The similarities between the mingling of sacred and profane objects in her room and in Lady Marchmain's point to this affinity.

Though the house is not a recusant one, Lady Marchmain comes from recusant stock. Waugh's description of her family is reminiscent of that of the Riversdales by Mrs Wilfrid Ward:

> The family history was typical of the Catholic squires of England; from Elizabeth's reign to Victoria's they lived sequestered lives among their tenantry and kinsmen, sending their sons to schools abroad, often marrying there, intermarrying, if not, with a score of families like themselves, debarred from all preferment.[13]

Another theme is that of the incursion of the mean values of the modern world into the world of tradition. In this novel, all this is summed up in Hooper, Captain Ryder's subordinate. Hooper returns to Ryder's mind, when he thinks of Lady Marchmain's heroic brothers, who had died in the war:

> These men must die to make a world for Hooper; they were the aborigines, vermin by right of law, to be shot off at leisure so that things might be safe for the travelling salesman, with his polygonal pince-nez, his fat wet handshake, his grinning dentures.[14]

These are not the only traditional themes of the Catholic novel that we find in this work, however. As a far more central issue, the conflict in Julia's mind between Catholic duty and desire, culminating in her giving up her lover, would appear at first sight to be typical of the novels of renunciation to be found in the earlier period. We would be wrong, however, to classify Waugh as a mere continuator of old traditions. He uses them in a new way, subordinating them to the central theme of the novel, the operation of divine grace upon the various characters.

The most obviously devout Catholics, in the family at the centre of this novel, are strangely unsympathetic. 'Mummy is popularly believed to be a saint',[15] says Sebastian. Yet Lady Marchmain's single-minded devotion to her faith can lead her to dominate and manipulate others. Waugh's own view of her was a complicated one: 'Lady Marchmain, no, I am not on her side; but God is, who suffers fools gladly; and the book is about God.'[16] Her son Brideshead, whose unquestioning and unimaginative piety often appears dogged and blinkered, is clearly another 'fool of God'. His lack of concern for the feelings of others, his obsession with the minutiae of religion, make him appear at times uncaring (as when he precipitates Julia's crisis of conscience by his remarks). Yet he is admirable in his way. The important thing is that neither Lady Marchmain nor Brideshead change in any way during the course of the novel.

Nor does Cordelia, Lady Marchmain's youngest child. She grows older, but her religious attitudes remain constant. She has a simple uncomplicated faith which develops naturally over the years, She is depicted as a 'child of God' – full of natural piety, apparently naïve and yet alarmingly clear-minded about the forces at work within her brother and sister, as comes out particularly in her final interview with Charles (Waugh himself felt that 'the last conversation with Cordelia gave the theological clue'[17] to the whole book).

If we are to look for changes effected by divine grace, however, we must look to the other characters. The title of the final section of the novel, 'A Twitch upon the Thread', announces the beginning of the process. It refers to the concept we have already seen, in G. K. Chesterton, of 'the unseen hook and the invisible line'[18] that is long enough to bring someone back to God, once he twitches on the thread. At one point, Cordelia reminds Charles of the evening when Lady Marchmain read that Father Brown story to them.[19] And now, 'There's him [Lord Marchmain] gone and Sebastian gone and Julia gone. But God won't let them go for long', she says.[20] And now the thread is pulled in, for them all.

Neither Sebastian nor Julia seem at first sight a candidate for the working of grace. Yet it is as though they were marked for it from the start. Sebastian, the drunken wastrel, is tortured not so much by the actions of his mother (which are merely ancillary), as by a sense of loss (expressed through a sense of loss of childhood, but in fact something far deeper) – and by what Cordelia perspicaciously perceives as a vocation that he was resisting.[21] After many vicissitudes, he eventually tries to get taken on as a lay-brother at a monastery in North Africa, but is not accepted because of his alcoholism. Finally (just as Charles de Foucauld had in Jerusalem after his conversion), he ends up as a humble doorkeeper in the house of the Lord, 'a sort of under-porter'.[22] As Cordelia puts it, the Superior 'was a very holy old man and recognized it in others'. Gently, Cordelia explains to Ryder that what he has to understand about Sebastian is that he is holy and that his suffering has been necessary: 'One can have no idea what the suffering may be, to be maimed as he is – no dignity, no power of will. No one is ever holy without suffering. It's taken that form with him . . .'

Julia, too, appears to have a predisposition for self-destruction. When we see her again years later, she is already tortured by guilt at what her marriage to the worldly Rex Mottram has meant. She sees the death of her child as a punishment for her infidelities. Perhaps, she thinks, that is why she and Charles have now met: 'Perhaps this is why you and I are here together like this . . . part of a plan'.[23] That plan, via the drama of guilt and renunciation in the final stages of the novel, is to bring not only her, but also Charles, to God.

For it is in fact Charles Ryder, the narrator, who has the central role in the novel. He appears at first to be merely a first-person 'naïve' observer of the doings of the other characters, a conveniently non-Catholic commentator cast adrift in a Catholic world. Yet the shape of the novel, which begins and ends with a scene many years later, when Charles returns to Brideshead with the army, means that he is in fact a 'knowing' narrator who already knows the whole course of events. That narrator, from the start, gives us hints as to a change that has subsequently taken place in him. Gradually we begin to realize that the main theme of the novel is the workings of grace in *him*. The subtitle of the book, *The Sacred and Profane Memories of Captain Charles Ryder*, which is so often ignored, points clearly to this.

Lord Marchmain's return to Brideshead, to die, brings matters to a head not just for him, but for Julia and Charles. The dispute over whether a priest should be brought to him as he is dying is not just about the old man's soul (though that is of course of importance). As Charles says, there was 'the sense that the fate of more souls than one was at issue.'[24] In the event, Marchmain gives a sign, before dying, that he has become reconciled to God and the Church. But the high drama of the deathbed scene also affects Charles and Julia, in different ways. Charles, the sceptic who has declared that all these things are 'such a lot of witch-craft and hypocrisy'[25] has found himself praying for the dying man in suitably sceptical terms: 'O God, if there is a God, forgive him his sins, if there is such a thing as sin.' But as the man on the bed opens his eyes and sighs, Charles finds himself asking for more and in different terms:

I suddenly felt the longing for a sign, if only of courtesy, if only for the sake of the woman I loved, who knelt in front of me, praying, I knew, for a sign. It seemed so small a thing that was asked, the bare acknowledgement of a present, a nod in the crowd. I prayed more simply: 'God forgive him his sins' and 'Please God, make him accept your forgiveness.'

And when Marchmain has made the sign of the cross,[26] Charles knows 'that the sign I had asked for was not a little thing, not a passing nod of recognition, and a phrase came back to me from my childhood of the veil of the temple being rent from top to bottom.'[27]

It has brought matters to a head for Julia, too. However, her reactions are strangely inadequate, compared to Charles'. When she tells Charles that this scene has finally made her decide to renounce him, her choice of words shows not only a certain self-centredness, but also her complete incomprehension of where Charles stands. She asks herself (with the Catholic conviction of the *difference* that separates them from non-believers) why it is that she has been allowed to understand these things, when Charles hasn't. Perhaps, she simplistically muses, it is because her whole family have kept her in their prayers, or 'it may be a private bargain between me and God, that if I give up this one thing I want so much, however bad I am, he won't quite despair of me in the end.'[28] The irony in this statement is that she does not realize that Charles, too, whom she so lightly dismisses, has begun to understand, perhaps more fully than she does.

Charles has begun to learn the Claudelian lesson that suffering can bring one to God, and that human love, when thwarted, can be a stepping-stone on the way to knowledge of God,[29] as, disappointed in our search, we find ourselves 'each straining through and beyond the other, snatching a glimpse now and then of the shadow which turns the corner always a pace or two ahead of us.'[30]

The epilogue brings us back to the present day, with Charles Ryder and his troops at Brideshead. Charles goes to visit the chapel and finds the lamp once more burning before the altar. And we realize that he is now a Catholic: 'I said a prayer, an ancient, newly learned form of words'. As he walks back to the camp, he muses on the building of the house, the passing of time, the destruction of the old and the coming of 'the age of Hooper', the vulgar subordinate who epitomizes for him all that is wrong with the modern age. 'Vanity of vanities', he thinks. And yet there is cause for hope. Just as the lamp has been relit, so the faith will continue, and the traditions of heroism from the former ages:

> Something quite remote from anything the builders intended, has come out of their work, and out of the fierce little human tragedy in which I played; something none of us thought about at the time; a small red flame – a beaten-copper lamp of deplorable design relit before the beaten-copper doors of a tabernacle.

And he imagines the soldiers, far from home like the crusaders who had seen that flame, which is now 'burning anew among the old stones'. His final mood is a happy one, full of hope: '"You're looking unusually cheerful today", said the second-in-command.'[31]

Brideshead Revisited was the climax of Waugh's writing up to that stage.

It is his one major Catholic work. After it, anything was likely to be an anti-climax.

The Later Novels

In 1945, at the time when *Brideshead Revisited* was appearing in the bookshops, Waugh was already starting work on another book. This, the novel *Helena*, was to appear some years later. In the meanwhile, however, he returned to the satirical mode of his pre-war secular novels, first with *Scott-King's Modern Europe* (1947), a short work in which an unworldly scholar is invited to a conference in a Left-wing dictatorship (loosely based on Yugoslavia) and then *The Loved One* (1948) a satire on Californian funeral practices which competes brilliantly with the work of his first period. Neither of these books address Catholic themes, so *Helena*, which appeared in 1950, was Waugh's first post-*Brideshead* Catholic work.

The novel, though it has brilliant moments, is marred by an evident desire to edify and by a concentration on Waugh's own very rigid view of Catholic faith and doctrine. By telling the story of the Empress St Helena, the finder of the True Cross, Waugh not only stresses the *reality* of the Christian religion through the importance of an actual object relating to the Gospel, but also, by skilful use of anachronisms, of modern speech and of sly, apparently unconscious, references to the future, gives a sense of the Church's role at all times and in all places. And Waugh's irrepressible sense of mischief enables him also to mock Modernist tendencies in his own time by depicting them as being eternally with us:

'You see none of the Western bishops have got a new idea in their heads. They just say: "This is the faith we were taught. It is what's always been taught. And that's that." I mean they don't realise they've got to move with the times . . . What they were taught may have been all very well in the catacombs, but now we have to deal with a much more sophisticated type of mind altogether . . . I mean, we must have Progress. Homoousion is definitely dated.'[32]

Brilliant as some of these individual scenes are, they do not combine to create a satisfactory whole. Waugh thought that this was one of the best books he had written. Unfortunately, neither his contemporaries nor posterity have agreed.

Shortly thereafter, Waugh started work on a major project, which would once more bring together a Catholic theme and a depiction of the contemporary world. This was the first volume, *Men at Arms* (1952), of a trilogy, to include *Officers and Gentlemen* (1955) and *Unconditional Surrender* (1961), which was later to be gathered together under the title *Sword of Honour* (1965). The material for these novels comes from Waugh's wartime experiences, first in Britain, then in the commandos, then in the ill-fated Crete campaign and finally with the partisans in Yugoslavia. The hero, who binds the whole thing together, is Guy Crouchback, the last remnant of a recusant family, whose brothers have both died and who has himself divorced, thus preventing any chance of an heir. From the start, we realize that Guy is out of tune with his times. Waugh sums this up in a phrase that has overtones both of Benson's Elizabethan novels and of the last scene of *Lord of the World*:

> Often he wished that he lived in penal times when Broome [the family home] had been a solitary outpost of the Faith, surrounded by aliens. Sometimes he imagined himself serving the last mass for the last Pope in a catacomb at the end of the world.[33]

Guy has been living, in Italy, a useless life 'set apart from his fellows by his own deep wound, that unstaunched, internal draining away of life and love.' All he has are 'a few dry grains of faith.'[34] But now, with the advent of war, he feels that 'eight years of shame and loneliness were ended'.[35] The enemy is in view, 'huge and hateful' and there is 'a place for him in that battle.'[36] Guy is a romantic, like Tony Last in *A Handful of Dust*. The novels gradually depict his disillusionment with the world and with the war, as he undertakes increasingly futile activities and as he sees cowardice rewarded and protected, virtue ignored and the values for which he had thought the war was being fought being gradually undermined by *Realpolitik*.

The introduction of characters from Waugh's secular novels increases the sense of corruption. Lord Copper's newspapers distort the truth and make of the cowardly Trimmer (a new avatar of Hooper) a war hero. Julia Stitch, exerting in Alexandria the same powers of influence that she had in London, saves the coward Ivor Claire (whom Guy had formerly seen as a pattern of chivalry) and has Guy sent back to England in order to hide his knowledge of it all.

But what of religion? Some commentators have seen the trilogy as not being in any sense a 'Catholic novel'. Others have seen it as unrelentingly pessimistic. At first sight, both judgements seem possibly to be justified. The occasional mentions of 'Catholic pieties and practice' do, as Bernard Bergonzi suggests,[37] seem at best peripheral to the main themes. With Guy's father, and the ancestral home, we seem to have returned to the old recusant romanticism. Though Mr Crouchback has left Broome, he has leased it to a convent and 'the sanctuary lamp still burned at Broome as of old.'[38] The depiction of this 'innocent, affable old man'[39] recurs at various stages of the book. At times, too, we are told of various acts of religious conformity performed by Guy himself; they seem strangely disconnected from the plot. One might think that these interludes were a mere adjunct to a story that could just as well have otherwise been a purely secular tale, with Guy a secular man initially full of ideals and then disillusioned by his experience – but that would be wrong. While it is often thought that the trilogy represents the destruction of the hope evoked at the end of *Brideshead Revisited*, that would be to ignore an underlying, unobtrusive religious dimension.

Religion, in this trilogy, is not just the evocation of a romantic past, nor is it found merely in occasional acts of religious conformity on the part of the hero. The latter are there to remind us of Guy's religious basis for belief and action. And the whole point of the book, which Waugh described as 'the humanizing of Guy',[40] is reached when Guy, who no longer sees the war as the opportunity for heroic redemption of his wasted life, finds a humbler and more unexpected way to do something of use. At his father's funeral, 'In the recesses of Guy's conscience there lay the belief that somewhere, somehow, something would be required of him; that he must be attentive to the summons when it came . . . One day he would get the chance to do some small service which only he could perform, for which he had been created.' And he wonders whether his father is at that moment clearing the way for him. 'Show me what to do and help me to do it', he prays.[41]

Soon the opportunity comes. His flighty, divorced wife Virginia is expecting a baby by Trimmer, the working-class figure who stands for all that Guy, and Waugh himself, dislike in the modern world. And she is destitute. Guy asks her to remarry him. In an argument with a mutual friend, he points out that he has never, until now, done a single positively unselfish action:

> Of course Virginia is tough. She would have survived somehow. I shan't be changing her by what I'm doing. But you see there's another –' he was going to say 'soul'; then realized that this word would mean little . . . 'there's another life to consider. What sort of life do you think the child would have, born unwanted in 1944'.[42]

It is at this point that we realize that his father *has* 'cleared the way' for him. In his last letter to Guy, he had written of the Lateran Treaty in the following terms:

> 'Did you consider how many souls may have been reconciled and have died in peace as a result of it? How many children may have been brought

up in the faith who might have lived in ignorance? But quantitative judgments don't apply. If only one soul was saved that is full compensation for any loss of "face".'[43]

Sword of Honour was a great opportunity for Waugh to give vent to his feelings about the conduct of the war and more generally about the 'modern world'. It also enabled him to indulge in his love and admiration for the recusant aristocracy. But the trilogy is more than this. Despite the apparent aimlessness of its plot, it has a serious Catholic point to make and a serious examination of the development of a character to undertake. And, despite the tenor of so much of the trilogy, like *Brideshead Revisited* it ends on a note of hope.

Like Greene, Waugh gives a bleak picture of the human condition. His vision, however, is conditioned by a nostalgia for a better time that had once, he believed, existed. On the pattern of many of his predecessors both in France and in Britain, he conceived of the 'modern world' as being an evil force that had undermined the virtues of the past. Like them, he saw the continuity of the faith as being its major strength and its traditions and liturgy as being inviolable. His reliance on the authority of the Church was as rigid as that of any of the early British converts. His (approving) comments on R. H. Benson's faith illustrate his own attitudes:

> What he sought and found in the Church was authority and catholicity. A national church . . . could never speak with universal authority.[44]

Vatican Two, which to Greene and to many of the post-war generation brought hope, was to Waugh a disaster. As he gloomily said in the preface to the 1965 edition of *Sword of Honour*, on re-reading the book he realized that, unknowingly, he had 'written an obituary of the Roman Catholic Church in England as it had existed for many centuries', and that 'all the opinions here described are already obsolete.'[45]

Nevertheless, his two major achievements in the Catholic novel give us, despite his later feelings, a possibility of hope. In Greene, that hope is based on the human characteristic of compassion, seen as present in believer and non-believer alike. In Waugh, it is based on the acceptance of Catholic truth, which can reconcile us to all the suffering and grief of the world, amidst which we each have our role to play, however strange or unsuitable that role may appear to be.

It is fascinating, when reading *Brideshead Revisited* and *Sword of Honour*, to see the technique whereby Waugh gradually introduces nuggets of

Christian truth into novels that at first sight appear predominantly secular. In *Brideshead*, of course, there is a gradual build-up and the Catholic theme predominates in the later part of the novel (though the message of Charles Ryder's greater understanding and more real faith, in comparison to Julia's more childlike and conventional attitudes, is introduced in a highly understated way). In *Sword of Honour*, Guy's eventual role is even more carefully hidden; yet it is the point of the whole trilogy. Waugh's great achievement is to have eschewed the surface treatment of matters of faith that had been so common in the English Catholic novel, and to have conveyed to us something of the complexity of the mysterious ways in which God moves.

Notes

1   Evelyn Waugh, *Vile Bodies*, p. 104
2   Michael Davie, editorial comments in *The Diaries of Evelyn Waugh*, p. 159.
3   See p. 88.
4   There seems to be some reminiscence, here, of Jefferies' *After London*.
5   For example, the form taken by the Mass from the sixteenth century onwards was not something that had not altered for 'twenty-five centuries'.
6   Reprinted in *The Complete Short Stories*, pp. 119–34.
7   In 'Fanfare' (*Life*, 1946), quoted in Frederick Stopp, *Evelyn Waugh: Portrait of an Artist*, p. 90.
8   A very unsatisfactory alternative 'happy' ending was written for an American serialization of this novel. In it, Tony returns from an uneventful cruise and is reunited with Brenda. All is forgiven, but Tony secretly takes over Brenda's London flat, presumably for affairs of his own. He has ceased to be a moral hero and has taken on the characteristics of the corrupt society around him. ('By Special Request', the alternative ending printed as an appendix in most modern editions.)
9   Evelyn Waugh, preface to *Brideshead Revisited* (revised edition, London: Chapman & Hall, 1960), p. 9.
10   Diary entry for 7 February 1947, in *Diaries*, p. 673.
11   *Brideshead Revisited*, ed. cit., pp. 47–8.
12   Ibid., p. 45, 141. Note the recurrence of a plaster statue of St Joseph.
13   Ibid., p. 155.
14   Ibid., p. 155.
15   Ibid., p. 102.
16   Waugh, letter to Nancy Mitford, 7 January 1945 (*Letters*, p. 196).
17   Waugh, letter to A. D. Peters, May 1944 (*Letters*, p. 185).
18   See p. 97.
19   Typical of Waugh's carelessness about such things is the fact that he has got his reference wrong: Lady Marchmain had been reading to them from *The Wisdom of Father Brown*, whereas the story from which this image comes figures in the earlier collection *The Innocence of Father Brown*.
20   *Brideshead Revisited*, p. 245.
21   Ibid., p. 246.

22 *Brideshead Revisited*, p. 338.

23 Ibid., p. 286.

24 Ibid., p. 358.

25 Ibid., p. 357.

26 This powerful scene is not in fact an invention, but an evocation (including the attitude of the family and the words of the priest), of the death of Waugh's friend Hubert Duggan (*Diaries*, 13 October 1943, pp. 552–3).

27 Ibid., pp. 370–1.

28 Ibid., p. 373.

29 In most of Claudel's plays, the separation of lovers is seen as a step on the path to redemption and to communion with God.

30 *Brideshead Revisited*, p. 333.

31 Ibid., pp. 380–1.

32 Waugh, *Helena*, pp. 95–6. Homoousion means 'of one substance'. In the Nicene Creed this expresses the relation between the Father and the Son. It was inserted in order to combat Arianism.

33 Waugh, *Sword of Honour*, p. 19.

34 Ibid., p. 38.

35 Ibid., p. 14.

36 Ibid., p. 15.

37 Bernard Bergonzi, 'The Decline and Fall of the Catholic Novel', in *The Myth of Modernism and Twentieth Century Literature*, p. 175.

38 *Sword of Honour*, p. 22.

39 Ibid., p. 39.

40 Letter to Cyril Connolly, 8 September 1952 (*Letters*, p. 383).

41 *Sword of Honour*, pp. 603–4.

42 Ibid., p. 699.

43 Ibid., p. 546.

44 Evelyn Waugh, introduction to R. H. Benson, *Richard Raynal Solitary* (Chicago, 1956).

45 Evelyn Waugh, preface to *Sword of Honour*, 1965.

13

David Jones: The Meaning of Signs

The writings of David Jones (1895–1974) received rapturous critical acclaim at their appearance. T. S. Eliot described *In Parenthesis* (1937), as 'a work of genius' and W. H. Auden said of *The Anathemata* (1952) that it was 'very probably the finest long poem written in English this century'. Eliot saw Jones as a writer on a par with James Joyce, Ezra Pound and (modestly) himself.[1] Clearly, as with Gerard Manley Hopkins, Graham Greene and Evelyn Waugh, we here have a writer who, over and above his status in Catholic literature, can be seen as a major force on the wider literary scene.

Yet Jones is strangely neglected nowadays. His paintings appear to be far better known than his literary works. Why is this? It may, of course, be because of the 'difficulty' of much of his writing, so typical of the Eliot-Pound generation. Auden, in a 1963 review, pointed to some of the problems for the average reader:

> It is certainly true that no reader is going to be able to make Mr Jones's 'nowness' his own without taking a great deal of trouble and many readings of *Anathemata*, and, if he says: 'I'm sorry, Mr Jones is asking too much, I have neither the time nor the patience which he seems to expect me to bring to his poem', I do not know what argument one could use to convince him otherwise. I can only state my personal experience, namely, that I have found the time and trouble I have taken with *Anathemata* infinitely rewarding.[2]

Yet that 'difficulty' is shared by the poetry of Eliot and Pound, which is still widely read and has not suffered the same neglect. It may be that the importance of the Catholic religion in Jones's later poetry and above all the major part played in it by the Mass, is what has deterred a great many ordinary readers. The average Catholic, more used to straightforward and uncomplicated treatments of Christian themes, may have failed to appreciate the complications of his thought.

Be that as it may, in the history of English Catholic literature Jones, a Welshman, has a very special place. In the nineteenth and twentieth centuries most other Catholic poets who had used the imagery and symbolism of the Catholic Church (with the grand exception of Gerard Manley Hopkins, whom Jones greatly admired), had tended to do so in a fairly banal way. The use of Catholic imagery had tended to be a surface application. In Jones, however, this imagery forms an essential part of a way of perceiving Christian truths.

The Mass had been a major theme in the Catholic narrative prose of the first part of the twentieth century, but Jones was the first British Catholic poet to give it a similar role in poetry. This was in large part due his experience as a visual artist and to early influences upon him in the years up to his late flowering as a writer (he was in his forties when his first book appeared).

Early Life: painter and sculptor

For many people, Jones is pre-eminently a visual artist and we will find that there are important resonances between his work in the visual arts and his writing. He was born in south-east London, of a Welsh father and before the First World War began studying at the Camberwell School of Arts and Crafts. In the War he served for four years as a private with a London Welsh battalion of the Royal Welch Fusiliers. On his return, he continued his study of art for another couple of years. In September 1921 he was received into the Catholic Church by Father John O'Connor (the original for Chesterton's Father Brown). O'Connor was very closely connected with the Catholic sculptor Eric Gill and his artistic community at Ditchling and had introduced Jones to Ditchling just before his conversion. For the next few years, Jones was to be strongly affected by the ethos of Gill's group, first here and later at Capel-y-ffin. This ethos was a mixture of Fabian and Chestertonian Distributist ideas and of theories about the connections between art, work and religion. In the frequent discussions the mixture was a heady one. They debated 'Usury, Private Ownership, Beauty, Goodness, Truth'.[3] The neo-Thomism of Jacques Maritain was central to the group's view of the relationship between religion and the arts (Father O'Connor produced a translation of Maritain's *Art et Scolastique*). Another important influence on Jones was the French Jesuit Maurice de la Taille's book *Mysterium Fidei* (1921), translated into English as *The Mystery of Faith: Regarding The Most August Sacrament and Sacrifice Of the Body and Blood of Christ*. This book argued that Christ's sacrifice, beginning from his self-offering at the Last Supper, completed in the Passion and continued in the Mass, was all one act, with there being only one immolation, that of Christ at Calvary to which the Supper looks forward and the Mass looks back. La Taille's theory shed, for Jones, 'a sort of reflected radiance upon the sign-world in general', because of 'his French understanding of an artistic wholeness.'[4]

For Jones, it was through 'the sign' that art and religion came together. In this he was much affected, also, by those French artists the Gill circle most appreciated – the Nabis, or Symbolists. One or two of this group, including Jan Verkade and Maurice Denis, had of course become Christian artists, but what affected Jones far more was the importance of *symbol* in the paintings of this group and also some of their theories in relation to the re-creation and re-ordering of reality through the medium of painting. For Maurice Denis, a painting 'should look like paint', and should be 'a flat surface covered with colours assembled in a particular order'. For Sérusier, what was important was non-natural deformation of reality, the aim of art being 'to idealise nature by inserting it into a mathematical order'.[5]

The re-creation of reality, a form of 're-incarnation', became the essence of Jones's painting and also, eventually, of his writing. The important thing was to 'signify'. Maritain's philosophy had shown him that the artist should not merely 'reveal this or that object under the form of paint', but also 'make the universal shine out from the particular' so that 'what is represented becomes a sign of something else.'[6]

In this early period Jones's art, whether in the form of painting, engraving or sculpture, hieratically re-created reality in a way that owed much to Gill. Where it went beyond Gill, however, was in its ability, through symbol and sign, to point to mysterious truths. A very good example of this is a carved wooden Crucifixion of 1925, in which a figure on the right of Christ is collecting the mingled blood and water from his side in a chalice, while another figure on his left is swinging a censer and censing the dying Christ. Not only does this sculpture, as Miles and Shiel have pointed out,[7] illustrate La Taille's vision of the single act whereby Christ offers himself at the Last Supper, dies on the Cross and himself celebrates the Mass which recollects the sacrifice, it also vividly evokes the mystical bringing-together of the blood of the Crucifixion and the wine of communion which is 'broached' by the soldier's lance, as in George Herbert's *The Agony*:

> Who knows not Love, let him assay
> And taste that juice, which on the cross a pike
> Did set again abroach; then let him say
> If ever he did taste the like.
> Love is that liquor sweet and most divine,
> Which my God feels as blood; but I, as wine.

Such early works of art as this point the way to the similar techniques that Jones will use in his writings.

In Parenthesis (1937)

Jones's time in the front line in the War had been a traumatic experience and in the years thereafter he suffered continually from what was then known as 'shell shock'. His attempted solution to these problems had been a hectic work-schedule, which in turn aggravated them. This was to lead to serious depression in 1931 followed by a complete mental breakdown in 1932–3. During this time he found it impossible to paint, finally starting again only in late 1936. He had another major breakdown in 1946–7 and was never entirely to escape from nervous depression.

Despite the trauma of his war experiences, Jones had since 1928 been working on a book about the war, which was to become In Parenthesis (1937). In some senses, the writing of it can be seen as some kind of effort at catharsis. In the process, however, Jones created a remarkable work of art unlike any other. It is an epic poem (though most of it is not written in verse), which describes the experiences of a group of men flung together by war, whom we follow from their embarkment to France, to the terrible experience of Mametz Wood. As with his visual art, he produces a 're-creation' of reality. Our attention is drawn to the universality of the war experience, as a whole range of cultural allusions are brought into play. These include Welsh and Celtic myths (many from the Mabinogion), Welsh history (as depicted in Y Gododdin, the early Welsh epic about the battle of Catraeth, which provides the quotations at the beginning of each of the seven parts of the book), Arthurian history (much of it from Malory), the Chanson de Roland, Roman history, medieval warfare, and Christian and specifically Catholic themes, intermingled with themes from earlier religions. All this, amid the down-to-earth, day-to-day conversation of the present-day soldiers.

The men in this company, Jones tells us in his preface, were 'mostly Londoners with an admixture of Welshmen, so that the mind and folk-life of these two differing racial groups are an essential ingredient to my theme . . . Together they bore in their bodies the genuine tradition of the Island of Britain, from Bendigeid Vran to Jingle and Marie Lloyd. These were the children of Doll Tearsheet. Those are before Caractacus was.'[8] The vivid depiction of their conversation, their jokes, their fears, is the basis for a deeper evocation of a past that is common to all, whatever the varying cultural expression of it.

Typical of Jones's techniques is the great 'set-piece' in Part Four, 'Dai's boast', in which a Welsh soldier makes a 'boast' (a medieval Welsh art-form), which, in a footnote, Jones relates to the boast of Taliesin at the court of Maelgwyn ('I was with my Lord in the highest sphere, on the fall of Lucifer into the depth of hell. I have borne a banner before Alexander . . .'). Here, the boast is intermingled with the comments of the Cockney soldiers. The first few lines of this remarkable, and lengthy, piece give the tone of the whole:

> This Dai adjusts his slipping shoulder-straps, wraps close his misfit
> outsize greatcoat – he articulates his English with an alien care.
> My fathers were with the Black Prinse of Wales
> at the passion of
> the blind Bohemian king.
> They served in these fields,
> it is in the histories that you can read it, Corporal – boys
> Gower they were – it is writ down – yes.
> Wot about Methusulum, Taffy?
> I was with Abel when his brother found him,
> under the green tree.
> I built a shit-house for Artaxerxes.
> I was the spear in Balin's hand
> that made waste King Pellam's land.

This recital has started with an actual historical situation in which the Welsh had taken part, in this very part of France, during the Hundred Years' War and then rapidly moves between other ancient examples of strife, in the Bible, in Malory's *Morte d'Arthur* and far further afield. All this is interspersed with mocking comments by the listeners and with comic side-references. The techniques are the same as in the rest of the book: the extensive footnotes, as in T. S. Eliot's *Waste Land*; the often obscure references, which as in Eliot even the footnotes only too often fail to illuminate; the sense that the actual, the present, is a part of a greater and more universal and timeless whole.

Catholicism is one among many cultural references here – but a particularly resonant one. It figures not only in the Christian themes of the Arthurian legends, or the direct references to the Passion ('You can't believe the Cup wont pass from / or they wont make a better show / in the Garden').[9] It is also ever-present in side-references to Catholic language and ritual (often with direct quotation from the liturgy). Part Three, for example, for which the title 'Starlight Order' is fittingly taken from Gerard Manley Hopkins's poem *The Bugler's First Communion* – a poem which brings together military and religious themes – starts with a version of the rubrics for the Good Friday Office: 'Proceed . . . without lights . . . prostrate before it . . . he begins without title, silently, immediately . . . in a low voice, omitting all that is usually said. No blessing is asked, neither is the kiss of peace given . . . he sings alone.'[10] The solemnity of this Good Friday opening, which stresses the sacrifice to which the soldiers are going, is intensified at the opening of Part Seven, where extracts from the *Tenebrae* for Good Friday and from the psalms are quoted in Latin and the *Songs of Degrees* from the Little Office of the Blessed Virgin Mary are paraphrased in English.

> Invenimus eum in campis silvae
> and under every green tree
> Matribus suis dixerunt: ubi est triticum et vinum? Cum deficerent quasi
>   vulnerati . . . cum exhalarent animas suas in sinu matrum suarum . . .
> In the Little Hours they sing the Song of Degrees
> and of the coals that lie waste.
> Soul pass through torrent
> And the whole situation is intolerable.

This solemn beginning is the prelude to the slaughter of Mametz Wood. Typically, we are immediately thereafter brought back to the stark reality of the situation, as a soldier suffering from shell-shock is described:

> He found him all gone to pieces and not pulling himself together nor mak-ing the best of things. When they found him his friends came on him in the secluded fire-bay who miserably wept for the pity of it all and for the things shortly to come to pass and no hills to cover us.[11]

The main concern for Jones, in the writing of *In Parenthesis*, was the descrip-tion and the 'signifying illumination' of the experience of the First World War. In that process, Catholic references had an important but subordinate part to play, amid the myriad other cultural and spiritual references. In this context, it is significant that the book ends, not with Christian or Catholic themes, but with a paraphrase of a passage from a medieval Welsh poem, followed by the solemn last lines of the *Chanson de Roland*, which stress the participation of the writer in the action of his own poem and at the same time the universality of the lessons to be learned:

> The geste says this and the man who was on the field . . . and who wrote the book . . . the man who does not know this has not understood anything.

This is an extremely powerful book. T. S. Eliot later said that he had been 'deeply moved'[12] when reading it and that has been the experience of many.

Other Writings before *The Anathemata*

During a visit in 1934 to Palestine, Jones was struck by the British soldiers he saw there, who seemed to him reminiscent both of his comrades from the trenches and of the Roman soldiers occupying Judaea in the time of Christ. This idea continued to ferment within him and he was to develop it more fully in a series of fragments written over the next fifteen years or so, which were eventually to be published in the 1950s and 1960s in various outlets. Of them, 'The Wall', 'The Fatigue' and 'The Tribune's Visitation' are all, in Jones' own words, 'concerned with the Roman troops garrisoned in Syria Palaestina at the time of the Passion.'[13]

'The Fatigue' deserves particular attention. In it the fatigue party that was detailed to accompany Jesus to the Cross is depicted. The inscription in Roman capitals at the beginning is a solemn introduction, which through a whole series of disparate allusions stresses Jones' obsession with 'the wood of the Tree' and also the idea of the three crosses at Calvary being the 'vexilla regis', the military standards of the Roman legions which had now become the 'signs' of the triumph of the King, who was crucified upon one of them.[14] It ends with a quotation from Venantius Fortunatus' Good Friday hymn *Vexilla Regis*, as the poet hails the cross/standard: 'O CRUX AVE / AVE VEXILLUM.'

The fragment itself echoes many of the techniques used in *In Parenthesis*: the colloquial military language of the trenches, here used anachronistically; the use of images from later depictions of the Crucifixion, such as the Anglo-Saxon *Dream of the Rood*; further images from Norse and Roman mythology and so on. But suddenly, among the orders being given to the soldiers, we come to the cross itself. There is a high seriousness at this point, as Jones evokes the co-existence of the Supper, the Passion and the Mass, as the true meaning behind the words of the non-commissioned officer. The NCO is speaking to his men, ordering them to keep the crowds at bay from the *adytum*, the sanctuary, in which the *mensa*, the table, has been set up and where the soldier's lance will pierce Christ's side and 'drain the Cup':

> You will stand at the ready
> and hold them
> if need be
> at a pilium's length
> for sometimes the stouter
> more resolute or more slippy
> would trespass
> the marked-out *adytum*

> (where the stripped *mensa*
> is set up
> where the long *lancea*
> obliquely thrust
> must drain the Cup
> for here
> is *immolatio oblata*.)[15]

The parenthesis between brackets is described by Jones, in a footnote, as 'a hinge-passage'. The phrase '*immolatio oblata*', he says, 'is used to describe the actual bodily immolation on the Cross of what had already been oblated at the lighted and festal board in the Supper-Room, which oblative act committed the Offerand to his actual immolation on the morrow and by his command "Do this" committed his *ecclesia* to the offering at her lighted altars of what had been immolated once and for all on the dark Hill.' And he goes on to praise La Taille, who had 'provided what seemed to me an aesthetic wholeness, a comprehensible, almost tangible unity to various propositions of our religion touching the relationship between the Mass, Calvary, and the Supper.'[16]

The Anathemata (1952)

On first reading, this long poem can be disconcerting. It appears to wander at will and it is difficult to grasp any shape it may have. Yet eventually one realizes that it is a coherent whole, centred on the insistent theme of the Mass. The poet himself is the hub around which the many and varied themes revolve. He is a person present at Mass, whose mind wanders over a whole series of implications of what he is attending, creating allusions related to his many historical, literary and religious interests. Jones himself describes the process in his preface:

> In a sense the fragments that compose this book are about, or around and about, matters of all sorts which, by a kind of quasi-free association, are apt to stir in my mind at any time and as often as not 'in the time of the Mass'. The mental associations, liaisons, meanderings to and fro, 'ambivalences', asides, sprawl of the pattern, if pattern there is – these thought-trains (or, some might reasonably say, trains of distraction and inadvertence) have been as often as not initially set in motion, shunted or buffered into near sidings or off to far destinations, by some action or word, something seen or heard, during the liturgy.[17]

The poem does indeed begin at a celebration of the Mass and if we look at this first scene in detail, we get a sense of the techniques that will be used throughout the poem.

The priest's actions and words are described, as they follow the text and rubrics of the Roman Mass and we are already made aware of the mystery of his 'making this thing other' and of the importance of the 'efficacious sign' that he is lifting up. The ceremony is taking place in modern times, 'at the sagging end and chapter's close', in a church full of modern 'tat' ('between the sterile ornaments / under the pasteboard baldachins'), which contrast with earlier times, 'in the young-time, in the sap-years', when it had all been in more suitable surroundings ('between the living floriations / under the leaping arches).

Priests such as this, muses the onlooker, are a 'rearguard' in 'quaint attire, heedless of incongruity', oblivious to the way in which utilitarianism has been infiltrating even into this chancel. Standing in the 'waste land' of modern society, they are like the 'cult-man' standing alone 'in Pellam's land' (in Malory King Pellam is Lord of the Waste Lands),[18] as they guard the 'signa', standing amid 'the things come down from heaven together with the kept memorials, the things lifted up and the venerable trinkets'.

And now, suddenly (but very much in accordance with La Taille's view of the relationship between Supper, Crucifixion and Mass), we move to the Last Supper. Here, in the present, 'within the railed tumulus' the priest sings 'in a low voice / as one who speaks / where a few are, gathered in a high-room / and one, gone out.' And now we move further backwards, into the preparations of the room for the Supper. The preparations are being made for the apostles. Matthew and John (writers of Gospels), James (the other 'Son of Thunder'), Peter (the 'swordsman' who cut off the high priest's servant's ear) and Judas 'the man from Kerioth' (Is-cariot). are described elliptically through use of a popular song. The room (which is at the same time this church in which Mass is being celebrated) is described as being like a ship ('the high nave', later turned into 'the high cave'),[19] and they prepare 'the thwart-boards' till all is 'trim' and 'Bristol-fashion'. The theme of the ship recurs throughout the whole poem. The room is being prepared for the guest (hôte) who will be the victim or sacrifice (hostia) and ultimately the Host:

> In the high nave they prepare
> for guest to be the *hostia*.
> They set the thwart-boards
> and along:
> Two for the Gospel-makers
> One for the other Son of Thunder

One for the swordsman, at the right-board, after; to make him feel afloat.
One for the man from Kerioth, seven for the rest in order.

And now we come back to the priest, who, though imprisoned in time, is also performing a timeless act, an act that had been decided by the Word before the beginning of time, before the creation of the earliest creatures (oreogenesis) and before the creation of time itself; and the timelessness of Christ's sacrifice is shown by the fact that, 'before all oreogenesis', it was decided 'on this hill' (a clear reference to Calvary):

> In the prepared high-room
> he implements inside time and late in time under forms indelibly marked
>   by locale and incidence, deliberations made out of time, before all
>   oreogenesis
>   on this hill
> at a time's turn
>   not on any hill
> but on this hill.[20]

This leads into the first of the great digressions of the book – a long section on mountains across the ages and their mystical significance in a wide variety of cultures, which leads inexorably to the Hill.

This examination of the first five pages of *The Anathemata* has, I hope, given a taste of the tone and methods of this infinitely complex book. The first section, called 'Rite and Fore-time', comes back incessantly to the idea of the events 'before time' which are recalled 'in time' 'when we make the recalling of him / daily at the Stone'.[21] Several of the other sections take up the theme of the ship, but the underlying theme is still that of the inexorable tide of history leading to the great Event that is commemorated in the Mass. Throughout these sections, a multitude of cultural references, not just from the ancient world, but also from medieval Wales and Cockney London, seem at times to be moving in a vast number of directions, but all, aided by subtle references to scripture and to the liturgy, come back to the poem's main theme.

This theme is finally summed up in the last few pages. Christ's suffering on the 'axile stipe' (the tree-trunk around which the world revolves) is vividly described, with 'his cry before his *mors*-cry / Of his black-hoürs' cryings / his ninth-hour outcry'[22] (the agony of this being underlined by the reference to a phrase from one of Gerard Manley Hopkins's 'terrible sonnets', 'I wake and feel the fell of dark, not day. / What hoürs, O what black hoürs we have spent'). Finally, we come back to the priest celebrating Mass (his movements being, as Jones points out in a footnote, strictly according to the rubrics of the Roman rite):

> Here, in this high place
>   into both hands
> he takes the stemmed dish
>   as in many places
> by this poured and that held up
> wherever their directing glosses reads:
>   Here he takes the victim.

The victim, the Host, is Christ the dinner-guest, Christ the sufferer on the Cross, Christ in the bread – and Christ his own Celebrant. This message is stressed once more in the final lines of the poem:

> He does what is done in many places
> what he does other
>   he does after the mode
> of what has always been done.
> What did he do other
>   recumbent at the garnished supper?
> What did he do yet other
>   riding the Axile Tree?[23]

Where very many people, from whatever background, found *In Parenthesis* deeply moving because the poet's allusive techniques were there used to great effect in relation to a subject that was immediate to them (the sufferings of so many in the First World War), *The Anathemata* has a far more specialized appeal. To most Christians of a sacramental bent, whether Roman Catholic or not, it is even more moving than the earlier book and stands as the author's masterpiece. Jones's reputation as a visual artist rests on innumerable pictures and sculptures. His fame as a writer rests solely on two major works. These two long poems have, however, arguably made of him not only a great writer, but the greatest Catholic poet of his age.

Notes

1   T. S. Eliot, 'A Note of Introduction', in David Jones, *In Parenthesis*, 2nd ed. (1963), p. vii.
2   W. H. Auden, 'Adam as Welshman', *New York Review of Books*, 1, 1 (1 February 1963).

3 Ferdinand Valentine, OP, *Father Vincent McNabb, OP*, p. 289, quoted in Jonathan Miles and Derek Shiel, *David Jones: The Maker Unmade*, p. 48.

4 David Jones, 'Art and Sacrament', in *Epoch and Artist*, p. 163.

5 Quoted in Charles Chassé, *Les Nabis et leur temps*, p. 66.

6 Miles and Shiel, *David Jones*, p. 49.

7 Ibid., p. 80.

8 David Jones, preface to *In Parenthesis* (London: Faber and Faber, 1937, reprinted in 1963), p. x.

9 Jones, *In Parenthesis*, ed. cit., p. 158.

10 Ibid., p. 27.

11 Ibid., p. 153.

12 T. S. Eliot, 'A Note of Introduction', in *In Parenthesis*, ed. cit., p. vii.

13 Jones, *The Sleeping Lord*, p. 24.

14 This is the title of one of Jones's best paintings, *Vexilla Regis* (1947), which depicts three trees in a forest, but which, as he explained in a letter, contained elaborate symbolism relating both to the decline of the Roman Empire and to the Crucifixion. (Letter to Mrs Ede [Jim Ede's mother], 28 August 1949, quoted in Miles and Shiel, *David Jones*, p. 196.)

15 The similarity of this to his early sculpture of the Crucifixion, described earlier, is clear.

16 *The Sleeping Lord*, p. 36.

17 Jones, preface to *The Anathemata*, pp. 31–2.

18 Jones uses this as one of many references, in his poetry, to the modern world as the 'Waste Land' of T. S. Eliot's poem.

19 The 'nave' or *nef* is a term for the body of a ship, given to the nave because it looks like an upturned ship.

20 *The Anathemata*, pp. 49–53.

21 Ibid., p. 81.

22 Ibid., pp. 237–8.

23 Ibid., pp. 242–3.

SECTION SIX

New Wine in New Bottles: Catholic Writers of the Late Twentieth Century

14

A Revival of Religious Poetry

The second half of the twentieth century was marked by a major revival in the writing of English religious poetry, in which Catholic poets played an important part. What marks most of this poetry is a lack of that certainty, that firm acceptance of the teachings of the Church, that calm repose in the Faith, that had marked so much of the Catholic literature that had preceded it. We have entered a new period of questioning, in which certainties are out of place. Doubt exists here alongside faith, and the sufferings of the world, and of the poet, remain unexplained by any pious platitudes. This suffering is now caused not so much, as in the Catholic novels of the earlier period, by the conflict between human desires and a settled Catholic morality, as by a sense of the futility of existence and of the problems religion has in explaining or palliating the suffering of the world. The expression is often tortured, reminding us of the similar forms of expression in the 'terrible sonnets' of Gerard Manley Hopkins, who in this as in so many other things had been ahead of his time.

Indeed, Hopkins hovers over much of this poetry. David Jones was, as we have seen, greatly influenced by him and a number of the Catholic poets we will now be considering show a constant awareness of, and indebtedness to, the nineteenth-century Jesuit – not only to the tortured anxiety of his later poems, but also to his *modernity*, his ability to cut across old concepts of form and expression and to create something that was new and revolutionary.

These poets are a refreshing departure from the 'Georgian' lack of adventure or experiment that had till then marked Catholic poetry in the twentieth century. What marks our purveyors of 'new wine' is their acceptance of modern trends in literature. Just as David Jones owed much to the secular poetry of Eliot, and to Pound, Joyce and the other Modernists of the early part of the century, these other poets were similarly involved in the secular poetic trends of their day – and shared much with Christian poets of other denominations.

The British poets who, in the late 1930s and early 1940s, appeared to show the way to a new Christian poetry were the Anglican T. S. Eliot and the Catholic David Jones. Though Eliot was influential in Modernist poetic technique and in expressing disaffection with the 'waste land' of modern life and culture, his specifically Christian poetry (particularly *Four Quartets*) has little in common with that of his post-war successors. There is a sense of detachment, of measured consideration of philosophical and theological issues, of a 'rhetoric of profundity', which differs fundamentally from the emotionalism, and indeed anguish, of a number of the poets we will be considering. One might be tempted to say that this was perhaps the difference between a certain type of Anglicanism and a certain kind of Catholicism. Geoffrey Hill has told us how unsatisfactory he has found 'the specifically Anglican spirituality which opens the *Four Quartets*'. He describes Eliot as 'float[ing] on the surface of the language and serv[ing] us spiritual platitudes from the credo of the Church of England' in the form of repetitions which, 'in addition to being tiresome, ring false, in a tonality of false humility and of a special pleading.'[1] While some might disagree with the finality of Hill's dismissal of Eliot's Christian expression, there is no denying that Eliot's poetry on Christian themes lies far from the *Angst* of the post-war generation, whether Anglican or Catholic. David Jones, on the other hand (who in his poetic techniques owed so much to the earlier Eliot), was far more in tune with that post-war generation and was to exert a profound influence upon a number of widely differing poets.

While the Catholic authors of the post-war generation shared a number of common characteristics, they were also a widely disparate body of authors and are impossible to categorize in the same way as one could their predecessors of the nineteenth century. Several of them, while clearly Christian poets, have varying relationships with conventional Catholicism. Certain strong influences and personal relationships did exist (as among the friends and admirers of David Gascoyne), but it is as individuals with widely different aims and backgrounds that we must consider these poets. Let us start with David Gascoyne, a major poet who was another forerunner of this post-war generation.

David Gascoyne (1916–2001)

David Gascoyne would have reacted against being described as a 'Catholic poet'. While he stressed the necessity of religion as an integral part of human existence, his approach to Christianity came from a variety of sources, theological, philosophical and psychological and one of his constant themes was the inability of rites and religious forms to deal with the problems of the human condition. Yet his poetry extensively uses Catholic liturgical and devotional imagery, and the early religious influences upon him were French and Catholic.

His literary career started at a remarkably early age. His first collection of poetry, *Roman Balcony*, was published in 1932 when he was sixteen and in the following year his novel *Opening Day* appeared. In 1933 he made his first visit to Paris, where over the next few years he was to spend a lot of his time. He met there many of the major surrealists, mixing with André Breton, Salvador Dali, Paul Éluard and others. In 1935, at the age of nineteen, he published in London *A Short History of Surrealism* and in 1936 his own volume of surrealist poetry, *Man's Life is this Meat*. From 1937 to 1939 he spent long periods of time back in Paris. Members of the Parisian literary scene from this period have recalled their impression of a shooting star of genius, a young phenomenon reminiscent of Rimbaud – and also the sense he gave of a Rimbaldian capacity for self-destruction.[2] It was about this time that he appears to have developed the dependence on amphetamines that was to cost him so dearly in later life.

By now he was disenchanted with surrealism and was searching for new forms of expression. In late 1937 he came into contact with the writer who was to be central to his literary and religious development – the Catholic poet and novelist Pierre-Jean Jouve (1887–1976). On a bookstall Gascoyne found, and was bowled over by, Jouve's translations of Hölderlin's poems, *Poèmes de la Folie de Hölderlin*. More importantly, he made contact with Jouve himself and with Jouve's wife the psychiatrist Blanche Reverchon, with whom he underwent analysis for several months in 1938. Gascoyne, speaking of Jouve, has described 'the enormous influence that his poetry, outlook and conversation were to have on me for many years to come.'[3]

In the 1920s Jouve had discovered Freudian psychoanalysis and had also read widely in the mystics (particularly St Teresa of Avila and St John of the Cross, both of whom experienced for periods of time the suffering of God's absence). His poetry collection entitled *Les Noces* (published in various forms between 1925 and 1931) established his break with atheistic surrealism, which in his view had produced a caricature of mysticism, neglecting its religious dimension. Jouve's next collection *Sueur de Sang* (published in various editions between 1933 and 1935), shows by its very title his identification of Christ's suffering with that of humankind.[4] In his preface, entitled 'The Unconscious, Spirituality, Catastrophe', he defines man, in Freudian-cum-Christian terms, as a being in whom eroticism and suffering are inextricably intermingled.[5] The titles of the three poetic sections in the 1934 second edition sum up the mixture of religion and despair within them: 'Bloody sweat' (*Sueur de Sang*), 'The Wing of Despair' (*L'Aile du désespoir*) and 'Pieta'.

Under this influence Gascoyne's poetry was utterly transformed. His poems from the period 1937–42, gathered together in an edition in 1943,[6] expressed the tortures of depression and despair in religious terms. An epigraph from Jouve sets the scene for the collection, linking despair, love and the hope that society may change ('Le désespoir a des ailes / L'amour a pour aile nacré / le désespoir / Les sociétés peuvent changer'). In the poems in the sequence 'Miserere', Christ's suffering on the Cross (and his mother's as she stands there 'upholding as a text / Her grief-scrawled face for the ensuing world to read') is linked to that of humankind. Christ is 'Him God has forsaken, Word made flesh / Made ransom . . . / Till the catharsis of the race shall be complete.'[7] Gradually, in this sequence of poems, the spotlight shifts from Christ to the suffering of the poet himself as he fails to 'conceive God's throne', all this depicted in graphic terms reminiscent of Hopkins:

> Out of these depths:
>
> Where footsteps wander in the marsh of death and an
> Intense infernal glare is on our faces facing down:
>
> Out of these depths, what shamefaced cry
> Half choked in the dry throat, as though a stone
> Were our confounded tongue, can ever rise:
> Because the mind has been struck blind
> And may no more conceive
> Thy Throne . . .
>
> Because the depths
> Are clear with only death's
> Marsh-light, because the rock of grief
> Is clearly too extreme for us to breach:
> Deepen our depths
>
> And aid our unbelief.[8]

Cyril Connolly described these poems of Gascoyne's as taking us 'as near the precipice as a human being is able to go and still turn back.' Yet, like Teresa of Avila, Gascoyne is still able to pray to the God in whom he finds it so difficult to believe. And, paradoxically, as we see in another poem, it is that very doubt that may go towards creating a more authentic certainty. By clearing away all the unreal certainties of an unquestioning faith, a solid base will be found on which to found a true faith:

> . . . Far from Thy face I nothing understand
> But kiss the Hand that has consigned
> Me to these latter years where I must learn
> The revelation of despair, and find
> Among the debris of all certainties
> The hardest stone on which to found
> Altar and shelter for Eternity.[9]

It is not just his own suffering that concerns the poet, however. How does one explain the suffering of the entire world? In 'Ecce Homo' Gascoyne depicts the suffering Christ in all the realistic horror that he had seen in the paintings of the Crucifixion by Mathias Grünewald ('Whose is this horrifying face, / This putrid flesh, discoloured, flayed, / Fed on by flies, scorched by the sun'). This suffering is not just of one place and time. Christ, he says, is 'in agony till the world's end'. He draws parallels with the horrors of the present time, as he describes the centurions wearing the uniform of fascism and greeting each other with 'raised-arm salutes' and evokes the suffering of oppressed minorities. Christ, who wept for Jerusalem, 'must watch this drama to the end'. Yet the poem ends on a note of hope. 'The turning point of history / Must come.' Christ is a figure of Revolution, who, despite the often sterile appurtenances of human worship of him, can redeem us by his sharing of 'the tree of human pain':

> Not from a monstrance silver-wrought
> But from the tree of human pain
> Redeem our sterile misery,
> Christ of Revolution and Poetry,
> That man's long journey into night
> May not have been in vain.[10]

Poems 1937–1942 was the high point of Gascoyne's poetic achievement. In 1950 he produced a slim volume entitled *A Vagrant and Other Poems*. The poems in it are of uneven value, though probably the most successful are those which continue his exploration of the relationship between religion and the scandals of present-day life. In particular, a series of short 'Fragments towards a Religio Poetae' deal with the contrast between God's justice and truth and those of Man. The tone in some of these fragments is now far more quirky, the paradoxes expressed in everyday prosaic language:

> Really religious people are rarely looked upon as such
> By those to whom religion is secretly something unreal;

And those the world regards as extremely religious people
Are generally people to whom the living God will seem at first an appalling
    scandal;
Just as Jesus seemed a dangerously subversive Sabbath-breaker
Whom only uneducated fishermen, tavern talkers and a few blue-stockings
    of dubious morals
Were likely after all to take very seriously,
To the most devoutly religious people in Jerusalem in Jesus' day.

And then, in other fragments, the tone becomes more intense and the expression more succinct:

Always, wherever, whatever, however,
When I am able to resist
For once the constant pressure of the failure to exist,
Let me remember
That truly to be man is to be man aware of Thee
And unafraid to be. So help me God.[11]

Shortly after the appearance of this volume Gascoyne went to live in France, where he remained for ten years. During this time he suffered from serious writer's block (probably caused by his addiction to amphetamines over many years) which made him completely incapable of writing poetry. Then in 1964 he had a major breakdown. He had further breakdowns in 1969 and in the early 1970s and during this period spent considerable time in a psychiatric hospital. There he met a volunteer for Mind (a leading mental health charity), Judy Lewis, whom he married. She restored his confidence and he began to write again, but very little, and that mainly in the form of reviews and translations. He died in 2001.

Gascoyne once described himself as 'a poet who wrote himself out when young and then went mad'.[12] Yet for a short period he produced some of the most remarkable poetry of his time. Kathleen Raine declared: 'We have only one great poet, David Gascoyne'.[13] But can we call it 'Catholic poetry'? Yes, if we look at the context in which it was written, the *via negativa* which it shares not just with the Spanish mystics but also with his predecessor Gerard Manley Hopkins, and the Catholic imagery and language which he uses. No, if one believes that one has to be a card-carrying Catholic to be a Catholic poet (and yet, so many card-carrying Catholics have written poetry and prose that it would be hard to call Catholic!). His influence on other problematic 'Catholic poets' would seem to justify the use of the term in his case.

Catholics and 'Fellow Travellers': a variety of other poets

The religious poets of the post-war period do not present a coherent picture. The only thing they had in common was a shared attitude of questioning all that had seemed most certain to most of their predecessors. The most remarkable among them failed to remain within the categories 'Catholic' or 'Anglican'. Lines of influence and communication had now become open between Christian poets of varying forms of belief. It is worth looking closely at four of the most outstanding of the 'Catholic' poets among them.

Kathleen Raine (1908–2003) converted to Catholicism in 1941. She is reported to have later felt that to have been a mistake, but a variety of sources indicate that towards the end of her life she again seems to have thought of herself as Catholic. Her poetry, some of the most remarkable Christian poetry of her time, is written far less within a Catholic tradition than even that of Gascoyne had been. As a literary scholar, she had devoted herself to the study of Blake and of the English Platonists, and her own poetry is heavily in the Platonist tradition. Some of her best poems address the poet's role in breaking through to a world beyond the reality around us and bringing back to us some glimpse of that 'otherness'. One of her most moving expressions of this is in her poem 'For David Gascoyne, Fallen Silent', in which, mingling Christian and classical imagery, she at first laments his loss of the ability to bring a message to the 'chattering shadows of shadows' of this 'post-real world', but then shows how within each one of us Christ, 'the holy deathless one', lies awaiting resurrection and that Gascoyne's silence may itself be eloquent for those awaiting 'the still small voice of the divine'.[14]

Her founding, in 1981, of the review *Temenos*, followed by the creation of the Temenos Academy in 1990, illustrated the all-embracing universalist nature of her religious commitment. Temenos stood, in her words, for the age-old wisdom that 'Man is a spiritual being . . . and the Arts . . . are the flowering of a vision of the Sacred enshrined in some form of spiritual teaching.'[15] Buddhism, Hinduism, Judaism, Christianity and Islam all had their place in it. In this sense, Raine is less a Catholic author than a poet of the universal human aspiration to the spiritual.

Elizabeth Jennings (1926–2001), on the other hand, stands firmly within the Catholic tradition. A cradle Catholic, while at St Anne's College Oxford she became a close friend of Philip Larkin and Kingsley Amis, and she was later to be associated with the 'Movement' School, the 'loose aggregation'[16] which contained among others Larkin, Amis, Donald Davie, John Wain, Robert Conquest and D. J. Enright. She was rather unhappy with being classified in this way, however, in part because her Catholicism was somewhat out of place amid the witty, sardonic tone of much of what was written by the others. Indeed, she often seemed a romantic marooned among anti-romantics.

Her own poetry is straightforward, succinct in expression and completely lacking in irony. David Gascoyne praised the economy of her style as follows: 'In an era dominated by vacuous verbiage, such poetry as Elizabeth Jennings continues to produce is indeed a triumphant anomaly.'[17] Much in her early poems is highly personal, particularly her accounts of her mental breakdown and hospitalization in 1961. The collection that she devoted to this experience was called *The Mind has Mountains* (1966), a clear reference to Hopkins's 'terrible sonnet', 'No worst, there is none'.[18]

Hopkins was a major influence on her, as were a number of other Christian poets, Catholic and non-Catholic. She was vastly impressed by David Jones, whose vision of 'art as gesture and as sacrament . . . / Much like the Presence under wine and bread' she evokes in a poem published in 1961.[19] But she also appreciated the poetry of seventeenth-century Anglicans like George Herbert, Henry Vaughan and Thomas Traherne and the modern Anglican poets T. S. Eliot and W. H. Auden.

Her own faith has been described as 'vexed but sustaining'.[20] Teresa of Avila was for her a great example of constancy in uncertainty. Following Jones, Jennings saw the creation of art, the writing of poetry, as a sacramental act, to which she devoted her often tortured life. She saw it as being a form of prayer. At its best, her poetry achieves an amazing calm, aided by the framework of Catholic liturgy, but above all by the sacraments. It is invidious to choose one poem among so many, but a sonnet written towards the end of her life, when she was in hospital, sums up not only her debt to Hopkins, but also the power of the sacrament for her and her belief in the sacramental role of the poet:

> Hopkins, I understand exactly now
> What you meant when you told us that the sick
> Endear us to them. I know this is true
> Because I am a sick one and God's quick,
>
> Saving principle has come to me,
> A tiny piece of bread unleavened saves
> The soul. I feel its power immediately.
> Stammering my thanks, I know my flesh behaves
>
> Oddly, but I know also I am
> Within Heaven's confines. You, O Hopkins I
> Commend for showing me how close I came

To our Redeemer in his healing, high
Offices. My thanksgiving is home
And Jesus Christ is with me where I lie.[21]

Jennings's description of Peter Levi (1931–2000) strikes true for all who knew this remarkable Jesuit priest and poet:

You seem close to fragility yet have
A steel-like strength . . .
You are on the strong side of life, yet also the brittle,
I think of blown glass sometimes but reject the simile.
Yet about your demeanour there is something frail,
The strength is within, won from simple things
Like swimming and walking.
Your pale face is like an ikon, yet
Any moment, any hour, you break to exuberance,
And then it is our world which is fragile:
You toss it like a juggler.[22]

Peter Levi came of a Jewish family in North London, which had originated in Istanbul. His father had become a Catholic convert under the influence of his wife, a devout Catholic from a Spanish background. Peter and his brother Anthony both became Jesuits (while their only sister became a nun). Peter trained for the priesthood at Heythrop College and then read classics at Campion Hall, Oxford. He was left with an abiding love for Greece and things Greek both ancient and modern, which form the subject matter of a great deal of his best poetry and prose.

In the late 1960s Peter and his brother Anthony were teaching at Campion Hall and enlivening the place with their witty, urbane and often irreverent conversation. Peter delighted to shock. Yet one could be misled by outside appearances. There was a high seriousness in him and his religious commitment was very real. It came as a shock to many when Peter resigned from the priesthood and from the Order in 1977.[23]

That, despite this, his faith remained intact is shown by various religious works he produced after this date, including translations of the Bible, an anthology of Christian poetry and a book on monks and monasteries.[24] Religious poetry had admittedly made up only a small part of his entire poetic output; but he wrote more poems on religious themes in the last six years before he left the Order and in the years after leaving it, than he had in the many years before that. In particular, the 1971 collection *Death is a Pulpit*, and the separate long poem *Good Friday Sermon 1973*, reveal a highly original voice. They consist of a series of long poems. In them, as Levi put it, 'Traditional forms – mainly the heroic couplet – are used in a new way under a new necessity.'[25] That new necessity was expressed in the anguish that appears so clearly in these poems.

Among Levi's literary and artistic heroes were Gerard Manley Hopkins and David Jones. He devoted a short monograph to Hopkins and in his sermon at Jones's requiem in 1975 echoed Jones's vision of the Mass as 'what has already been done once for all on another hilltop . . . and also done many times from the beginning of mankind'.[26] He also had a great admiration for David Gascoyne, who he described as an 'authentic visionary poet'.[27] The new voice which we hear in Levi's 1971–3 poems owes, however, little to any of these. 'Christmas Sermon', for example, starts like a traditional sermon: 'God so loved us he sent his only son. / In the name of the Spirit of God. Amen'. Yet almost immediately one is caught up in a panic-stricken series of apparently disconnected experiences, expressed in disjointed phrases. This is strongly reminiscent, both in tone and in content, of the long poem by Blaise Cendrars, 'Les Pâques à New York' (Easter in New York), the bulk of which was similarly written in couplets.[28]

> I am frightened by sanctity and light.
> Somewhere it is all starting again,
> worse than a dream. Christmas starting again,
> lamplight choking to twilight on my table
> I am colder than Christ was in his stable.
> The house-walls shiver and sweat in the back-street,
> grimy town-halls repeat and repeat
> what my mouth drops, what English cannot say,
> pink motor-tyres of roses, Christmas day.
> I am terrified by what is beginning.[29]

The tortured expression in the rest of this poem, which recurs in the other long poems 'Whitsunday Sermon' and 'Good Friday Sermon 1973', leads eventually, however, through the saving grace of the events that are being commemorated, to a resolution in God's love. In 'Good Friday Sermon 1973', for example, the poet's inadequacy is expressed ('I am rotten wood, there is no fruit in me'), but the figure of Christ's sacrifice is immediately contrasted with this; and, though the state of the world is so appalling and 'the murder of the just men continues', our way to deal with this is to join Christ in his suffering:

We can never again repair that loss
but by nailing ourselves to the same cross.

The poem ends with a resounding and joyful affirmation of hope:

Justice shall be like the snow and the sea.
Christ is the end of all calamity,
and what is true and strong shall come to birth.
There shall be no more wickedness on earth. Amen.[30]

In 1981, at the untimely death of his friend and colleague Anne Pennington, Levi devoted to her an elegy which included an Easter Sermon. It is one of his most moving pieces of Christian verse (particularly for those who remember the 'profound simplicity' of this remarkable young woman). It is also a calm proclamation of his own faith:

The lark ascending when Christ has risen
is our mind on any simple morning,
and the chorus at dawn in blushing light
and the last bird calling through evening light
repeat the happy wishes of childhood;
mysterious trees flower deep in the wood.
Because Christ is risen and his mountain
is streaming water and will never die,
and we are overshadowed by his tree.
Spirit or star chiming one silver note
Anne you are singing of the love of God
mediated in the breaking of bread.[31]

Nobody could have been more different from the urbane, urban Peter Levi than the Orcadian poet George Mackay Brown (1921–96); yet Levi, reviewing one of his collections, wrote that it gave him 'hope for poetry and for the language'.[32] Brown is one of the most powerful and original voices in post-war Catholic poetry in the English language.

He spent almost all his life, apart from two short ventures to the mainland, in his native Orkneys. He had a strong interest in the history of the islands and particularly their Norse years as a fief of Norway (875–1471). His imagination had been fired by his reading of the *Orkneyinga Saga*, a collection of stories and poetry handed down from generation to generation and probably compiled in Iceland some time in the early thirteenth century. The influence of this work is found throughout his poetry, in the themes and characters treated therein, and in his adoption of the succinct, pure and matter-of-fact poetic style of the saga. The story which had most impact on him was that of St Magnus, Earl of Orkney, who was martyred in 1117 on the island of Egilsay, having been inveigled there under the pretext of a parley of peace. Part of the pull of the story, for Brown, was its religious element, which included Magnus' hearing of Mass in his last hours and his offering of his suffering in order to bring peace to Orkney after years of war. In his autobiography, Brown described the martyrdom of Magnus as having shone out, amid the Viking stories of intrigue and revenge, 'like a precious stone'.[33] The story continually recurs in Brown's poetry and prose.

Brown was received into the Catholic Church in 1961, after many years of interest and attraction (and reaction against his family's grim Protestantism). His religion was from then on at the centre of his poetic creation. Two major influences upon him had been John Henry Newman, a reading of whose *Apologia pro Vita Sua* had, as early as 1947, impressed him by its 'magnificent devastating logic'[34] and made him think of becoming a priest; and Gerard Manley Hopkins, whose influence is evoked at length in his autobiography and on whom he had an abortive attempt to write a thesis for Edinburgh University. It is not these influences that stand out most powerfully in his writings however. Instead we find an original blending of the liturgy of the Mass, of Norse Christian elements, of the experience of Orkneys fishermen over the ages, of the ordinary life of Orcadians in the modern world and of the Biblical story of the Passion.

As in David Jones's *Anathemata*, the sea and the liturgy are continually brought together and the Mass is a timeless enactment rather than a re-enactment. In 'Feast of Candles' the priest, speaking 'in Latin whispers', with a boy replying 'hesitant with the Latin syllables, / in country whispers', celebrates Candlemas 'in the stone ship' of the nave, while outside further candles light the ship that 'would weigh that night for Trondheim, with news of Magnus.'[35] And, in 'Corpus Christi', the Mass is again at the centre of the poem. All is given us through the mouth of a fisherman of Galilee who, as a young man, had accompanied Peter and the others (with great detail being given of the fishermen's craft) and who had then accompanied them to the events of Christ's mission and finally to the Crucifixion. He muses now, as an old man in the Orkneys, that time has set him 'on a distant shore', but that 'Today, in a western island, at least / on a summer morning / I can kneel at the Mass of Corpus Christi'. The central part of the poem brings together (in a manner reminiscent of Jones) the Mass itself, the events on 'the Hill' and the previous events in the 'high room', as this observer remembers these events (while still using the imagery of the fishing boat to describe the descent from the Cross):

HOC EST ENIM CORPUS MEUM
HIC EST CALIX SANGUINIS MEI

    The net-minder was too young
    To be in the high room that night

    But I was at the gate
    When the treasurer left for the city by a secret door

    And the mother of sorrows
      Stood outside, under a tree, alone.

    And I was at the last hill
      When he was notched with five wounds

    I stayed to watch (unregarded)
      When Corpus Christi
    Was unhooked from the black wave
    And wrapped, dripping, in the death net

    When bread bakers and fishermen
    Came and lingered at dawn
      Beside the stone of time's ending.[36]

The technique of the humble observer of great events recurs time and again in these poems. In 'The Gardener: Easter', for example, Christ's journey to the Cross and his entombment, are viewed uncomprehendingly by Joseph of Arimathaea's gardener, who is far more concerned with the fate of his rosebush.[37] Often, we see one scene through a variety of eyes, as in 'Tryst on Egilsay', a poem which celebrates the events of Easter Monday, 1117, 'as seen by some of the people on the island'.[38]

    Not all Brown's poetry has a religious theme. Commentators have noted though that as time went by, 'the religious note becomes increasingly dominant'.[39] It is the basis for some of his most powerful poems.

These poets give some idea of the diversity that was found, not just in Catholic poetry, but in religious poetry in general, in the post-war period. The old distinctions no longer seemed to hold water. As well as these Catholics there were a number of other outstanding religious poets, with whom they often found great affinity. Two of the most important British religious poets of the late twentieth century have been non-Catholics: Geoffrey Hill and R. S. Thomas, both of whom epitomize the questioning and often anguished approach to their God and their religion that is typical of their Catholic counterparts. To look more closely into this relationship is outside the scope of the present volume; but it is a great temptation.

Though in its questioning, its doubts, its concerns as to the role of God in a suffering universe, this Catholic poetry has this affinity with the other religious poets of its time, it also contains much that is specifically Catholic and sacramental. This Catholic quality, at its best, is an integral part of the poetry and has little in common with the often purely external use of Catholic imagery and language in so much nineteenth-century English Catholic poetry. At the heart of the poetry of Jones, Jennings and Mackay Brown, for example, we find a profound meditation upon the meaning of the Mass and of Christ's sacrifice.

It is this mixture of the traditional and the modern, of believing and doubting, of the sacramental and the everyday, that renders this poetry so vital and so exciting and which presents us with a way forward for Catholic literature.

Notes

1   Geoffrey Hill, interview with Anne Mounic, Paris, 19 March 2008, and letter to her elucidating certain points, 31 March 2008.
2   For example, Maxime Alexandre and others, in conversation with the present writer in the early 1960s.
3   Gascoyne, 'Introductory Notes' to *Selected Poems* (1994), p.xiv.
4   Lk. 22.44 (The Agony in the Garden): 'And being in agony he prayed more earnestly: and his sweat was as it were great drops of blood falling down to the ground.'
5   Pierre-Jean Jouve, 'Avant-propos dialectique' to *Sueur de Sang*, 1933.
6   Gascoyne, *Poems 1937–1942*, 1943.
7   Gascoyne, 'Pieta', the second poem of 'Miserere', in *Poems 1937–1942*.
8   Gascoyne, 'De Profundis', in ibid.
9   Gascoyne, 'Ex Nihilo', in ibid.
10 Gascoyne, 'Ecce Homo', in ibid.
11 Gascoyne, 'Fragments towards a Religio Poetae', in *A Vagrant and Other Poems* (1950), pp. 32–6.
12 Quoted in *The Independent* obituary by Sebastian Barker, 28 November 2001.
13 In conversation with the Indian writer Raja Rao in 1986; quoted in Philippa Bernard, *No End to Snowdrops*, p. 160.
14 Kathleen Raine, 'For David Gascoyne, Fallen Silent', in *Collected Poems* (2008), pp. 345–6.
15 Quoted in obituary of Kathleen Raine by Shusha Guppy, *The Independent*, 8 July 2003.
16 Michael Schmidt, preface to Elizabeth Jennings, *New Collected Poems* (2002), p. xix.

17 *The Tablet*, 14 September 1985.

18 See p. 41 for this sonnet.

19 Elizabeth Jennings, 'Visit to an Artist', in *Song for a Birth or a Death* (1961), republished in *New Collected Poems*, p. 45.

20 Michael Schmidt, preface to Jennings, *New Collected Poems*, p. xx.

21 Jennings, 'Homage to Gerard Manley Hopkins: After Receiving Communion in Hospital', in *Timely Issues* (2001), reprinted in *New Collected Poems*, p. 346.

22 Elizabeth Jennings, 'A Letter to Peter Levi', in *The Animals' Arrival* (1969), reprinted in *New Collected Poems*, p. 86.

23 This was at a time when a number of other Jesuits were following the same path, including Peter's brother Anthony, Peter Hebblethwaite and, in France, Michel de Certeau.

24 Peter Levi, *The Frontiers of Paradise: A Study of Monks and Monasteries* (1988).

25 Peter Levi, blurb on dust-jacket of *Death is a Pulpit*, 1971.

26 Peter Levi, 'Requiem Sermon for David Jones', in *The Flutes of Autumn* (1983), pp. 187–91. ('Hopkins a'i Dduw' [Hopkins and his God], 1990.)

27 Peter Levi, 'Visionary Poets', one of his public lectures as Oxford Professor of Poetry, printed in: *The Art of Poetry: The Oxford Lectures, 1984–1989.*

28 Blaise Cendrars, 'Les Pâques à New York' in *Du monde entier*, 1912. While we have no actual proof that Levi necessarily was inspired by this poem, Cendrars was very much a subject of conversation in Oxford in those years, in circles such as Levi's; and it is striking that two such different poets should produce an impression of complete disorientation by such similar, and original, poetic means.

29 Peter Levi, 'Christmas Sermon', in *Death is a Pulpit* (1971), p. 14.

30 Peter Levi, 'Good Friday Sermon 1973', in *Collected Poems 1955–1975.*

31 Peter Levi, *The Echoing Green: Three Elegies* (London: Anvil Press, 1983).

32 *Catholic Herald*, 8 September 1989 (quoted in Maggie Fergusson, *George Mackay Brown: The Life*), p. 269.

33 Brown, *For the Islands I Sing*, p. 52 (quoted in Fergusson, *George Mackay Brown*, p. 63).

34 Letter to Ernest Marwick, 26 April 1947 (quoted in Fergusson, *George Mackay Brown*, p. 84).

35 George Mackay Brown, 'Feast of Candles', in *The Wreck of the Archangel* (1989), reprinted in *Collected Poems*, pp. 286–7.

36 Brown, 'Corpus Christi' (uncollected 1993), in *Collected Poems*, pp. 313–6.

37 Brown, 'The Gardener: Easter', in *The Wreck of the Archangel* (1989), *Collected Poems*, pp. 288–9.

38 'Tryst on Egilsay' (1989), in ibid., pp. 291–7.

39 Archie Bevan and Brian Murray, introduction to George Mackay Brown, *Collected Poems*, p. xvi.

15

Developments in the Catholic Novel

In the Catholic poetry of the post-war period we have been able to distinguish, despite all the differences between individual poets, certain underlying common characteristics which contribute to a feeling that there is still a future for the genre. The novel, however, presents a far less coherent picture. Despite some observers' predictions of the imminent demise of the Catholic novel, it still had life in it in the second half of the twentieth century and there were a good number of writers who could be described as 'Catholic novelists'. In certain outstanding figures, such as David Lodge and Muriel Spark, we can see an ability to use the techniques of modern secular literature in a way that breathes new life into the genre and goes some way towards releasing it from the traditional stereotypes. There were also some other highly successful and original figures, including Antonia White, Alice Thomas Ellis and George Mackay Brown. And then there were a considerable number of writers who continued to write novels of the traditional type, as always happens in the years following the time when a literary genre has been established. These latter have this in common with their more adventurous contemporaries: they can, through their subject matter, give us some insight into changing attitudes in the Church.

Changes in the Subject Matter of the Catholic Novel

Probably the thing that hits one most forcibly when looking at the wide array of novels on Catholic subjects in this period is the almost complete absence of most of the major themes of the traditional English Catholic novel. Heroic renunciation, based on a conflict between human desire and Catholic morality, is no longer a major concern. It has given way in many cases to a questioning of the basis for that morality, with the Church's authority being brought into question. The main preoccupation appears to be with the effects of the Church's traditional teachings upon people living in contemporary society. Case histories of young people beleaguered within traditional Catholic education, of priests finding it difficult to remain within their vocation,[1] of the Catholic laity grappling with problems raised by Catholic birth control teachings, take the place of the battles that individuals, in the traditional Catholic novel, had waged with themselves, as they strove to conform their lives to what was expected of them. The refuge that the earlier converts had taken in the authority of the Church was replaced for many, in the heady atmosphere of the build-up to Vatican Two, and in its immediate aftermath, by a mistrust of authority and a thirst for change.

At the same time, of course, there was a strong reaction to all these changes and to what was seen as moral and religious laxity. A number of writers entrenched themselves in a last-ditch defence of traditional values, particularly after what they saw as the pernicious effects of the Council. High among the causes for disgust were the changes in the age-old liturgy of the Church – and in particular the change from Latin to the vernacular. Alice Thomas Ellis is typical in this respect. In her novel *The Sin Eater* (1977) she puts into the mouths of her characters devastating – and often very funny – criticisms of the new trends in the Church.

Writing in 1991, Woodman succinctly described post-war British Catholic fiction as being 'at present split into "post-Catholic" and neo-conservative modes'.[2] There were also, however, as he noted, intermediate positions. Piers Paul Read, for example, in his novel *Monk Dawson* (1969), depicts a monk who, carried away by the new ideas fermenting within the Church, gradually loses his faith because of his failure to make any impact and leaves the priesthood to live a trendy and self-indulgent life as a journalist. This might seem to be a typical novel dealing with a 'spoiled priest'. However, Read has a surprise for us at the end, when Dawson, his lover having committed suicide, returns to the priesthood and becomes a Trappist monk. In the last pages, Dawson states to the narrator his rationale:

> He spoke of the soul and of God as though the soul was the only facet of his identity and God the only person of any account . . . He said he thought that there was great confusion in our generation between social and religious morality – between the exigencies of human life and the deference that was due to God.[3]

Read in many ways straddles the divide between the two sides in the debate – often showing sympathy with the aspirations of the new thinkers within the Church, but, in his later writings in particular, showing a strong attachment to traditional Catholic values. At all events, the wide spectrum of attitudes that were held in this area by the various Catholic writers merely underlines that *these* questions have become the major issues in Catholic fiction, replacing so many of the themes of the pre-war Catholic novel.

Politically, too, the Right-wing tendencies of earlier generations, though they remained in some quarters, had now become replaced by a presumption among a good number of Catholic intellectuals that the Church should stand for ideas of the Left, both in this country and abroad. Graham Greene was still at the forefront of such political trends, both in his novels and in his innumerable letters to the Press about topics ranging from Vietnam to liberation theology, in which the Church's official attitudes often came in for particular criticism.[4]

In social terms, too, the emphasis had changed. For the first time, English Catholic literature began to deal with lower middle-class and working-class Catholic culture, viewing it *from the inside*. There had, admittedly, been occasional treatments of these classes in previous Catholic literature,[5] but even in these rare cases there had been a tendency to describe them from outside, through upper middle-class eyes.[6] Now however, notably in the novels of David Lodge (in which this 'cradle Catholic' describes things from his own experience), ordinary non-aristocratic Catholicism could take centre stage in its own right.

Whatever the shades of opinion expressed in Catholic novels in this period, there is no denying the fact that the content had changed beyond recognition.

Greene as Literary Model: a mixed picture

A key to some of the attitudes of the new Catholic literature of the post-war period can be found in the impact Greene had upon a number of authors. Several of the new generation of Catholic novelists looked to him as a literary model, either for attitudes to religion or for novelistic techniques, or for both. There is a clear impact of Greene on the writing of David Lodge's early novels (as Bernard Bergonzi, and Lodge himself, have pointed out). Later, in *How Far Can You Go?* (1980), Lodge was to use Greene as an intertextual theme running through the whole novel, with a series of explicit references to his works illustrating the attitudes of the various characters by reference to the changing nature of Greene's own output over the years. Muriel Spark, too, owed a great deal to Greene's practical encouragement right from the start of her career and found inspiration in his work. Even for Catholic writers who did not find themselves inclined to follow Greene's example in their work, it was impossible to ignore this colossus who spanned the Catholic literature of his epoch. Someone like George Mackay Brown, who appears to owe so little to him in his novels, nevertheless gives evidence of having read him avidly and having taken his novelistic situations as parallels to his own experience.[7]

The influence of Greene is hardly surprising, given the nature of his Catholic novels from *The Quiet American* onwards and given the compatibility of his political and religious views with those of the new generation. What does take one aback is Piers Paul Read's (b. 1941) clear debt not to the later Greene, but to the traditional French-style Catholic novels of Greene's 1938–51 period; a debt that makes some of Read's works something of a throwback to the old-style Catholic novel. This is particularly evident in *The Upstart* (1973) and *A Married Man* (1979).

The epigraph to *The Upstart*, though taken from the French Catholic novelist Julien Green, clearly places the novel in the 'literary space' of the English Greene: 'In each of us there is a sinner and a saint. The one and the other develop, each to his own plane. The one and the other, not the one or the other. Both at the same time.'[8] The novel is, however, something of a disappointment, even in these terms. It has none of Greene's subtlety when dealing with the Maistrian paradox. Instead, we have a horrifying story of complete evil, as the hero takes violent revenge on an upper-class family that he believes to have patronized and thwarted him. This revenge includes the cold-blooded seduction of the youngest daughter, the crippling of another person and even the murder of a newborn baby. In the process the hero also becomes a pimp and a thief. There seems no let-up. At the end of the novel, predictably, the hero repents. In prison, under the influence of a 'good' thief, he begins to feel 'more and more intolerably what I must call remorse. I wished, I wished even to God, that I had not done these things.'[9] One is left feeling that it is all too neat. There is no psychological preparation for the change and no examination, in Greene style, of the implications of good and evil.

Greene's techniques are used far more successfully in Read's *A Married Man*. John Strickland, a successful barrister, while on holiday with his wife's Catholic parents in Norfolk, reads Tolstoy's *The Death of Ivan Ilych* and like Tolstoy's hero asks himself what he has done with his life, nothing of which now satisfies him. He takes up political life once more and then uses his political activities as a cover for seeing other women. However, amid all this he still sees himself as 'a married man', thus underestimating the women with whom he has to deal (both his wife and his mistress). Eventually his mistress, Paula, has his wife Clara murdered, alongside Clara's new lover (a friend of John's). It is here that Greenian themes take over, in a form reminiscent of *The End of the Affair*. John finds some letters Clara had received from a Jesuit, which make it clear that she had been confiding in him. Eventually, he gets the Jesuit to send him her letters to which these had been replies. In them she describes her life with her husband and her love for him, her temptations to adultery because of their situation and her even greater desire to renounce everything for God. Yet she had given in and it was with her lover that she had been murdered. There is, however, a sign that she might have repented at the moment of her death – a sign of the cross, written on the wall in her own blood. This novel is, in its ending, as melodramatic as *The Upstart*, but there is greater complexity in the psychological handling of the characters' motivation. It is fascinating to see the techniques of Greene's middle period taken up once more at this late stage in the history of the Catholic novel.

Three Disparate Novelists: Antonia White, Alice Thomas Ellis and George Mackay Brown

It is very difficult to make generalizations about these three successful novelists. Each treads his or her own path.

Antonia White (1899–1980), whom we have already seen as the author of *Frost in May* (1933), returned to the Catholic Church in 1940.[10] After the war, she produced three sequels to her early autobiographical novel: *The Lost Traveller* (1950), *The Sugar House* (1952) and *Beyond the Glass* (1954). They trace the author's often anguished relationship with other people – and with her religion. *The Lost Traveller* takes up the story as the young girl (now called Clara Batchelor) returns home from her convent school. In the final volume, *Beyond the Glass*, White graphically depicts herself as having been imprisoned behind a 'glass wall' of her own guilt and repression. She descends into insanity. The book movingly describes the process, from onset to recovery. Autobiographical fiction is a notoriously difficult genre. But, as Elizabeth Bowen said in a review, Antonia White carried it off 'infallibly'[11] in her very moving depiction of her own problems. The novels are written in a traditional manner, though at certain moments (particularly the ending of *The Lost Traveller*) there are techniques which are similar to those of the French Catholic novelist Georges Bernanos, whose novels White greatly admired.[12]

Though the novels of Alice Thomas Ellis (1932–2005) at first sight appear to owe much to Ronald Firbank, they do however differ from him in the clear religious commitment that exists beneath the surface glitter of Catholic paraphernalia. Typical of her techniques is *The 27th Kingdom* (1982), in which an eccentric household in Chelsea is joined by Valentine, a young West Indian novice from a convent at which the Russian landlady Aunt Irene's sister is the Mother Superior. She has temporarily been expelled from the convent because she has been performing miracles. The novel shows the effect of Valentine on this extraordinary little community. The tone in this and most of Ellis's other novels is brittle, the views expressed by the characters are intentionally depicted as simple and often apparently naïve and the action is caricatured and unreal, with perpetual contrast being drawn between Catholic glamour and the surrounding Protestant incomprehension. But here, as in *The Sin Eater* (1977), the author, despite predictable sideswipes against the modern Church, also succeeds in providing a kind of allegory of good and evil

George Mackay Brown's novel *Magnus* (1973) powerfully tells the story of the twelfth-century martyr St Magnus, making extensive use of details from the *Orkneyinga Saga* (including a vivid depiction of a Viking raid on Anglesey). Much of the style echoes the terse narrative techniques of the sagas. The tone reminds one forcibly of his poetry on the same themes. The whole book leads up to the chapter entitled 'The Killing', in which Magnus is martyred. Central to this chapter is the depiction of the last Mass attended by Magnus before his betrayal, at which Magnus becomes aware of the sacrifice he must make to create peace. This description of the Mass lies within the tradition of the Catholic novel. Later in the chapter, the author muses on the pagan and pre-Christian history of human sacrifice. And, in an imaginative leap, we find ourselves at the murder of Bonhoeffer, in a Nazi concentration camp. Explaining it all, the sacrifice of Christ is seen as 'the one only central sacrifice of history':

> *I am the bread of life.* All previous rituals had been a foreshadowing of this; all subsequent rituals a re-enactment. The fires at the centre of the earth, the sun above, all divine essences and ecstasies, come to this silence at last – a circle of bread and a cup of wine on an altar . . .
>
> At the moment of consecration, the bread – that is to say, man and his work, his pains, his joys and his hopes – is utterly suffused and irradiated with the divine. *Hic est enim corpus meum.*[13]

Though he is a very different writer from David Jones, Mackay shares some of Jones's universal view of human experience, centred on the Mass – and *Magnus* can, in certain respects, be seen more as a poem than as a novel. It stands completely outside the norms of the post-war Catholic novel and harks back to earlier values. In an earlier novel, *Greenvoe* (1972), he had honed those same skills on a novel of contemporary Orkneys life, which interwove the present and the past. Mackay Brown is one of the most original voices in the post-war Catholic novel – a writer in whose work poetry and prose are usually indistinguishable.

David Lodge

David Lodge (b. 1935) is best known, to the general public, as the author of some devastatingly funny satirical novels about university campus life, including *Changing Places* (1975), *Small World* (1984) and *Nice Work* (1988). He is an academic specializing in English literature and his novels are marked by a fascination with narrative techniques, which he uses self-consciously in postmodern games with reality.

Apart from academe, the other major theme in his novels, throughout his novelistic career, has been Catholicism. While studying at University College London he had prepared an MA thesis on the Catholic novel and when he himself set out to write Catholic novels he was well aware of the history of the genre and of its dangers. He has described himself as an 'agnostic Catholic' – a Catholic with doubts – which as Bergonzi has pointed out must mean something different from Graham Greene's description of himself as a 'Catholic agnostic' (the relative importance of noun and adjective being significant).[14] This places him very much among most other Catholic poets and novelists of this period.

David Lodge's development as a Catholic novelist shows us a rapid transition from more traditional modes of thought and expression in his first novel, to a completely new approach. The first novel, *The Picturegoers* (1960), begins to redefine the subject matter of the Catholic novel by its depiction of a working-class Catholic family, the Mallorys. Yet, strangely enough, this picture is not significantly different from the literature that had preceded it. For example, those elements that are taken to epitomize the nature of this society turn out to be the same 'tawdry paraphernalia' that, in the earlier period, had been singled out by the converts from the middle classes and upper classes as essential components of British Catholicism and, though they are seen through the eyes of a non-believing, middle-class observer, retain their role as essential components of British Catholic life.

Lodge, when rereading the novel in later years, declared himself to be surprised at the traditional Catholic elements within it. In particular, the description of a conversion. The main character Mark is shown as having a mystical experience during the course of a Mass. The Mass is described at length, with – as in earlier Catholic novels – quotations from the liturgy playing a prominent part. Mark reads in his Missal the English translation of the crucial section of the prayer of consecration. This is followed by the elevation, at which point Mark has his experience:

> The priest stretched up, lifting the Host on high. Mark stared at it, and belief leapt in his mind like a child in the womb. The pale disc was snatched

down by the priest, but Mark continued to stare at the space in the air that it had occupied. The chalice rose in its place, containing the conse-crated wine.[15]

Though the whole question of Mark's faith and commitment, in the latter part of the novel, is admittedly an ambiguous one, there is no doubt that here Lodge is using the liturgy in the emotive way typical of his predecessors. Indeed, his text is very close to that of Compton Mackenzie, in his similar description of a conversion at the Mass in *The Heavenly Ladder* (1924)[16] (with Mackenzie's 'Truth speaking with the voice of a little child' being matched by Lodge's 'Belief leapt in his mind like a child in the womb' and with both protagonists being called Mark). A further element of tradi-tional religious melodrama is added by the fact that this conversion comes in answer to a prayer that another character, Clare, has earlier made (and which specifies the form that the conversion should take):

Tomorrow he would be kneeling beside her at Mass . . . God must do something to help. Please God, you must do something to help. When the priest elevates the Host at Mass, You could appear to Mark. You've done it before. Sister Veronica had told them of many such miracles.[17]

With knowledge of Lodge's later writings, it is naturally tempting to see irony or even parody here. But there was clearly, from Lodge's own later reaction, no such intention. Writing thirty-three years later, Lodge wrote that he was surprised at 'the seriousness with which the hero's "conversion" is treated' and suspected 'that the source was primarily literary'.[18] He pointed, in this context, to the extensive reading of Catholic novels that he had done for his MA dissertation.

There *are*, of course, elements of humour and parody in this novel, but they are seen above all in Lodge's treatment of fairly ridiculous minor fig-ures, such as the parish priest Father Kipling, with his narrow view of the cinema-going culture of the young as being 'sin'. The central story of Mark's progression from disbelief to belief appears to have been treated seriously.

Lodge's next 'Catholic' novel, *The British Museum is Falling Down* (1965) moves away from such traditional themes. It is a hilariously funny book which nevertheless deals with a serious topic, that of the problems ordinary Catholics were having with the Church's policy on contraception. It was written at the time of the Second Vatican Council, on which people like the hero Adam Appleby and his wife and Barbara 'pinned their hopes for a humane and liberal life in the Church'.[19] Contraception had been entrusted to a special commission which was expected to pronounce before long. There were high hopes of this, too (later to be dashed by Pope Paul VI's encyclical *Humanae Vitae* [1968]). The humour in this novel is not bitter, but contemptuous of the 'old attitudes' which it was believed were changing.

It is the story of one day in the life of Adam Appleby, 'a postgraduate student preparing a thesis he was unlikely to complete',[20] short of money and the father of three children. He has just realized that his wife Barbara's period is overdue. The description of their previous agonized attempts to use the rhythm method, which was 'in accordance with the Natural Law', sets the tone within the first pages of the book.

Adam's capacity for literary daydreaming is one essential component in the complex system of intertextuality that dominates the book. As he crosses Albert Bridge on his scooter, for example, on his way to do his research at the British Museum, the notice telling soldiers to break step while marching over it leads him into a fantasy based on military adventure stories. Sitting outside the Museum after reading a newspaper article about the conflicting attitudes on contraception held in Rome, he has a fantasy based on Rolfe's *Hadrian the Seventh*, about the election as Pope of the 'unknown Padre Appleby, secretary to the English cardinal'. His first encyclical 'is concerned with the role of sexuality in marriage and related problems of birth control, world population problems *etcetera* . . . The Pope concluded by asserting that, in the present state of theological uncertainty, the practice of birth control by any method was left to the discretion and conscience of the Faithful.'[21]

Such literary allusions are not restricted to Adam's daydreams, however. The author subtly introduces similar intertextuality on several occasions, making of the whole book something of a literary playground. Bergonzi lists, among these references, 'Kafka, Conrad, James, Lawrence, Woolf, Hemingway, C. P. Snow and Graham Greene'.[22] Critics have noted, too, that the whole shape of the novel is in itself a form of intertextual joke: it is based on the events of one day, like Joyce's *Ulysses* and its ending, a long soliloquy by Adam's wife Barbara, is clearly based on Molly Bloom's soliloquy at the end of that novel. What does not seem to have been remarked is that the way in which Adam's daydreams are introduced is clearly based on James Thurber's 'The Secret Life of Walter Mitty' (1939).[23]

Fifteen years later Lodge was to produce another Catholic novel, *How Far Can You Go?* (1980). Much had happened in between. In 1968 Pope Paul VI had, with *Humanae Vitae*, retained the ban on contraception. And in 1978, as Lodge was writing his last chapter, Pope John Paul I was elected, closely followed by John Paul II. Lodge's novel takes us through the period from 1952 to 1978, charting the varied experiences of a group of young students who at the start of the novel are attending a Mass conducted by a young priest, Father Austin Brierley. We see them (and Brierley) in their varied relationships and careers, but also in their attitudes to a changing Church. All this is underlined by the comments of an omniscient narrator strangely like Lodge himself. This narrator specifically draws attention to his function, with comments such as:

> The omniscience of novelists has its limits, and we shall not attempt to trace here the process of cogitation, debate, intrigue, fear, anxious prayer and unconscious motivation which finally produced that document [*Humanae Vitae*].[24]

At times indeed, in a manner reminiscent of Laurence Sterne or of Diderot, he even addresses the reader directly, as in 'Let me explain. (Patience, the story will resume shortly)',[25] and 'But enough of this philosophizing'.[26]

Much of the novel, as one might expect, is extremely funny (one of the highest moments being the grotesque depiction of the 'Catholics for an Open Church Paschal Festival' towards the end. Lodge makes indiscriminate fun of both tendencies within the Church). The overall tone, however, is more serious than in *The British Museum* and the narrator's tone is at times quite acerbic and his *parti pris* clear, as in the following:

> Contraception was the issue on which many lay Catholics first attained moral autonomy, rid themselves of superstition, and ceased to regard their religion as, in the moral sphere, an encyclopaedic rule-book in which a clear answer was to be found to every possible question of conduct. They were not likely to be persuaded to reverse their decision by the tired arguments of *Humanae Vitae* . . . *Humanae Vitae* itself is a dead letter to most of the laity and merely an embarrassing nuisance to most of the clergy.[27]

In his next novel to contain major elements of Catholicism, *Paradise News* (1991), Lodge combined some of the best of his secular satire with a serious examination of the problems raised for ordinary Christians by the whole question of death and the afterlife, in an age when academic theologians had questioned all the bases of traditional belief. His central character, Bernard, is a former priest who has lost his faith, but who teaches part-time in an ecumenical theological college. Much of the plot takes place in Hawaii, where Bernard takes his father to visit his father's dying sister, who wishes to make her peace with him. Much of the description of the various holidaymakers in Hawaii (and the lack of satisfaction with this supposed 'paradise on earth') is devastatingly funny. In Hawaii Bernard, who had given up hope of leading a fulfilling life, finds love. He also finds himself discussing fundamental truths (or untruths) with his dying aunt. Amid the many forms of narrative technique (third-person narrator, first-person narrator, short extracts from holiday letters juxtaposed with each other, etc.), we have an account, written by Bernard, of his priestly vocation and his doubts and final departure from the priesthood – together with his sexual hangups and his personal difficulties – which he sends to the girl, Yolande, with whom he has fallen in love. This could almost be taken as an intertextual reference to the similar accounts of 'spoiled priests' in so many post-war Catholic novels.

In the final chapter Bernard, who has returned to his college thinking that he had lost his love for ever, gives a lecture which analyses the dilemma of academic doubt and notes that fundamentalism is flourishing in the present day precisely because of the scepticism of theologians. In this context, he quotes from W. B. Yeats: 'The best lack all conviction, while the worst / Are full of passionate intensity.'[28] The fundamental pessimism of this message is, as Bergonzi has suggested, palliated by the sense of hope at the end of the novel, as Bernard receives a letter which gives the possibility for a life with Yolande. The novel ends with words which are a conscious reference to the hopeful ending of Waugh's *Brideshead Revisited*, as Bernard, asked if Yolande's message contains good news, replies: 'Very good news'.

The good news is not just his future life with Yolande, however. Her letter contains far more important news. In it Yolande, who has attended Bernard's aunt's funeral Mass, speaks of her conviction that they had 'secured repose for Ursula's soul' and of her feeling that there must be some future for that soul:

> It's funny, this dying business, when you're close to it. I always thought of myself as an atheist, a materialist, that this life is all we have and we had better make the most of it; but that evening it seemed hard to believe that Ursula was totally extinct, gone for ever. I suppose everyone has these moments of doubt – or should I say, faith?[29]

She includes a cutting from Unamuno's *The Tragic Sense of Life* which speaks of the possibility of the afterlife in similar terms, as an 'uncertainty' without which we would find it hard to live.

Lodge shares with many modern Christians a sense of an incompatibility between their beliefs and the traditional words that have always been used to clothe them. This sense of the inadequacy of theological expression chimes well with modern literary and philosophical theory's mistrust of words in relation to meaning. Though one might be tempted to see, in the later Lodge, someone who was rejecting traditional belief, this is not necessarily so. It is the *expression* of that belief that had changed; also the sense of *certainty* that has been lost, giving place to what he described in 1984 as 'a more honest and profound but also a more provisional and metaphorical belief.'[30] He shares this sense, of the mixture of faith and doubt within us all, with many; but he is unusual in his determination to meet these problems head on. *Paradise News* is the most important of Lodge's Catholic novels. In it he leaves the contingent concerns of Catholics faced by moral problems of behaviour in face of the Church's teachings, and grapples with some of the fundamental problems of belief in an age of questioning. In this he comes closer to the concerns of modern Catholic poets than to most of his novelist contemporaries.

Lodge gives the lie to those who believe that modern changes in the nature of religious belief must be incompatible with the writing of Catholic novels. He has revivified the genre, both in content and in form. He expresses through his characters many of the problems Catholics face in the modern age, which are so different from those treated by his predecessors. He also makes very effective use of the whole gamut of techniques of the modern novel, including that *Verfremdungseffekt* that postmodern techniques can so effectively achieve, to describe all this.

This is, too, what in a very different way Muriel Spark (1918–2006) was able initially to achieve. One of Spark's greatest tools has, as with Lodge, been a very modern use of the omniscient narrator.

David Lodge, Muriel Spark and the Role of the Narrator

David Lodge has drawn our attention[31] to the fact that, amid all the stress on ambiguity and objectivity that marked secular novelistic theory in the early part of the twentieth century, it was 'the convention of the omniscient and intrusive narrator' that had above all lost favour. Yet there was one area where, for obvious reasons, this fashion had not been followed: 'Most of the significant modern novelists who have persevered with this convention have been professed Christians.'[32] This is because, if one has a specific message to convey, ambiguity has difficulty in conveying it.

In France, as we have seen,[33] there was some discomfort about this among the Catholic novelists of the interwar period, such as Mauriac, who prided themselves on being part of the literary establishment. In Britain, there had been no such worries – though, even when they used such techniques, some authors appeared to try to disguise them in a rather shamefaced manner.

Now, in the post-war period, the postmodern rejection of 'realism' in literature enabled writers like Lodge and Spark to *build on* the convention of authorial omniscience, rather than react against it. As we have seen, Lodge at times makes full use of such techniques in order openly to stress the unreality of the role of the narrator. 'Reality' is, in this context, an unreliable

concept and attempting to recreate 'reality' by literary techniques, which are
by nature (whatever form they take) unreal, with an 'author/narrator' who is
equally unreal, is a thankless task unless these uncertainties are accepted.

Both Lodge and Spark are capable of consciously incorporating the creation of a novel into their text, using the technique the French call '*mise en
abyme*'.[34] Lodge's narrator in *How Far Can You Go?* is in the process of
writing the novel as the novel itself progresses. And a number of characters
in Lodge's novels are writers who share his literary concerns. As one critic
has said about the hero of *Deaf Sentence* (2008) 'The academic in him is
uneasy with experience until he has trapped it in a web of literary anteced-
ents.'[35] In an unsettling variant on '*mise en abyme*', the heroine of Spark's
first novel *The Comforters* (1957) (written shortly after her 1954 conversion), believes that there is a mysterious narrator typing up the novel of her
experiences and commenting on them. At the end of the novel, cured of this
fantasy, she goes off to write a novel of her own, about imaginary characters.
From being created and ordered by another, she has now decided to create
and order her own world.

David Lodge draws our attention to the fact that in Spark's *The Prime
of Miss Jean Brodie* there is 'a highly original and effective exploitation of
the convention of authorial omniscience', with her use of 'daring time-shifts
backwards and forwards across the chronological span of the action'.[36] Yet,
paradoxically, this omniscience serves, not to confirm a clear interpretation
of events, but to unsettle the reader, who continually has to readjust amid
a series of 'elusive and ambiguous' hints and clues that defeat 'the reader's
expectation of clear and simple judgements.'[37] There are multiple possible
meanings, behind which one essential truth gradually emerges:

> Buried in this largely comic novel there is a severe and uncompromising
> dogmatic message: that all groups, communions and institutions are false
> and more or less corrupting except the one that is founded on the truths
> of Christian orthodoxy – and even that one is not particularly attractive
> or virtuous.[38]

Similarly, amid the depiction of the day-to-day life of the 'bed-sit-land' inhabited by so many of Spark's characters in her other novels, important elements
of Catholic experience are incorporated, even if their import for any kind of
overall 'message' is often rather more obscure. It is clear, for example, that
Ronald Bridges, in *The Bachelors* (1960), who has been unable to become
a priest because of his epilepsy, nevertheless on occasion fulfils a kind of lay
priestly role in relation to the other characters. He repeats a passage from
Philippians to himself at times of stress, has discussions about original sin

with his friends, and in a central conversation with the character Elsie, tells her that 'everyone tells me their troubles', and later that 'the best kind of love to give is sacrificial.'[39] And, given Spark's habitual use of allusion, the fact that Ronald is a professional graphologist seems to suggest that he may be able to interpret the events around him with insight. But, at the end of the novel, any such interpretation is seen to be pessimistic, as he enumerates his friends, 'fruitless souls, crumbling tinder, like his own self which did not bear thinking of' and as he imagines all the other aimless souls throughout the world:

> And there are others beside ourselves, he thought, who lie in their beds like happy countries that have no history. Others ferment in prison; some rot, maimed; some lean over the banisters of presbyteries to see if anyone is going to answer the telephone.[40]

Such ambiguities do not prevent one from noting something important about the themes that play a major part in Spark's Catholic world. They seem strangely imbued with the values of a previous Catholic generation. Evil can be seen as a material, palpable force, as in *The Ballad of Peckham Rye* (1960), where it is personified in the central character, Dougal Douglas, who appears to be possessed by some kind of demonic force (he even appears to have some kind of horns on his forehead). His impact upon the ordinary people of Peckham seems to bear this out, as he is the cause of a murder, a stroke and a marriage baulked at the altar. At the end of the novel we are told that after he left Peckham he went to Africa to sell tape-recorders to witch doctors and then became a novice in a Franciscan monastery, causing the Prior to have a nervous breakdown and several of the monks to break 'their vows of obedience in actuality, and their other vows by desire.'[41] He ended up by writing 'a lot of cockeyed books' about his own experiences (Spark thus reintroducing, as in *The Comforters*, the idea of the novelist as creator of a parallel universe). The fact that he then 'went far in the world' appears to be a proof of the success of evil in the world; but on the last page of the novel we find that everything now seems to be going right once more in Peckham and one of the characters, looking at the Rye, sees it 'for an instant looking like a cloud of green and gold, the people seeming to ride upon it' and he muses that 'as you might say there was another world than this.'[42]

As can be seen from this ending, Spark's often zany sense of fantasy tends to make the reader uncertain of the seriousness of what is being described. There is little doubt, however, that one of the major themes of her novels is, as here, an almost Manichaean view of the solid presence of good and evil in the world, together with a belief in original sin. As Ronald, in *The*

Bachelors, puts it: 'The Christian economy seems to me to be so ordered that original sin is necessary to salvation'.[43]

Muriel Spark's novels have been described as 'short, elegant, eccentric and sophisticated, with touches of the bizarre and the perverse.'[44] Within this format, her skilful use of modern techniques of ambiguity, including a highly sophisticated use of the convention of narrative omniscience, has unobtrusively managed to convey a series of Catholic messages. Her Catholicism is, however, of a traditional type, untouched by the modern tendencies that we have seen in so many other Catholic writers of this period. Indeed, in *The Abbess of Crewe* (1974) and *The Takeover* (1976) we find elements of satire at the expense of modern trends within the Church which are reminiscent of the kind of thing that Alice Thomas Ellis was writing in the same years.

Sadly, towards the end of her career Spark, while continuing to use Catholic themes in her novels, appears to have done so merely as an exotic adjunct, a kind of added *frisson* produced for novelistic effect. Woodman noticed this tendency in embryo as early as the 1970s. 'Style in the later novels', he writes, 'has become . . . a moral virtue in itself. It is largely severed from religious values.'[45] This decline in the way Catholicism was used was gradually matched by a more general decline in her novelistic creation, culminating in *Aiding and Abetting* (2000), in which Spark luridly imagines what has happened to Lord Lucan in the years since his disappearance. The Catholic element is provided by a phoney stigmatic who, every menstrual cycle, had covered herself in blood and pretended to have the five wounds of Christ. She inspired a cult following, especially in 'Ireland, the great land of believers'. Miracles did happen, 'as in fact they sometimes do.'[46] After she was exposed, she became a psychiatrist, to whom Lord Lucan comes and attempts to blackmail her about her past. The Lucan story is treated in a particularly sensational manner. It ends with a blatant reminiscence of Waugh's *Black Mischief*, with Lucan being eaten by cannibals. The weakness of Spark's later output, typified by this novel, should not however blind us to her remarkable achievement in the earlier part of her career.

Bernard Bergonzi has written that after Greene and Waugh the Catholic novel 'declined quite rapidly.'[47] Others have agreed with him. The basis for this belief lies in a particular conception of what necessarily made up its subject matter. Thomas Woodman, seeing Catholic conservatism as having been the 'cultural base' for the Catholic novel, has suggested that that conservatism's decline must mean that 'its influence as a cultural base for Catholic fiction must surely continue to shrink.'[48] David Lodge himself felt as early as the 1960s that the traditional Catholic novel was now imperilled by the 'confused – and confusing' nature of current Catholic beliefs and said that it was impossible to 'talk of the Catholic novel in quite such sharply-defined terms any more'.[49] In his statement, however, the possibility was left open that some form of Catholic novel, not in such 'sharply-defined terms', might still be possible.

It is true that the traditional Catholic novel always depended strongly on a particular form of belief. That belief was translated into particular forms of action and interpretation, whether on the French or on the English model, so that it was 'as much the embodiment of a literary convention as the enactment of religious experience.'[50] When it is viewed in this way, it is hardly surprising that so many critics should refer to Greene's novels of the 1948–51 period as his 'Catholic novels' and should refuse that description to what he produced thereafter. Yet, as we have seen, these later works were 'Catholic novels' in a very different sense. They epitomized the modern belief that alongside 'doctrinally informed and committed Christianity' there is another form of Christianity, 'virtual and implicit'.[51] David Lodge's later novels fall within this same mould and show that it is possible to create new forms to match the new ideas.

What of the future, though? Have we reached another dead end? Muriel Spark faded out before the end of her career and though Lodge goes from strength to strength (his most recent novel, *Deaf Sentence* (2008), being among the best he has written), there is no sign of any plausible successor to him. Perhaps the Catholic novel (which at any rate, even at its height, took root less successfully in Britain than in France) relied more heavily than one might suppose on a specific religious climate, and the new climate fits it less than Lodge's brilliant creations might have led one to believe. We can only wait and see.

Notes

1 For example, Piers Paul Read's Monk Dawson (1969) and John Cornwell's The Spoiled Priest (1969). It is also a theme touched on in David Lodge's novels *How Far Can You Go?* (1980) and *Paradise News* (1991).
2 Woodman, *Faithful Fictions*, p. 164.
3 Piers Paul Read, *Monk Dawson*, p. 200.
4 See Graham Greene, *Yours etc.: Letters to the Press, 1945–1989*, passim. Typical of Greene's criticisms of the Church is the following: 'In his unfortunate visit to Nicaragua the Pope proved himself a politician rather than a priest and yet he condemns other priests for playing a similar role in politics . . . Unlike John XXIII he himself seems to take a political and partisan line. To him, as to President Reagan, Marxism is the great enemy, and the word Marxist becomes more and more a vague term of abuse.' (Letters to *The Tablet*, 25 August 1984, and to *The Times*, 11 September 1984, ibid., pp. 223–5.)

5 For example, Mary Blundell's *Tyler's Lass* (1926), which depicts Lancashire working-class Catholics.

6 See, for example, Bruce Marshall, *All Glorious Within* (1941).

7 See, for example, Brown's letter to Stella Cartwright, 17 September 1974, quoted in Maggie Fergusson, *George Mackay Brown*, p. 197.

8 Epigraph to Piers Paul Read, *The Upstart*.

9 Ibid., p. 260.

10 Her spiritual journey at this time is brilliantly illustrated in her correspondence with a Jesuit friend, later published as *The Hound and the Falcon: The Story of a Reconversion to the Catholic Faith*.

11 Quoted in Carmen Callil, introduction to Virago edition of Antonia White's *Beyond the Glass* (1979).

12 For this admiration, see *The Hound and the Falcon*, pp. 102–8, 130.

13 George Mackay Brown, *Magnus*, p. 150.

14 Bernard Bergonzi, *David Lodge*, p. 43.

15 Ibid., pp. 110–11.

16 See p. 112.

17 *The Picturegoers*, p. 98.

18 David Lodge, introduction to *The Picturegoers* (1993), p. viii.

19 Ibid., p. 27.

20 David Lodge, *The British Museum is Falling Down*, p. 9.

21 Ibid., p. 64.

22 Bernard Bergonzi, *David Lodge*.

23 This was made into a famous 1947 film starring Danny Kaye, which was a favourite with most youngsters of Lodge's age at the time (including the present writer).

24 David Lodge, *How Far Can You Go?* p. 114.

25 Ibid., p. 115.

26 Ibid., p. 121.

27 Ibid., p. 118, 120.

28 David Lodge, *Paradise News*, p. 353.

29 Ibid., p. 363.

30 C. Walsh, 'David Lodge interviewed', *Strawberry Fare* (Autumn 1984, pp. 3–12), quoted in Bergonzi, *David Lodge*, p. 43.

31 See David Lodge, 'The Uses and Abuses of Omniscience: Method and Meaning in Muriel Spark's *The Prime of Miss Jean Brodie*', *Critical Quarterly*, 1970, reprinted in *The Novelist at the Crossroads*, pp. 119–44.

32 Ibid.

33 See p. 162.

34 A term from heraldry, 'meaning the reduced reproduction of an image within itself' (*The New Oxford Companion to Literature in French*, Oxford University Press 1995). It was Gide who first used it to refer to literature (a play within a play, a novel within a novel).

35 Jane Shilling, review of Lodge's *Deaf Sentence*, in *The Times*, 25 April 2008.

36 David Lodge, 'The Uses and Abuses of Omniscience', in *The Novelist at the Crossroads*, pp. 119–44.

37 Ibid., p. 122, 130.

38 Ibid., p. 135.
39 Muriel Spark, *The Bachelors*, p. 160, 165.
40 Ibid., p. 214.
41 Spark, *The Ballad of Peckham Rye*, p. 142.
42 Ibid., p. 143.
43 Spark, *The Bachelors*, p. 85.
44 Margaret Drabble (ed.), *The Oxford Companion to English Literature* (Oxford: Oxford University Press, 1985), p. 925.
45 Woodman, *Faithful Fictions*, p. 75.
46 Spark, *Aiding and Abetting*, p. 24.
47 Bernard Bergonzi, 'The Decline and Fall of the English Catholic novel', in *The Myth of Modernism and Twentieth Century Literature*, p. 175.
48 Woodman, *Faithful Fictions*, p. 164.
49 'David Lodge interviewed by Bernard Bergonzi', *Alta: University of Birmingham Review*, No. 7, Winter 1968–9), quoted in Bergonzi, 'The Decline and Fall', p. 177.
50 Bergonzi, 'The Decline and Fall', p. 178.
51 Ibid., p. 177.

Conclusion

'All generalizations are dangerous, even this one.' This statement by Dumas *fils* should serve as a warning to anyone attempting a conclusion to a book such as this. English Catholic literature over the last hundred and fifty years has been so varied that it is impossible to encapsulate it in a few sentences.

It has been much easier to generalize about French Catholic literature. Perhaps that is because the fairly rigid apparatus within the French Catholic novel remained far more constant (as late as the 1930s, as we have seen, with Mauriac's *Les Anges noirs*).[1] Theorizing is more difficult in relation to the English experience, partly because of the wide disparity that exists between the various successful English practitioners of the novel of modern life (Mrs Ward, Baring, Waugh, Greene, Lodge, Spark). What one can say is that, though most of the English Catholic novelists were individuals and in no way formed a 'movement', they were also intensely aware of each other's writings, to the extent that one can continually cross-reference between them.

Another difference between French and English Catholic literature lies in the field of poetry. Apart from certain outstanding individuals like Claudel, Péguy and Jouve, French Catholic poetry on the whole failed to get beyond the sentimental piety of the mid-nineteenth century. English Catholic poetry was far more successful, not just because of outstanding figures like Hopkins and Jones but also because of a solid backdrop of other fine poets, from Patmore, Thompson, Johnson and Meynell in the early period to Gascoyne, Raine, Jennings, Levi, Mackay Brown and others in more modern times.

In order to appreciate adequately the work of the major novelists, it is necessary to look at a whole range of other writers who provided the norm from which they emerged. The Catholic novel suffered in the late nineteenth century from a whole succession of lesser writers, most of whom fell into traps of sentimentality, didacticism and banality. This genre, unlike its French equivalent, eschewed the mystical and the miraculous and dealt with contemporary situations in which Catholic principles found themselves

242

in conflict with the modern world. Benson, while in some respects a more accomplished writer than many of these lesser authors, nevertheless had a lot in common with them. It is interesting to note how many Catholic novelists in this country (as opposed to in France) were priests (usually converts), for whom teaching and proselytism were central aims. These aims were usually pursued single-mindedly and with little concern for psychological realism, to the detriment of literary quality. Amid all these writers, Mrs Wilfrid Ward stands out as someone who, pursuing the same ends, was capable of doing so with subtlety and a proper regard for the intelligence of her readers. She proved that it was possible to convey Catholic truths without deciding everything for the reader in advance.

From the First World War onwards, the history of the English Catholic novel (unlike the French novel, except for a short and abortive period in Mauriac's writing in the late 1920s)[2] has been that of an attempt to combine the best in contemporary secular literary trends with specifically Catholic concerns. Baring led the way in this, and then Greene and Waugh became the most highly successful exponents of this new Catholic art. Greene, whose irony had helped to subvert the apparatus of the traditional Catholic novel and who had thereby already raised fundamental questions about the relevance of traditional Catholic teachings to human behaviour and morality, later moved even further in this direction, with novels which, dealing with the same dilemmas, avoided all easy solutions. The changes in Catholic thought in the post-war period enabled writers like David Lodge to create truly Catholic novels. These novels, dealing as they do with questions of truth and of behaviour, stimulate real thought by avoiding the easy answers, in a way that the earlier proselytizing novels had been completely incapable of doing. *Pace* those who believe that the survival of the Catholic novel depended on the continuance of traditional beliefs, Greene and Lodge have shown that a new, vital, more literary Catholic novel can be created on the basis of dialogue and uncertainty, which equally reflect Catholic concerns.

Many of the successful English Catholic poets expressed similarly complex problems, often in a highly personal and anguished way. We find examples of this as early as the late nineteenth century, in some of Hopkins' later poetry and in certain poems by Lionel Johnson. From the 1930s onwards, with poets like Gascoyne, Jennings and Levi, this was to be the dominant tone, which was shared with a number of non-Catholic Christian poets of the same generation. Not that it was the only original tendency in English Catholic poetry. From the complicated, highly original expression of Gerard Manley Hopkins's poems of praise to God within nature, to the simple, quiet, meditative verse of Alice Meynell and to the fierce, athletic poetry of Francis Thompson; from the highly devotional, Mass-centred poetry of David Jones and George Mackay Brown to the neo-Platonist poems of Kathleen Raine; from the simple, straightforward expression of Elizabeth Jennings to the elaboration of Peter Levi; English Catholic poetry is not only highly diverse, but also extremely successful in purely literary terms. So much so, that where in France the Catholic novel has been the flagship of modern Catholic literature, in Britain Catholic poetry is a major challenger for the same position.

Strangely, the theatre, which in France had a prominent position in the Catholic revival (mainly because of Claudel's dramas), played almost no part in the English equivalent. The plays of Greene are negligible in relation to his novels and the only British Christian dramatist of any worth has been an Anglican, T. S. Eliot.

English Catholic literature would not have been worth studying if it had not contained works of high literary value such as we have seen both in the novel and in poetry. These works, by their preoccupations and by the complex systems of imagery that they use, single out this genre from the secular literature surrounding it. It has therefore been worth examining these qualities, both in the great and in the lesser writers, in order to appreciate more fully just what they were attempting to achieve.

The close examination of the literature of this period has exposed the danger of artificially applying religion to the surface of texts, without inserting it more deeply. It has also proved that truly inspired and well-crafted writing can convey religious messages in depth, which can leave an indelible impression on the mind of the reader.

Notes

1 See pp. 162–5.
2 See p. 168.

Select Bibliography

A bibliography containing all the works read while studying this subject would be excessively long and of little use to either the scholar or the general reader. The works listed here are those that have been the most use. In the cases where readily available modern editions have been used, these editions are also mentioned (and will be quoted in the footnotes to the chapters).

Primary Sources

Agnew, Emily C., *Rome and the Abbey: A Tale of Conscience* (London: Dolman, 1849). Kessinger Publishing's Rare Reprints, n.d.
Allen, William (Cardinal) (with Henry Walpole), *A Briefe Historie of the Glorious Martyrdom of Twelve Reverend Priests: Father Edmund Campion and his Companions* (reprinted, London: Burns and Oates, 1908, ed. J. H. Pollen, SJ). Kessinger Publishing's Rare Reprints, n.d.
Baring, Maurice, *A Triangle* (London: Heinemann, 1923)
——*C* (London: Heinemann, 1924). Oxford: Oxford University Press, 1986
——*Cat's Cradle* (London: Heinemann, 1925)
——*Daphne Adeane* (London: Heinemann, 1926). House of Stratus, 2001
——*Comfortless Memory* (London: Heinemann, 1928)
——*The Coat Without Seam* (London: Heinemann, 1929). House of Stratus, 2001
——*Robert Peckham* (London: Heinemann, 1930)
——*In My End Is My Beginning* (London: Heinemann, 1932). House of Stratus, 2001
——*The Lonely Lady of Dulwich* (London: Heinemann, 1934)
——*Letters*, ed. Jocelyn Hillgarth and Julian Jeffs (Norwich: Michael Russell, 2007)
Barnes, James Strachey, *The Universal Aspects of Fascism* (London: 1928)
——*Fascism* (London: Home University Library, 1931)
——*Half a Life* (London: 1933)
——*Half a Life Left* (London: 1937)
Barry, William, *Arden Massiter* (London: Fisher Unwin, 1900)
Belloc, Hilaire, *Emmanuel Burden* (London: Methuen, 1904)
——*Mr Clutterbuck's Election* (London: Nash, 1908)
——*Pongo and the Bull* (London: Constable, 1910)
——*Europe and the Faith* (London: 1920). Rockford: Tan Books, 1992
——*The Jews* (London: 1922). Palmdale: Omni Publications, 1998
——*Essays of a Catholic* (London: Macmillan, 1931). Rockford: Tan Books, 1992
——*Letters from Hilaire Belloc*, ed. Robert Speaight (London: Hollis and Carter, 1958)

Benson, E. F., 'The Confession of Charles Linkworth' (1912), reprinted in *The Oxford Book of English Ghost Stories*, ed. Michael Cox and R. A. Gilbert (Oxford: Oxford University Press, 1986)

Benson, R. H., *The Light Invisible* (London: 1903). Once and Future Books, 2004

——*By What Authority?* (London: 1904) Wildside Press, 2006

——*The King's Achievement* (London: 1905). Burns, Oates and Washbourne, 1944

——*A Mirror of Shalott* (London: 1905). Burns, Oates and Washbourne, 1928

——*Richard Raynal, Solitary* (London: 1905). Aegypan Press, n.d.

——*The Queen's Tragedy* (London: Pitman, 1906). Burns, Oates and Washbourne, n.d.

——*The Sentimentalists* (London: Pitman, 1906). Once and Future Books, 2005

——*Lord of the World* (London: Pitman, 1907). Echo Library, 2005

——*The Conventionalists* (London: Hutchinson, 1908). Kessinger Publishing's Rare Reprints, n.d.

——*The Necromancers* (London: Hutchinson, 1909). Kessinger Publishing's Rare Reprints, n.d.

——*A Winnowing* (London: Hutchinson, 1910). St Louis: Herder, 1910

——*None Other Gods* (London: Hutchinson, 1911). Wildside Press, 2006

——*The Dawn of All* (London: Hutchinson, 1911). Aegypan Press, n.d.

——*Come Rack, Come Rope!* (London: Hutchinson, 1912). Echo Library, 2005

——*The Coward* (London: Hutchinson, 1912)

——*An Average Man* (London: Hutchinson, 1913)

——*Initiation* (London: Hutchinson, 1913)

——*Confessions of a Convert* (London: Longmans, Green, 1913). Sevenoaks: Fisher Press, 1991

——*Oddsfish!* (London: Hutchinson, 1914). Aegypan Press, n.d.

——*Lourdes* (London: Mauresa Press, 1914). Echo Library, 2006

Bergonzi, Bernard, *The Roman Persuasion* (London: Weidenfeld and Nicolson, 1981)

Bloy, Léon, *La Femme pauvre* (Paris: Mercure de France, 1897)

Blundell, Mary, *Tyler's Lass* (London: Sands, 1926)

Bourget, Paul, *L'Étape* (Paris: Plon, 1902)

Brown, George Mackay, 'The Broken Heraldry', in *Memoirs of a Modern Scotland*, ed. Karl Miller (London: Faber and Faber, 1970)

——*Greenvoe* (London: The Hogarth Press, 1972). Edinburgh: Polygon, 2004

——*Magnus* (London: The Hogarth Press, 1973). Edinburgh: Polygon, 2008

——*Collected Poems* (London: John Murray, 2006)

Caddell, Celia, *Home and the Homeless* (London: Newby, 1858)

——*Wild Times* (London: Newby, 1872)

Camm, Dom Bede, *Forgotten Shrines: An Account of some Old Catholic Halls and Families in England* (London: Macdonald and Evans, 1910). Leominster: Gracewing, 2004

Cendrars, Blaise, *Du monde entier* (Paris: Nouvelle Revue Française, 1912)

Chesterton, G. K., *The Napoleon of Notting Hill* (London: Bodley Head, 1904). Dover Publications, 1991

——*The Man Who Was Thursday* (London: Bodley Head, 1908). Penguin, 1986

——*Orthodoxy* (London: Bodley Head, 1908). New York: Doubleday, 1959

——*The Ball and the Cross* (London: Wells Gardner, 1909)

——*The Everlasting Man* (London: Dodd, Mead, 1925). San Francisco: Ignatius Press, 1993

——*The Father Brown Stories* (London: Cassell, 1947)

——*The Collected Poems* (London: Methuen, 1933)

Claudel, Paul, *Poëmes de Coventry Patmore* (Paris: NRF, 1912). Reprinted in *Oeuvre Poétique* (NRF Pléiade 1957)
——*Corona Benignitatis Anni Dei* (Paris: NRF, 1915) Reprinted in *Oeuvre Poétique* (NRF Pléiade 1957)
——*Le Soulier de Satin* (Paris: NRF, 1930). Reprinted in *Théâtre*, Vol. 2 (NRF Pléiade 1956)
Cornwell, John, *The Spoiled Priest* (London: Longman, 1969)
Dering, Edward, *Sherborne* (London: Art and Book Co., 1875)
——*The Ban of Mablethorpe* (London: Art and Book Co., 1894)
Donnolly, Gabrielle, *Holy Mother* (London: Gollancz, 1987). New York: Atlantic Monthly Press, n.d.
Dowson, Ernest, *Verses* (London: Bodley Head, 1896)
——*Decorations in Verse and Prose* (London: Bodley Head, 1899)
——*The Poems of Ernest Dowson*, with a Memoir by Arthur Symons, four illustrations by Aubrey Beardsley, and a portrait by William Rothenstein (London: Bodley Head, 1905)
——*Collected Poems*, ed. R. K. R. Thornton and Caroline Dowson (Birmingham: Birmingham University Press, 2003)
Ellis, Alice Thomas (Anna Haycraft) *The Sin Eater* (London: Duckworth, 1977). Akadine Press, 1998
——*The 27th Kingdom* (London: Duckworth, 1982)
——*The Other Side of the Fire* (London: Duckworth, 1983)
Faber, Frederick William, *Jesus and Mary* (London: Jo Burns, 1849)
——Most of his hymns are to be found in the *Church Hymn Book*, 1872, and in modern hymnals
Firbank, Ronald, *Valmouth* (London: 1919)
——*Prancing Nigger* (London: 1924)
——*Concerning the Eccentricities of Cardinal Pirelli* (London: G. Richards, 1926)
——*The Complete Ronald Firbank* (London: Duckworth, 1961). Picador, 1988, with Introduction by Anthony Powell
Fullerton, Lady Georgiana, *Constance Sherwood* (London: Moxon, 1865)
Gascoyne, David, *Poems 1937–1942* (London: Poetry London, 1943)
——*A Vagrant and Other Poems* (London: John Lehmann, 1950)
——*Collected Poems* (London: Oxford University Press, 1965)
——*Selected Poems* (London: Enitharmon, 1994)
——Pierre-Jean Jouve, *Despair Has Wings: Selected Poems Translated by David Gascoyne* (London: Enitharmon, 2007)
Gray, John, *Silverpoints* (London: Bodley Head, 1893)
——*Spiritual Poems, Chiefly Done Out of Several Languages* (London: Ballantyne Press, 1896)
——*Silverpoints* and *Spiritual Poems*, ed. R. K. R. Thornton and Ian Small (Oxford and New York: Woodstock Books, 1994)
——*St Peter's Hymns* (London: The Cayme Press, 1925). Published anonymously
——*Poems* (London: Sheed and Ward, 1931)
——*Park: A Fantastic Story* (250 copies) (Oxford: Blackfriars, 1932). Manchester: Carcanet, 1984 (ed. Philip Healy)
Greene, Graham, *Stamboul Train* (London: Heinemann, 1932)
——*A Gun for Sale* (London: Heinemann, 1936). Penguin, 1963
——*Brighton Rock* (London: Heinemann, 1938). Penguin, 1971
——*The Power and the Glory* (London: Heinemann, 1940). Penguin, 1962
——*The Heart of the Matter* (London: Heinemann, 1948). Penguin, 1962
——*The End of the Affair* (London: Heinemann, 1951). Vintage, 2004

——*The Quiet American* (London: Heinemann, 1955). Penguin, 1962
——*The Potting Shed* (London: Heinemann, 1958). Penguin, 1971
——*Our Man in Havana* (London: Heinemann, 1958)
——*A Burnt-Out Case* (London: Heinemann, 1961). Penguin, 1963
——*The Comedians* (London: Bodley Head, 1966)
——*Collected Essays* (London: Bodley Head, 1969)
——*A Sort of Life* (London: Bodley Head, 1971)
——*Ways of Escape* (London: Bodley Head, 1980)
——*Collected Plays* (London: Penguin, 1985)
——*Collected Short Stories* (London: Penguin, 1986)
——*Yours, etc.: Letters to the Press, 1945–1989* (London: Reinhardt/Viking, 1989) Penguin, 1991
——*Articles of Faith: The Collected* Tablet *Journalism of Graham Greene*, ed. Ian Thomson (Oxford: Signal Books, 2006)
——*A Life in Letters*, ed. Richard Greene (London: Little, Brown, 2007). Abacus, 2008
Harland, Henry, *The Cardinal's Snuff-Box* (London: Lane, 1900). Kessinger Publishing's Rare Reprints, n.d.
Harris, Elizabeth Furlong Shipton, *From Oxford to Rome: And How It Fared With Some Who Lately Made the Journey* (London: Longman, Brown, Green and Longmans, 1847). Kessinger Publishing's Rare Reprints, n.d.
Hobbes, John Oliver (Pearl Craigie), *Some Emotions and a Moral* (London: Fisher Unwin, 1891)
——*A Study in Temptations* (London: Fisher Unwin, 1893)
——*The School for Saints* (London: Fisher Unwin, 1897)
——*Robert Orange* (London: Fisher Unwin, 1900)
Hollis, Christopher, *The Monstrous Regiment* (London: Minton Balch, 1930)
Hopkins, Gerard Manley, *Poetry and Prose*, ed. Walford Davies (London: Everyman, 1998)
Huysmans, Joris-Karl, A Rebours (Paris: Charpentier, 1884)
——*En route* (Paris: Tresse et Stock, 1895)
——*La Cathédrale* (Paris: Stock, 1898)
——*Sainte Lydwine de Schiedam* (Paris: Stock, 1901)
——*Les Foules de Lourdes* (Paris: Stock, 1906)
Jefferies, Richard, *After London: or Wild England* (London: 1885). Echo Library, 2005
Jennings, Elizabeth, *New Collected Poems* (Manchester: Carcanet, 2002)
Jerrold, Douglas, *Storm over Europe* (London: Benn, 1930). Burns, Oates and Washbourne, 1943
——*Georgian Adventure* (London: Right Book Club, 1937)
Johnson, Lionel, *Poems* (London: Elkin Mathews, 1895)
——*Ireland and Other Poems* (London: Elkin Mathews, 1897)
——*Poetical Works* (New York: Macmillan, 1915). Reprinted in Bibliobazaar Reproduction Series, n.d.
Jones, David, *In Parenthesis* (London: Faber and Faber, 1937). Reprinted in paperback, 1963
——*The Anathemata* (London: Faber and Faber, 1952)
——*Epoch and Artist: Selected Writings* (London: Faber and Faber, 1959)
——*The Sleeping Lord, and Other Fragments* (London: Faber and Faber, 1974). Paperback edition, 1995
——*The Kensington Mass* (London: Agenda Editions, 1975)
Jouve, Pierre-Jean, *Sueur de sang* (Paris: Cahiers Libres, 1933)

Kingsley, Charles, *Westward Ho!* (Cambridge: Macmillan, 1855). Edinburgh: Birlinn, 2009 (ed. Malcolm Day)

La Taille, Maurice de, *The Mystery of Faith: Regarding the Most August Sacrament and Sacrifice of the Body and Blood of Christ*, 2 vols (London: Sheed and Ward, 1941)

Leslie, Sir Shane, *The End of a Chapter* (1916; revised and rewritten for the Travellers' Library, London: Heinemann, 1929)

——*Shane Leslie's Ghost Book* (London: Hollis and Carter, 1955)

——'The Cambridge Apostolate', in *Memorials of Robert Hugh Benson* (London: Burns and Oates, 1915)

Levi, Peter, *Death is a Pulpit* (London: Anvil Press, 1971)

——*Collected Poems 1955–1975* (London: Anvil Press, 1976)

——*The Echoing Green: Three Elegies* (London: Anvil Press, 1983)

——*The Flutes of Autumn* (London: Harvill Press, 1983). Arena edition, 1985

——*The Frontiers of Paradise: A Study of Monks and Monasteries* (London: Collins Harvill, 1988)

——'Hopkins a'i Dduw' (Hopkins and his God) (North Wales Arts Association, 1990)

——*The Art of Poetry: The Oxford Lectures, 1984–1989* (New Haven: Yale University Press, 1991)

Lodge, David, *The Picturegoers* (London: MacGibbon & Kee, 1960). Penguin, 1993

——*Ginger, You're Barmy* (London: MacGibbon & Kee, 1962). Penguin, 1984

——*The British Museum is Falling Down* (London: MacGibbon & Kee, 1965). Penguin, 1983

——*Changing Places: A Tale of Two Campuses* (London: Secker and Warburg, 1975). Penguin, 1978

——*How Far Can You Go?* (London: Secker and Warburg, 1980). Penguin, 1981

——*Small World: An Academic Romance* (London: Secker and Warburg, 1984). Penguin, 1985

——*Nice Work* (London: Secker and Warburg, 1988). Penguin, 1989

——*Paradise News* (London: Secker and Warburg, 1991). Penguin, 1992

——*Deaf Sentence* (London: Harvill Secker, 2008). Penguin, 2009

——*Graham Greene* (New York: Columbia University Press, 1966)

——*Evelyn Waugh* (New York: Columbia University Press, 1971)

——*The Novelist at the Crossroads, and Other Essays on Fiction and Criticism* (London: Routledge & Kegan Paul, 1971)

——*Working with Structuralism: Essays and Reviews on Nineteenth- and Twentieth-Century Literature* (London: Routledge & Kegan Paul, 1981). Paperback, 1982

Macaulay, Rose, *Letters to a Friend, 1950–1952* (London: Collins, 1961)

Mackenzie, Compton, *The Altar Steps* (London: Cassell, 1922)

——*The Parson's Progress* (London: Cassell, 1923)

——*The Heavenly Ladder* (London: Cassell, 1924)

——*Catholicism and Scotland* (London: Routledge, 1936)

Maistre, Joseph de, *Les Soirées de Saint-Pétersbourg, suivi d'un traité sur les sacrifices* (Seconde édition, Lyon et Paris: Rusand, 1831)

Marshall, Bruce, *Father Malachy's Miracle* (London: Heinemann, 1931). Fontana Books, 1962

——*All Glorious Within* (London: Constable, 1941)

Mauriac, François, *Le Roman* (Paris: L'Artisan du livre, Cahiers de la Quinzaine, 1928). Republished in: *Oeuvres Romanesques et Théâtrales Complètes* (NRF Pléiade, 1979, Vol. 2, 751–73)

——*Le Noeud de vipères* (Paris: Grasset, 1932). Republished in ibid., Vol. 2, 381–544

——*Les Anges noirs* (Paris: Grasset, 1936). Republished in ibid., Vol. 3 (1981), 215–367

Meynell, Alice, *Poems* (London: Burns and Oates, 1893)

——*Later Poems* (London: Burns and Oates, 1901)

——*Poems: Collected Edition* (London: Burns, Oates and Washbourne, 1913)

——*Last Poems* (London: Burns, Oates and Washbourne, 1923)

Milburn, J. B., *A Martyr of Old York: Being a narrative of the Life and Sufferings of the Venerable Margaret Clitheroe* (London: Burns and Oates, 1900)

Newman, John Henry, *Callista: A Sketch of the Third Century* (London: Burns & Lambert, 1856) New York: Cosimo, 2007

——*Loss and Gain: The Story of a Convert* (London: Burns & Oates, 1848) (6th ed., Burns and Oates, 1874). Echo Library, 2008

——*Apologia Pro Vita Sua* (London: Longmans, 1864). Oxford: Clarendon Press, 1967

——*Prayers, Poems and Meditations*, ed. A. N. Wilson (London: SPCK, 2007)

——*Verses on Various Occasions* (London: Burns and Oates, 1868)

'Pater, Roger' (Dom Roger Hudleston), *Mystic Voices* (London: Oates & Washbourne, 1923). Ashcroft, British Columbia: Ash-Tree Press, 2001

Pater, Walter, *Marius the Epicurean* (London: Cape, 1885)

Patmore, Coventry, *The Poems of Coventry Patmore* (Oxford: Oxford University Press, 1949)

Péguy, Charles, *Jeanne d'Arc* (Paris: Librairie de la Revue Socialiste, 1897). Reprinted in *Oeuvres Poétiques Complètes*, Paris, NRF Pléiade, 1960, pp. 21–324

——*Le Mystère de la Charité de Jeanne d'Arc* (Paris: Cahiers de la Quinzaine, 1910). Reprinted in *Oeuvres Poétiques Complètes*, Paris: NRF Pléiade, 1960, pp. 361–523

——*Notre Jeunesse* (Paris: Cahiers de la Quinzaine, 1910). Reprinted in *Oeuvres en prose 1909–1914*, Paris: NRF Pléiade, 1957

Petrie, Sir Charles, *Mussolini* (London: The Holme Press, 1931)

——*Lords of the Inland Sea* (London: Right Book Club, 1937)

Raffalovich, Marc-André, *Uranisme et Unisexualité* (Paris: Stock, 1896)

Raine, Kathleen, *Collected Poems* (Ipswich: Golgonooza Press, 2008)

Read, Piers Paul, *The Upstart* (London: Secker and Warburg, 1973). Pan Books, 1979

——*Monk Dawson* (London: Secker and Warburg, 1978). Pan Books, 1978

——*A Married Man* (London: Secker and Warburg, 1979)

——*The Free Frenchman* (London: Secker and Warburg, 1986)

——*On the Third Day* (London: Secker and Warburg, 1990)

Redmon, Anne, *Emily Stone* (London: Secker and Warburg, 1974)

——*Second Sight* (London: Secker and Warburg, 1987)

Rolfe, Fr. (Baron Corvo), *Hadrian the Seventh* (London: Chatto and Windus, 1904). New York: New York Review of Books, 2001

——*The Desire and Pursuit of the Whole* (London: Cassell, 1934). New York: New York Review of Books, 2002

Simpson, Richard, *Edmund Campion: A Biography* (1866: reprinted London: John Hodges, 1896). Kessinger Publishing's Rare Reprints, n.d.

Spark, Muriel, *The Comforters* (London: Macmillan, 1957)

——*Memento Mori* (London: Macmillan, 1959). Penguin, 1961

——*The Bachelors* (London: Macmillan, 1960). Penguin, 1963

——*The Ballad of Peckham Rye* (London: Macmillan, 1960). Penguin, 1963

——*The Prime of Miss Jean Brodie* (London: Macmillan, 1961). Penguin, 1965

——*The Girls of Slender Means* (London: Macmillan, 1963)

——*The Abbess of Crewe* (London: Macmillan, 1974)

——*The Takeover* (London: Macmillan, 1976). Penguin, 1978
——*Aiding and Abetting* (London: QPD, 2000)
——*Curriculum Vitae* (London: Constable, 1992)
Stewart, Agnes, *Eustace: or Self-Devotion* (London: Catholic Publishing Co., 1860)
Surin, Jean-Joseph, *Correspondance*, ed. Michel de Certeau (Paris: Desclée de Brouwer, 1966)
Symons, Arthur, *The Symbolist Movement in Literature* (London: 1899)
Thompson, Francis, *Collected Poems*, ed. Wilfrid Meynell (London: Burns, Oates and Washbourne, 1913). Sevenoaks: Fisher Press, 1992
Vere, Aubrey de, *English Misrule and Irish Misdeeds* (London: John Murray, 1848)
——*May Carols* (1857)
Voynich, Ethel Lilian, *The Gadfly* (1897). Amsterdam: Fredonia Books, 2001
Ward, Josephine Mary (Mrs Wilfrid Ward), *One Poor Scruple* (London: Longmans, Green, 1899). Padstow: Tabb House, 1985, with Introduction by Bernard Bergonzi
——*Out of Due Time* (London: Longmans, Green, 1906). Kessinger Publishing's Legacy Reprints, n.d.
——*Great Possessions* (London: Longmans, Green, 1909). Bibliobazaar, 2007
——*The Job Secretary* (London: Longmans, Green, 1911). Kessinger Publishing's Legacy Reprints, n.d.
——*Horace Blake* (London and New York: Putnam's, 1913). Kessinger Publishing's Legacy Reprints, n.d.
——*In the Shadow of Mussolini* (London: Sheed and Ward, 1927)
——*Tudor Sunset* (London: Sheed and Ward, 1931)
Waugh, Evelyn, *Decline and Fall* (London: Chapman and Hall, 1928)
——'Ronald Firbank', in *Life and Letters*, March 1929
——*Vile Bodies* (London: Chapman and Hall, 1930)
——*Black Mischief* (London: Chapman and Hall, 1932)
——'The Man who Liked Dickens', in *Hearst's International*, September 1933. (See *Complete Short Stories*)
——'Out of Depth', in *Harper's Bazaar*, December 1933. (See *Complete Short Stories*)
——*A Handful of Dust* (London: Chapman and Hall, 1934)
——*Edmund Campion, Jesuit and Martyr* (London: Longmans, Green, 1935)
——*Scoop* (London: Chapman and Hall, 1938)
——*Put Out More Flags* (London: Chapman and Hall, 1942)
——*Brideshead Revisited: The Sacred and Profane Memories of Captain Charles Ryder* (London: Chapman and Hall, 1945). Revised edition, Chapman and Hall, 1960
——*The Loved One* (London: Chapman and Hall, 1948)
——*Helena* (London: Chapman and Hall, 1950)
——Introduction to R. H. Benson, *Richard Raynal Solitary* (Chicago: Henry Regnery, 1956)
——*Men at Arms* (1952), *Officers and Gentlemen* (1955) and *Unconditional Surrender* (1961), forming the trilogy *Sword of Honour* (London: Chapman and Hall, 1965)
——*Ronald Knox* (London: Chapman and Hall, 1959)
——*The Diaries of Evelyn Waugh*, ed. Michael Davie (London: Weidenfeld and Nicolson, 1976). Penguin, 1979
——*The Letters of Evelyn Waugh*, ed. Mark Amory (London: Weidenfeld and Nicolson, 1980). Penguin, 1982
——*The Complete Short Stories* (London: Everyman's Library, 1998)

Wells, H. G., *The Time Machine* (London: 1898). London: Everyman Paperbacks, 2002
White, Antonia, *Frost in May* (London: Harmsworth, 1933). Virago Press, 1978
——*The Lost Traveller* (London: Eyre and Spottiswoode, 1950). Virago Press, 1979
——*The Sugar House* (London: Eyre and Spottiswoode, 1952). Virago Press, 1979
——*Beyond the Glass* (London: Eyre and Spottiswoode, 1954). Virago Press, 1979
——*The Hound and the Falcon: The Story of a Reconversion to the Catholic Faith* (London: Longmans, Green, 1965). Virago Press, 1980
Wilde, Oscar, *The Picture of Dorian Gray* (London, 1890)
——*The Works of Oscar Wilde*, ed. G. F. Maine (London and Glasgow: Collins, 1948)
Wiseman, Nicholas, *Fabiola: A Tale of the Catacombs* (London: Burns and Lambert, 1854). Burns and Oates, 1962, with Introduction by Bernard Basset, SJ

Secondary Sources

Agenda *Peter Levi Special Issue*, Vol. 24, No. 3 (Autumn 1986)
Allitt, Patrick, *Catholic Converts: British and American Intellectuals Turn to Rome* (Ithaca and London: Cornell University Press, 1997)
Atkin, Nicholas, and Tallett, Frank, *Priests, Prelates and People: A History of European Catholicism since 1750* (London: I. B. Tauris, 2003)
Benson, Arthur Christopher, *Hugh: Memoirs of a Brother* (London: Smith, Elder and Co., 1915)
Bergonzi, Bernard, Introduction to Mrs Wilfrid Ward, *One Poor Scruple* (Padstow: Tabb House, 1985)
——*The Myth of Modernism and Twentieth-Century Literature* (Brighton: Harvester Press, 1986)
——*David Lodge* (Plymouth: Northcote House, 1995)
Bernard, Philippa, *No End to Snowdrops: A Biography of Kathleen Raine* (London: Shepheard-Walwyn, 2009)
Bibesco, Princesse, *Le Confesseur et les poètes: avec des lettres inédites de Jean Cocteau, Marcel Proust, Robert de Montesquiou, Paul Valéry et Maurice Baring* (Paris: Grasset, 1970)
Caparrini, B. R., 'A Catholic public school in the making: Beaumont College during the Rectorate of the reverend Joseph M. Bampton, SJ', *Paedagogica Historica* 39, 6 (2003), 737–757
Chassé, Charles, *Les Nabis et leur temps* (Paris: La Bibliothèque des Arts, 1960)
Cornish, Blanche Warre and Leslie, Shane, *Memorials of Robert Hugh Benson* (London: Burns and Oates, 1915)
Diemert, Brian, *Graham Greene's Thrillers and the 1930s* (Montreal and Kingston: McGill-Queen's University Press, 1996)
Dilworth, Thomas, *Reading David Jones* (Cardiff: University of Wales Press, 2008)
Dunn, Jane, *Antonia White: A Life* (London: Jonathan Cape, 1998)
Duployé, Pie, *La Religion de Péguy* (Paris: Klincksieck, 1965)
Ellmann, Richard, *Oscar Wilde* (London: Hamish Hamilton, 1987). Penguin, 1988
Fergusson, Maggie, *George Mackay Brown: The Life* (London: John Murray, 2006)
Griffiths, Richard, *The Reactionary Revolution: The Catholic Revival in French Literature, 1870–1914* (London: Constable, 1966)
——*Le Singe de Dieu: François Mauriac entre le 'roman catholique' et la littérature contemporaine, 1913–1930* (Bordeaux: L'Esprit du Temps, 1996)

——'Quelqu'un qui ne sentait pas bon fit son entrée', in *Léon Bloy* (Paris: Editions de l'Herne, 1988), 241–50

——'Huysmans et le mystère du péché', *Bulletin Huysmans* 92 (1999), 5–14

——'Le sacré et le dé-sacré dans le roman catholique', in *Dimensions du sacré dans les littératures profanes* (Brussels: Éditions de l'Université de Bruxelles, 1999), 57–68

Guyard, Marius-François, 'De l'Eros Inconnu aux Grandes Odes', *Bibliothèque Française et Romane*, Série CVI (Strasbourg: Centre de Philologie Romane, 1963), pp. 75–107

Hale, Frederick, 'Moral Certitude and Moral Ambiguity in Bernard Bergonzi's *The Roman Persuasion*', *Revista Alicantina de Estudios Ingleses* 15 (2002), 95–108

Hanson, Ellis, *Decadence and Catholicism* (Cambridge, Massachusetts: Harvard University Press, 1997)

Kemp, Peter, *Muriel Spark* (London: Elek, 1974)

Ker, Ian, *The Catholic Revival in English Literature, 1845–1961: Newman, Hopkins, Belloc, Chesterton, Greene, Waugh* (Notre Dame, Indiana: University of Notre Dame Press, 2004)

Lesourd, Jean-Alain, *Les Catholiques dans la société anglaise, 1765–1865* (2 vols) (Lille: Université de Lille III, 1978)

Linklater, Andro, *Compton Mackenzie: A Life* (London: Chatto and Windus, 1987)

Maison, Margaret, *The Victorian Vision: Studies in the Religious Novel* (New York: Sheed and Ward, 1961)

——*John Oliver Hobbes: Her Life and Work* (London: The Eighteen Nineties Society, 1976)

Martindale, C. C., *The Life of Monsignor Robert Hugh Benson* (2 vols.) (London: Longmans, Green, 1917)

McCarthy, Patrick, 'Claudel, Patmore and Alice Meynell: some contacts with English Catholicism', in *Claudel: A Reappraisal*, ed. Richard Griffiths (London: Rapp & Whiting, 1968), pp. 175–87

Miles, Jonathan and Shiel, Derek, *David Jones: The Maker Unmade* (Bridgend: Seren, 2003)

Nicholson, Norman, Introduction to *An Anthology of Religious Verse, Designed for the Times* (London: Pelican, 1942)

Norman, Edward, *Anti-Catholicism in Victorian England* (London: Allen and Unwin, 1968)

——*A History of Modern Ireland* (London: Allen Lane the Penguin Press, 1971)

——*Roman Catholicism in England from the Elizabethan Settlement to the Second Vatican Council* (Oxford: Oxford University Press, 1985)

O'Brien, Conor Cruise, *Maria Cross: Imaginative Patterns in a Group of Modern Catholic Writers* (Revised edition, London: Universe Books, 1963)

Pearce, Joseph, *Wisdom and Innocence: A Life of G. K. Chesterton* (London: Hodder and Stoughton, 1997)

——*Literary Converts: Spiritual Inspiration in an Age of Unbelief* (London: HarperCollins, 1999)

Poulat, Émile, *Intégrisme et Catholicisme Intégral* (Paris: Casterman, 1969)

Prigent, Gaël, *Huysmans et la Bible: Intertexte et iconographie scripturaires dans l'oeuvre* (Paris: Honoré Champion, 2008)

Purcell, Edmund, *Life of Cardinal Manning* (2 vols) (London: Macmillan, 1895)

Scott, Malcolm, *The Struggle for the Soul of the French Novel: French Catholic and Realist Novelists, 1850–1970* (London: Macmillan, 1989)

Scotti, Dom Paschal, *Out of Due Time: Wilfrid Ward and the Dublin Review* (Catholic University of America Press, 2006)

Shuster, George N., *The Catholic Church and Current Literature* (London: Burns, Oates and Washbourne, 1930)

Sewell, Brocard, *In the Dorian Mode: A Life of John Gray 1866–1934* (Padstow: Tabb House, 1983)

Sharf, Andrew, *The British Press and Jews under Nazi Rule* (Oxford: Oxford University Press, 1964)

Sherry, Norman, *The Life of Graham Greene, Vol 1: 1904–1939* (London: Jonathan Cape, 1989)

——*Vol 2: 1939–1955* (London: Jonathan Cape, 1994)

——*Vol 3: 1995–1991* London: Jonathan Cape, 2004)

Sonnenfeld, Albert, *Crossroads: Essays on the Catholic Novelists* (York, South Carolina: French Literature Publications Company, 1982)

Speaight, Robert, *The Life of Hilaire Belloc* (London: Hollis and Carter, 1957)

Srebrnik, Henry Felix, *London Jews and British Communism, 1933–1945* (Ilford: Vallentine Mitchell, 1995)

Stannard, Martin, *Muriel Spark: The Biography* (London: Weidenfeld and Nicolson, 2009)

Sternhell, Zeev, *La Droite révolutionnaire: les origines françaises du fascisme* (Paris, 1978)

Stopp, Frederick, *Evelyn Waugh: Portrait of an Artist* (London: Chapman and Hall, 1958)

Sudlow, Brian, *Catholic Reaction to Secularization in France and England 1904–1914: The Cases of Adolphe Retté and G. K. Chesterton* (PhD thesis, Reading University)

Symons, A. J. A., *The Quest for Corvo* (London: Macmillan, 1934). New York Review Books, 2001

Thornton, Francis Beauchesne, *Return to Tradition: A Directive Anthology* (Fort Collins: Roman Catholic Books, 1948)

Valentine, Ferdinand, *Father Vincent McNabb, OP* (London: Burns and Oates, 1955)

Vidler, Alec, *The Modernist Movement in the Roman Church* (Cambridge: Cambridge University Press, 1934)

——*A Variety of Catholic Modernists* (Cambridge: Cambridge University Press, 1970)

Ward, Maisie, *The Wilfrid Wards and the Transition* (London: Sheed and Ward, 1934)

——*Insurrection versus Resurrection* (London: Sheed and Ward, 1937)

Weber, Eugen, *L'Action Française* (Paris: Stock, 1962)

Weekes, Philip, *A Great Wealth of Lack of Knowledge* (Cardiff: BBC, 1990)

Whitehouse, J. C., *Vertical Man: The Human Being in the Catholic Novels of Graham Greene, Sigrid Undset and Georges Bernanos* (London: St Austin Press, 1999)

Williams, Rowan, *Dostoevsky: Language, Faith and Fiction* (London: Continuum, 2008)

Wilson, A. N., *Hilaire Belloc: A Biography* (London: Gibson Square Books, 2003)

Woodman, Thomas, *Faithful Fictions: The Catholic Novel in British Literature* (Milton Keynes: Open University Press, 1991)

Index

This incisive and perceptive new
book concerns 'Catholic Literature' in
Britain since 1850. To many people,
Roman Catholicism is culturally foreign
and 'other'. And yet some of the most
outstanding writers of recent times
have been Catholics – often converts,
such as Evelyn Waugh, Graham Greene,
Muriel Spark and David Jones. In every
case these authors' Catholicism was
integral to their creative genius and they
represent an important strand in any
account of English literature.

Professor Griffiths' account is set against
a wide and varied canvas. It gives a full
account of the growth of Catholicism
as a cultural, social and political force in
Great Britain since Newman.

Griffiths is concerned also to relate his
story to movements on the continent
and examines on his way the impact
of French Catholic writers such as
Huysmans, Péguy and Mauriac on their
British counterparts and the influence of
British Catholic writers such as Newman,
Faber and Chesterton on Europe.